5,110 Days in Tokyo
and Everything's Hunky-Dory

5,110 Days in Tokyo and Everything's Hunky-Dory

The Marketer's Guide to Advertising in Japan

SEAN MOONEY

QUORUM BOOKS
Westport, Connecticut • London

Library of Congress Cataloging-in-Publication Data

Mooney, Sean, 1960–
5,110 days in Tokyo and everything's hunky-dory : the marketer's guide to advertising in Japan / Sean Mooney.
p. cm.
Includes bibliographical references and index.
ISBN 1–56720–361–2 (alk. paper)
1. Advertising—Japan. I. Title: Five-thousand one-hundred ten days in Tokyo and everything's hunky-dory. II. Title.
HF5813.J3M66 2000
659.1'0952—dc21 99–046060

British Library Cataloguing in Publication Data is available.

Library of Congress Catalog Card Number: 99–046060
ISBN: 1–56720–361–2

First published in 2000

Quorum Books, 88 Post Road West, Westport, CT 06881
An imprint of Greenwood Publishing Group, Inc.
www.quorumbooks.com

Printed in the United States of America

The paper used in this book complies with the Permanent Paper Standard issued by the National Information Standards Organization (Z39.48–1984).

10 9 8 7 6 5 4 3 2 1

This book is dedicated to
my mother, Tsuneko,
and my father, Russell.

One taught me to dream,
the other kept my feet
on the ground.

◆◆◆

Most of all,
I dedicate this book to
Jennie, Rei, and Jun.

You are my love, my life,
and my inspiration.

Contents

Illustrations

TABLES

FIGURES

PLATES

Preface

Foreign firms annually spend tens of millions of dollars on advertising in Japan. From a business perspective, the pressure on them to successfully market more of their products to Japan's wealthy consumers is never-ending. Advertising is critical to accomplishing that goal.

Today, Japan represents a market that cannot be ignored by multinational companies ranging from Ford to BVD. Japan's well-heeled population, well over 90% of whom are middle-class, are vital to these corporations' bottom lines.

The key to the marketing successes of these non-Japanese companies, still an area where they inevitably hit a proverbial stone wall, is understanding how to advertise in Japan.

Over the years, several books have been published that deal with "marketing in Japan" and "Japanese marketing." Most of these books touch only briefly on the difficult subject of advertising in Japan. Yet it is impossible to successfully market any product or service in Japan without an effective advertising campaign. Inevitably, advertising plays a crucial role in the ultimate success of a foreign firm in Japan, and entails a huge investment in personnel, time, and money.

Unfortunately, there is a lack of authoritative published information on advertising available in English. I hope this book fills that gap, providing non-Japanese marketers and advertisers in all industries with the basic knowledge necessary for successfully advertising their products and services in Japan.

5,110 Days in Tokyo and Everything's Hunky-Dory is based on over 250 presentations I've made to Western advertisers during the past 14 years. The book is designed to provide Western advertisers with the answers they have been seeking, regarding advertising in Japan. Each chapter focuses on one of the most commonly questioned areas of advertising in Japan.

Many Western marketers have come to Japan, plied their trade, and returned to their home country without ever having grasped the fundamentals of advertising in Japan—not for lack of effort or desire, but usually for lack of clear explanation. Nor is this absence of a clear explanation the result of stonewalling by their Japanese colleagues or advertising agency. Rather, it is usually due to the fact that their Japanese staff, regardless of their English ability, often cannot explain the ins and outs of the advertising industry in Japan satisfactorily.

Yet understanding advertising in Japan is not impossible. Neither is the advertising per se very different from that found in the West, as many would have us believe. The main differences are due more to the Japanese perception of the role of advertising and the limitations imposed by the differences in Japanese media. When these differences are understood, most Western marketers in Japan should have no problem getting their advertising to accomplish its task. This is presuming the advertising is good, for no amount of understanding the basics of advertising in Japan will make a bad ad good. Yet such understanding should go a long way toward helping in the creation of good ads. So what do you need to know? Basically, you need a solid grasp of the content of advertising in Japan, as well as the context in which advertising appears.

Advertising in Japan is at once similar and dissimilar to advertising in any other country. Understanding where the similarities end, and the dissimilarities begin, is of vital importance to non-Japanese executives newly posted to Japan, as well as to their colleagues in the head office who are involved with the company's ad campaign in Japan.

During my career in the ad business in Japan, the majority of the "final" decision makers at the foreign clients I've worked for have been expatriates based in Japan for a few years. Since the rotation of these expatriates is constant, I've found myself being repeatedly asked the same questions regarding various aspects of advertising in Japan. Nor have I found myself alone. Most of my friends at other agencies in Japan, who also deal with foreign clients, have had the same experience.

After 14 years of repeating this process, I allowed my colleagues and clients to talk me into writing this book.

I first moved to Japan as a child in the 1960s, and have since resided here five times, for a total of more than 24 years. Growing up in Japan with a Japanese mother and an American father, and with both Japanese and Western friends, I naturally assumed the role of a "diplomat," explaining cultural differences to one side or the other.

Having then spent the second half of my time in Japan working my way up through the Japanese ad industry ranks at several agencies, promoting the products and services of Western companies, I believe I am in a unique position to explain the subject of advertising in Japan. Only the reader will be able to judge if I've been successful.

My objective is not to include everything about advertising in Japan from A to Z. To do so would entail several volumes, which would defeat my purpose. I have focused on the main areas of advertising, deliberately omitting areas that foreign marketers have little involvement with. I have also avoided any attempt to analyze and give profound insights into Japanese advertising (although I must admit the temptation was a severe test of willpower!). Finally, it is not my objective to give advice. Each non-Japanese marketer will have different objectives, and/or limitations, in Japan. Each has different needs. My only objective is to give non-Japanese executives a foundation of the ins and outs of advertising in Japan, from which they can begin to build the special knowledge necessary for their company's situation.

This book's purpose is simple: to provide the non-Japanese marketer with an overview of advertising and the ad industry in Japan. For the sake of clarity and simplicity, I set two guidelines for myself when writing this book. One was to limit the content to what the average Japanese AE (account executive) with about five years of experience would know about the ad business in Japan. The second was to address the basic issues of advertising in Japan that non-Japanese marketers have often asked me about. If I've accomplished my purpose, upon finishing the book, the reader should have a solid foundation of how advertising works in Japan.

In no sense should the contents of this book be taken as the final word on advertising in Japan. Attempting to provide an overview of the entire ad industry has of necessity forced me into making many generalizations. Arguably, for each "fact" I give, there is an exception. As a matter of fact, I could provide a list of exceptions myself!

I hope this book will save you time, help you avoid misunderstandings, and prevent some unnecessary frustrations. In the end, I hope it will serve as a basis from which you will discover what additional information you wish to know. This will allow you to know what questions to ask your present ad agency, and/or which questions to ask potential agencies should you decide to put your account up for a pitch.

ACKNOWLEDGMENTS

I'd like to express my gratitude to all those who've worked with, and guided, me over the years, expecially Tajika-san, Matsunaga-san, Oki-san, Sekine-san, Echizen-san, and Satoh-san. I also want to thank all my friends and colleagues in the ad industry in Japan for encouraging me to write this book, and for taking the time to read the drafts and make suggestions. It goes without saying that any errors are mine, not theirs.

A BRIEF NOTE ON THE TITLE OF THIS BOOK

The "5,110 days" in the book title refers to the length of the author's career in the Japanese advertising industry, at the time of this book's publication.

And for those interested in etymology, "hunky-dory" is derived from Yokohama's "Honcho Dori" (Honcho street), a nightlife area favored by U.S. sailors prior to World War II, and again during the occupation. Being on Honcho Dori became synonymous with being "fine" or "excellent," and Honcho Dori entered American slang as "hunky-dory." Although much more subdued and refined, Honcho Dori exists to this day.

Chapter 1

Introduction

This book is for all non-Japanese involved with advertising in Japan, whether you are employed at the head office or stationed in Japan.

If you are an expatriate working in Japan, you will ultimately become involved in your firm's advertising. This is for a variety of reasons, not the least being the high cost of advertising in Japan and the fact that as an expatriate, you will have more opportunity to be in contact with the head office than your Japanese staff will. Naturally, expatriates who are heading their company's office in Japan are ultimately responsible for setting their advertising budget and acquiring the head office's approval. Chances are, they will also be involved in approving the advertising execution and explaining it to the head office.

When judging the planned advertising, the vast majority of expatriates are both "deaf" and illiterate. They have to depend on the explanations provided by their Japanese marketing staff and ad agency to make any sense of the advertising.

Can you imagine approving an ad budget when you can't read the copy on the proposed print ads? Or approving a TV commercial when you can't understand the narration? How do you justify your approval of an ad budget that will be spent on media you never look at (because you don't understand Japanese)? Worst of all, why is it that the few times you do happen to look at the magazines and/or newspapers you are placing ads in, you inevitably come across a picture of a naked woman on at least one page? How are you going to explain this to the head office, not to mention the woman there who is in charge of international advertising?

How, as an expatriate, do you explain to your head office that most of the magazines (about 97%) you are spending their millions on aren't audited? Television ratings are not much better. While household audience ratings are measured (although how they are measured is a story in itself), measurement of individual audience ratings is still in its infancy.

Every year, foreign firms spend a fortune on advertising in Japan. Is it money well spent? Is the advertising message being communicated to the target audience? Do you understand why certain things that are easily done in your home country are considered impossible here? Can you answer your boss's questions on the subject? You've probably opened this book because you have doubts.

Reading this book will not make you an expert on advertising in Japan. However, it will give you a better understanding of what is, and what is not, possible in the realm of advertising in Japan. More important, it will either provide you with the answers you require, or indicate what questions you should be asking.

ADVERTISING IN JAPAN

Japan's population of approximately 125 million (the vast majority of whom are considered middle-class) represents a sizable consumer market with powerful spending ability. It is this wealthy, sophisticated, and highly literate consumer base that offers attractive marketing opportunities for foreign firms.

After the U.S., Japan is the world's second largest advertising market, with a total advertising expenditure of U.S.$52.7 billion (¥5,970.5 billion) in 1997 (see Table 1.1). According to *Advertising Age* (21 April 1997), among all the world's cities the advertising expenditure of Tokyo alone was U.S.$32.4 billion, a close second to New York's U.S.$34.2 billion.

Japan's advertising industry is well developed and makes use of all major forms of mass-media advertising. Advertisements in Japan range from television commercials broadcast nationwide to ads in local newspapers. In addition to the traditional mass media, Japan boasts a variety of other media—such as transit, cinema, postcards, even the outsides of aircraft—that can carry advertisements.

Expertise in advertising to the sophisticated Japanese consumer is a vital part of business success in Japan. The sheer volume of commercial messages, and the large number of media vehicles that carry them, make it imperative to understand how to create a message that will attract consumers' attention, and how to deliver that message to them. This book outlines advertising methods and practices available in Japan, an understanding of which will greatly enhance Western companies' marketing and advertising strategies in Japan.

Foreign firms face several hurdles when advertising their products and services in Japan. These can be distilled into two major areas. The first is a confusion regarding how Japanese advertising works, and whether it really is different from advertising in the West. The second is a lack of basic information on Japanese mass media, how they function, and if there are viable alternatives available. The first

Table 1.1
Total Advertising Expenditure in Japan, 1997

	¥ Billion	%
Total	5,970.5	100.0
Mass media	3,935.7	65.7
Newspapers	1,263.6	21.1
Television	2,007.9	33.5
Magazines	439.5	7.3
Radio	224.7	3.8
Sales promotions	2,034.8	34.9
Transit	249.0	4.2
Flyers	417.4	7.0
Exhibitions, visual images, etc.	367.8	6.1
Outdoor	332.2	5.1
Telephone directories	183.0	3.1
DM	316.5	5.3
POP	168.9	2.8
New media	19.6	0.3

Source: Dentsu, Inc., *Japan 1999 Marketing & Advertising Yearbook* (Tokyo: Dentsu, Inc., 1998).

step in overcoming these hurdles is acquiring a basic understanding of the various aspects of advertising in Japan.

Successfully marketing foreign products and services to the discerning Japanese consumer is not an easy task. Many books have been written to help their readers understand the unique ins and outs of marketing to the Japanese consumer, from product presentation to distribution. Yet there has never been a book dedicated to the one component of the marketing mix that has perplexed foreign advertisers for decades . . . advertising. The purpose of this book is to give the reader a basic understanding of each area.

According to Toyo Keizai/Dun & Bradstreet (*Foreign Affiliated Companies in Japan*, 1998), there are 3,037 foreign companies operating in Japan, over half of which are fully owned. This figure does not take into account the hundreds of foreign firms that market and advertise their products in Japan through Japanese affiliates.

Individually, foreign firms spend tens of millions of dollars annually on advertising in Japan. According to the figures published during the spring of 1997 by Video Research/MRS, in 1996 the top 25 foreign advertisers in Japan spent U.S.$1.383 billion (¥142.59 billion) on mass-media advertising. Coca-Cola led the pack with U.S.$159.689 million, followed by Nestlé's ad spend of U.S.$122.873 million. Ford, the fifth largest foreign ad spender, used U.S.$78.252 million; Procter & Gamble (twelfth) spent U.S.$45.495 million. Even Master Foods (ranked seventeenth) invested U.S.$37.359 million. These figures don't begin to take into account the advertising expenditure of foreign firms not in the top 25, but give an indication of how large their combined advertising expenditure is.

Japanese advertising is at once similar to, and different from, advertising in the West, both in the execution of the advertising and in the approaches taken.

While considered a necessary component of advertising in the West, successfully communicating a product's emotional benefits can take priority over rational benefits in Japanese advertising. Although a unique rational product benefit is essential, it alone is not sufficient. The key to successful advertising in Japan is the ability to communicate far beyond what is actually said or written in ads/commercials.

Japanese advertising strives to foster a positive feeling toward the product and the company producing it rather than to stress multiple reasons for the product's purchase. Product desirability is based on consumers' perception of the manufacturer. Japanese consumers are influenced to choose a particular product not on its features alone, but rather on the favorable image of the product and the company manufacturing it.

Japanese companies in consumer product industries tend to spend heavily on advertising and promotion purely to build their corporate image. In Japan, consumers associate a product's quality, safety, and reliability with the image of the company that produces it. For all these reasons, how something is said in an ad is as important as what is said.

While many Japanese ads are accused of not clearly stating what they are advertising, the same accusation cannot be made regarding who is doing the advertising. Corporate branding is strongly evident in all Japanese advertisements. In all ads for Kirin's beers and soft drinks, it is clear that Kirin (a leading Japanese beverage company) is the advertiser. The same can be said of Sony's commercials for all its various products. They all end with the tag line "It's a Sony." In this sense, Japan has led the world in line extension. The difference is that Japanese firms use line extension on their corporate brand rather than on their product brands.

One of the most noticeable differences between Japanese and Western advertising is the Japanese media scene. Japanese media characteristics, strengths/weaknesses, audience, availability, and even measurement differ in both obvious and subtle ways from media in other developed markets. Experience gained in the West regarding the media's use, and the placement of advertising in them, is frequently turned upside down in Japan.

An example is newspaper advertising. The first difference is that Japan has five national newspapers, all with huge circulations. The two largest have morning circulations of over 8 and 10 million, respectively.

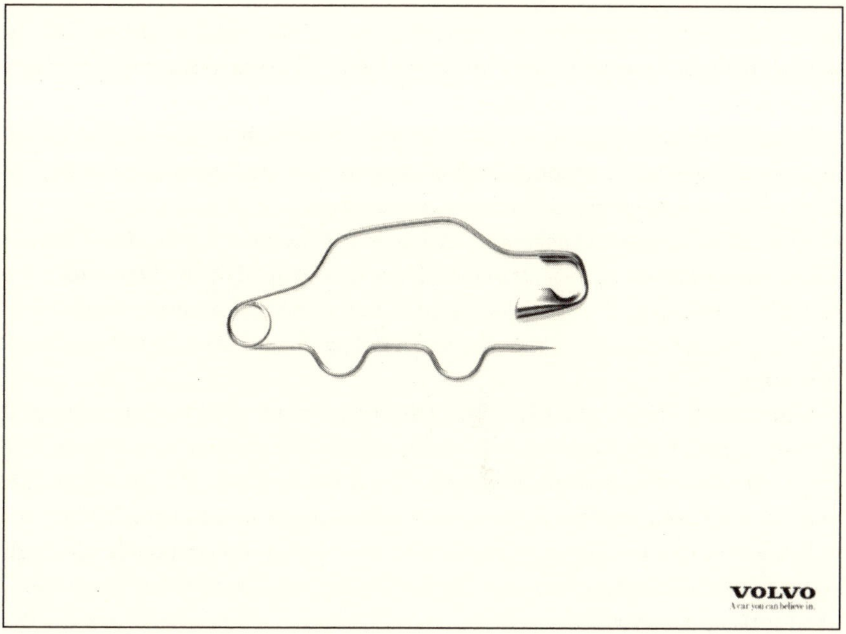

Plate 1.1
Volvo
A perfect illustration of the Japanese use of a visual so strong that no body copy is needed to supplement the message. The slogan under the logo reads, "A car you can believe in." *(By permission of Dentsu Young & Rubicam, Inc., Tokyo)*

More amazing is the fact that well over 95% of newspaper sales in Japan are by subscription. Since many households subscribe to both a national paper and a local paper, the average Japanese home receives 1.2 newspapers. Newspapers thus provide an effective, although expensive, way to blanket the nation with advertisements.

But with all major corporations in Japan vying to place their ads in the national newspapers, ad space is at a premium. At certain times, acquiring the desired space is extremely difficult. Compounding the problem is the fact that Japanese newspapers are thin (36 pages at most), and do not add pages to carry extra advertising. Furthermore, an advertiser has no guarantee that an advertisement will appear on the day desired. The ad could be pushed back to another day at the last moment, with no compensation provided by the newspaper.

Most magazines in Japan have circulations that are minuscule by Western standards. On the other hand, Japan has 4,000 magazine titles. This great variety allows advertisers to focus their campaign on specific target groups.

A major headache, however, is that magazine readership loyalty is very low. Almost all magazines in Japan are bought on a single-issue basis. Subscriptions are rare. Since readers choose each magazine based on that issue's contents, they do not buy the same magazine every week or month. Thus, advertisers are, in effect, always trying to hit a moving target.

For an advertiser in Japan, television basically refers only to the five nationwide networks. Cable and satellite television stations have such minuscule audiences that the ratings companies do not bother with them.

With only five national networks, airtime is at a premium. Even when Western advertisers can afford it, they often find that sponsorship of the highest-rated programs is locked up by the major Japanese firms. Buying airtime on the satellite and cable channels, with their relatively small number of subscribers, is not an attractive option.

Other foreign firms, which have budgeted money for television spots in their ad campaign, have been dismayed to find that the ads' effectiveness was swamped by the clutter of other commercials on air. The short length of TV spots (the vast majority are 15 seconds) forces advertisers to stress awareness, and provide time for only the scantiest description of product benefits. Many foreign brands, although major television advertisers in their home markets, long ago abandoned any hopes of advertising on television.

These are just a few examples of the different characteristics of Japanese media that must be understood before a decision on their effective use can be made.

Finally, foreign firms face the constraints of their advertising budgets. Without a doubt, the advertising budgets of foreign firms in Japan do not come close to those of their Japanese rivals. As in any other country, in the realm of consumer advertising the size of a media budget separates companies that can dominate mass-media ad space from those that cannot. In this sense, major Japanese firms, with more money to spend, have always enjoyed an advantage over their foreign competitors.

Indeed, many foreign advertisers find themselves unable to sustain a continuous, yearlong ad campaign in Japan's mass media.

Budget constraints also explain why many foreign advertisers concentrate their advertising on Kanto (the prefectures surrounding Tokyo) and Kansai (the prefectures surrounding Osaka). These two areas cover over 50% of the entire Japanese population. If the Chukyo area (surrounding Nagoya) is included, over 70% of Japan is covered.

Understanding the different approach taken to advertising by the Japanese is essential to the creation of an advertising message that is relevant to the consumer. Then, to get that message to the consumer, a solid understanding of Japanese media is essential.

For the reasons cited, the following chapters will concentrate on the two areas essential to successful advertising in Japan: the advertising and the media in which it is placed.

Chapter 2

Imēiji Kōkoku
Hard Sell versus Soft Sell

It is hard to believe that hard sell does not work in a country where the first recorded advertising catchphrase was *"Genkin Yasu-uri Kake-ne Nashi"* ("Cash only, cheap prices, no bargaining"). This catchphrase was used by Echigoya, the predecessor of today's Mitsukoshi department store. And that was back in the 1700s.

Yet, sooner or later, the foreign advertiser is inevitably informed by his or her Japanese staff, or his or her Japanese agency, that "hard sell does not work in Japan." At that point, the foreign advertiser can only make a judgment based on the ads he or she sees (but usually cannot read or understand). Certainly, most of the ads do not contain a hard sell. Actually, foreigners often find it difficult to tell what product is being promoted. Overall, it is true that the majority of ads in Japan are not hard sell in the Western sense. Yet that does not mean that the hard-sell approach cannot be, or is not ever, used. Nexnet, a digital mobile telephone service provider, uses a straightforward approach in its print ad, which says "Save Cost" in English.

THE MYTH OF JAPANESE "MOOD" ADVERTISING

The debate on the merits of Western-style hard-sell advertising versus Japanese-style soft-sell advertising has raged for years. Japanese-style soft-sell advertising has often been called mood, or image, advertising (*imēiji kōkoku*[1] in Japanese). Most foreigners believe that Japanese ads are vague, if not downright esoteric. Many foreigners, including those who have worked in Japan for a long time, seriously argue that many Japanese ads are purposely irrelevant or bizarre in order to gain attention and popularity, and to stand out from the clutter.

Others argue that Japan's unique culture allows ads to contain subtle nuances appreciated only by Japanese consumers. This is supposedly the mood or image advertising. Unfortunately, many self-serving Japanese agency personnel (both account staff and creative staff) have fed this myth by expounding in English-language speeches and articles on "Japanese mood advertising."

Various theories and explanations have been offered for the phenomenon of Japanese mood advertising, most of them nonsense. First of all, as in anything else, there is no single answer. A variety of factors combine to influence Japanese advertising. Second, it is debatable if such a thing as mood advertising, as described by many Western "experts" on Japanese advertising, even exists. That most of these foreign experts are not fluent Japanese speakers gives an indication of their understanding of Japanese advertising.

Nevertheless, it is true that Japanese advertising is mostly soft-sell, utilizing entertainment, celebrities, and attractive graphics rather than the hard sell of logic and product-specific commentary. Japanese advertisements are not as product-oriented as Western ads, nor are their messages given with the hard-hitting directness of Western ads.

Why Detailed Product Information Is Not Included in Ads

Some foreigners believe that Japanese ads are designed mainly to entertain rather than to sell the sponsor's product. Certainly Japanese ads contain less product benefit and more entertainment value than ads in the West. It can also be argued that even when they give reasons to purchase a product, their overall effect is a much softer sell than would be seen in the West. Take, for example, Kanebo's ad for Sala shampoo, which leads with the headline "Let's wash with good shampoo." Yet to suggest that major Japanese companies spend huge sums to entertain the populace through advertising is nothing short of ridiculous.

An often overlooked reason for the lack of product detail in Japanese advertising is the wealth of product detail already available from other sources. A direct result of Japan's extremely high literacy rate (99%) is the huge volume of print media. These regularly contain detailed product or service information in conventional articles. Certain magazines, for example, are dedicated exclusively to providing such information, and read like editorialized catalogs.

Specialized magazines cater to consumers eager for information about the latest gadgets. Separate "new product" magazines target male and female consumers. There are also videos (available at convenience stores) and TV programs on the latest cars. This kind of editorial product coverage in the media reduces the need for ads to communicate facts.

In addition, free pamphlets, brochures, and catalogs on any product or service are readily available throughout Japan. Walk into any retail outlet, and you can walk out with stacks of printed information. In other words, there is a wealth—if not an overwhelming amount—of product information available to the consumer.

Japanese companies consider the jobs of informing consumers of product details and benefits, and the selling of products, to be the responsibility of retail outlets. This is not difficult to understand when you consider the typical Japanese housewife. She does not do her grocery shopping once or twice a week, as do housewives in most other countries. She shops every day, buying necessities at small retail shops within walking distance of home. This is a central concept of shopping in Japan and explains why there are so many retail outlets. It makes the retail outlets perfect venues for disseminating product information and also shows why Japanese advertising does not have to be so hard-sell, nor does it have to pull the consumer into the retail outlet. To put this into perspective, Japan, with half the population of the U.S., and an area the size of California, has roughly the same number of retail outlets. For the reasons cited, there is not as pressing a need for an ad (whether print or television) to define or promote product features, as would be the case in the West.

Japanese consumers already have a lot of knowledge about products. They tend to believe that competing products from well-known companies are not really very different from each other on a technical level. Thus, in ads for well-known companies' products, the key creative issue often becomes how the message is conveyed, rather than the message itself.

On the other hand, when there is little outside information available on a product, Japanese advertising does tend to be more detail-oriented. Ads for detergents, cleansers, and personal hygiene items, which are often promoted on narrow technical merits, are good examples. Products in these categories are not covered in the specialist media mentioned earlier. Pamphlets and brochures on these types of products are not usually available. Though these ads do show how the product "can get your whites whiter than white," they are still a far cry from the Western definition of the hard sell. New products also require ads that explain their benefits to the consumer.

The Indirect Approach—The Importance of Images in Product Differentiation

In Japan, product differentiation is not explained with narration or showing the product in action, but by emphasizing subtle differences through the nuances and tone of the ads. This is accomplished by dramatizing those differences in the audio and/or visual elements of the ad. Rather than the product, the people who appear, their manner of speech, the background music, and the scenery are emphasized. The product's unique features and dissimilarities with other products are secondary. Japanese consumers are not influenced to choose a particular product on its features alone. Rather, they are influenced by the favorable image that ads convey of the product and the company manufacturing it, through the aforementioned elements.

The key to successful advertising is the ability to communicate beyond the message implicitly stated in the ads and commercials. Naturally, since Japanese ads rely more heavily on allusion than on direct messages, images are of key importance. Especially important are the mental associations that create the desired image and atmosphere.

The tendency to avoid directness in advertising is reflected in the Japanese language itself and is rooted in the homogeneity of Japanese society. Ambiguity in advertising can be traced to the Edo period (1603–1867). At that time, shops often hung a curtain called a *noren*, with the shop's name on it, over the front door. *Noren* are still used by Japanese restaurants. During the Edo period, instead of the shop's name, a symbolic depiction of what the shop sold would be written on the *noren*. For example, a shop selling wild boar meat would have *yama kujira* (mountain whale) printed on its *noren*. This was based on the idea that boar meat, which is dark red and oily, resembled whale meat (which is also dark red and oily). A shop selling horse meat would have *sakura* (cherry blossom) written on its *noren*. This was because horse meat is a light pink, resembling the color of a cherry blossom. Sometimes the symbolic explanation was too esoteric to immediately connect to what the shop sold. Shops selling deer meat, for instance, were called *momiji* (maple leaf), and sushi shops were called *kitsune* (fox).

Japanese advertising's indirectness also comes from an attempt to establish a positive feeling or atmosphere related to the product rather than citing multiple reasons for its purchase. Western-style logical sales messages are felt to be *kudoi*, an adjective that means tedious. Japanese advertisers prefer to communicate through intuition, indirect hints, and subtle suggestions rather than verbiage and logic. An example of how this is handled in copy can be found in a print ad for Ricola's Swiss Herb Candy, which shows just the front of the package. Superimposed is a headline that translates into English as "The wisdom of the Swiss." The implication is that since the Swiss have lived for centuries in the Alps, with clean water and air, they have hundreds of years of experience in mixing herbs to create the best throat lozenges.

A VISUAL SOCIETY—PRESENTATION IS AS IMPORTANT AS CONTENT

Another reason for the soft-sell approach of Japanese advertising is Japan's culturally ingrained avoidance of the direct approach. Japanese advertising is purposely designed to appeal to consumers' emotions and to produce a positive atmosphere. How something is said is as important as what is said. If the language of an ad is not right, the consumer will reject the product being promoted. Style

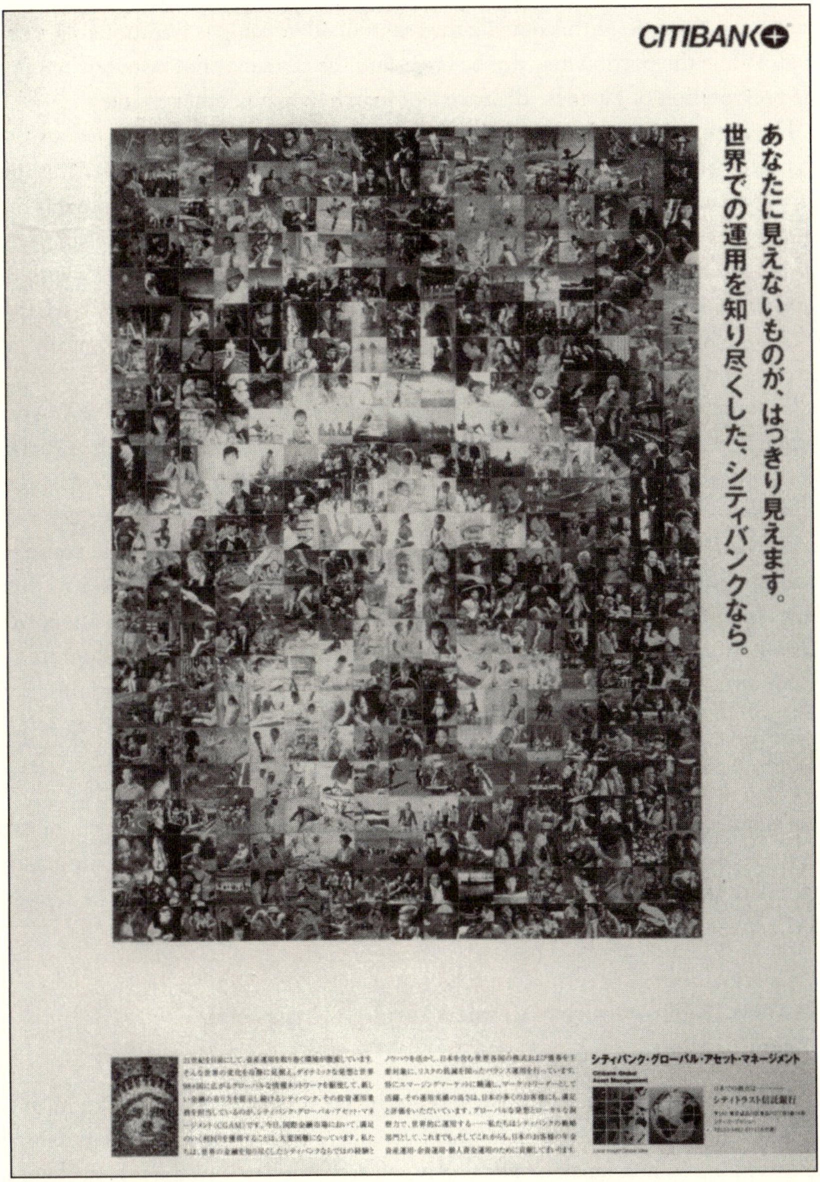

Plate 2.1
Citibank
A collage of photos of people from around the world that combine to form the Statue of Liberty enforces the message that Citibank's Global Asset Management sees things that are not readily seen. *(By permission of Dentsu Young & Rubicam, Inc., Tokyo)*

assumes a much heavier weight than in the West. This is a case for form over substance. An example of this outside the realm of advertising is traditional Japanese food. While the portion may not be large, and the taste may not be overwhelming, the presentation of Japanese dishes is not matched in any other country.

The importance of form, and how an ad states its message, cannot be overemphasized. Some argue that ad execution in Japan takes precedence over the content. *How* what is meant is stated is as important as what is meant. While this may be an exaggeration, there is an underlying truth in it. In Japan, advertising typically provides an emotional appeal for a product or service and supports it with the company's commendable image. This message is suggestive and indirect, whereas Western advertising presents its message in a more verbal, direct, and logically oriented manner.

Japanese television commercials in particular tend to make heavy use of symbolism and are calculated to make the consumer feel positive toward the product. They appeal to the consumer's emotions through intelligence or humor while containing very little product information. The Japanese understand these vague 15-second commercials partly because the Japanese language forces them to complete sentences, and/or fill in missing gaps in conversations, as a part of their normal daily communications. Another reason is that the entire Japanese population, with their daily use of *kanji* (Chinese characters), which are essentially pictograms, is highly visually attuned. Each *kanji* has several meanings and interpretations, each giving a different nuance and message, depending on the *kanji* preceding or following it. The Japanese visually interpret *kanji* on a daily basis.

Thus, in advertising, pictures are used to give messages that are quite clear to the Japanese but may not be clear to foreigners. In Japan, a picture really is worth a thousand words. Executed properly, a message sent to Japanese consumers through the use of visuals is much more effective than would be the case in the West.

Group Think—Desire Is Created Through Horizontal Identification

When trying to propagate a viewpoint, the Japanese avoid confrontation, aiming to include the other party and thereby maintain group integrity. Advertising is no exception. When Japanese ads do give clear reasons to buy, the reasons tend to be packaged in a softer way. The primary reason for this is that Japanese social organization revolves around the group rather than the individual.

In a society where "the nail that sticks up is hammered down," how does a marketer call attention to a product or build a brand? It seems like a contradiction in terms, but the Japanese have developed effective methods of standing out that are uniquely suited to their conformist culture. Group consensus and conformity are the basis for all activity in Japan. Before any new action is taken, all important members of the group must accept the proposal. Interestingly, this ideal of consensus recognizes that there exists a multiplicity of viewpoints and not necessarily just one correct interpretation.

This concept is clearly expressed in Akira Kurosawa's famous movie *Rashomon*, in which four people give differing, yet equally plausible, accounts of a violent crime. The ability of the Japanese to simultaneously accept diffuse viewpoints permits a multifaceted approach to advertising. It frequently encompasses the whole gestalt of the product, unlike the narrow, single-point perspective of traditional Western ads. In some cases, it may even take on aspects of surrealism, complete with subconscious imagery.

In Japan, a successful ad gains the concensus of the group. This gaining of group consensus is found in the Japanese technique of *nemawashi*, literally "turning the roots," which involves gradually changing the attitudes of each individual, based on personal empathy. In other words, desire is created through personal trust or fellow feeling, rather than authority—which, while respected, is also feared.

In advertising, this means that horizontal identification is important, whereas both top-down command and vertical aspiration to a higher station are suspect. A testimonial ad in the West might have a dentist promoting a toothpaste, or a famous actress singing the praises of a luxury soap. In Japan the speaker would more likely be a member of the target's group, such as a coworker or sister (although the role might be portrayed by a Japanese celebrity). Foreign brands have frequently stumbled on such points, thinking that in adapting their advertising to the Japanese market, it was enough simply to switch from foreigners to Japanese while retaining the same structure as their original ad.

Since the social organization of Japan puts primary focus on the group rather than the individual, ads in Japan must also address the group. Ads that present a product in a way that indicates each member of the group can benefit—directly or indirectly—are the norm. The most common technique for producing this is showing the product's acceptance by a peer. That peer is commonly played by a Japanese celebrity. People are the center of interest of Japanese ads—not the product. The people featured give the product its personality. For the most part, Japanese advertising works by building empathy with the consumer. To gain that empathy, Japanese advertising tends to be very friendly.

Successful ads target the group rather than individuals. An ad that shows an individual getting the better of his/her peers, or in a situation in which his/her peers would not find themselves, will not work. Avoidance of exclusivity is also one reason why comparative advertising is so rare; it is important not to make anyone lose face in Japan. Similarly, contempt or scorn—as in the famous American hair tonic ad with the line "Still using that greasy kid stuff?"—is uncommon. This ties in with the concept of *uchi* (family, company, the group) versus *soto* (others), which is

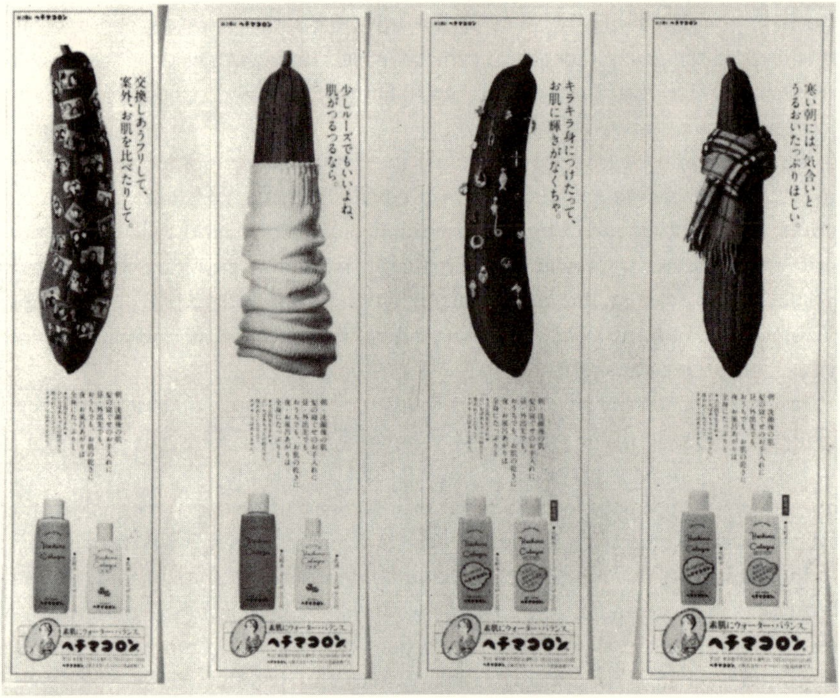

Plate 2.2
Hechima Cologne
This series of ads for Hechima Cologne's skin-care products demonstrates the Japanese sense of humor by stressing that no matter what you are covered with, you want to have healthy, smooth skin. *(By permission of Dentsu Young & Rubicam, Inc., Tokyo)*

basic to Japanese social organization. In Japan, there is little point in trying to gain cooperation from someone unless you have an introduction or are otherwise thought to be part of the same group.

Associating a product with the target group, rather than with an individual, is a way of maintaining interest. Unsuccessful ad campaigns for American products in Japan have ignored this. In a series of TV commercials for Kent cigarettes that was eventually dropped, one man, among many, ends up getting the girl. Since his success is exclusive, in the Japanese milieu this ad contained the unfortunate sub-message that men who smoke the brand are socially insensitive. In the replacement campaign, developed entirely in Japan, all members of the group of smokers benefit equally.

A successful approach in a series of commercials for Lark cigarettes portrayed James Coburn winning safe passage through dangerous situations by flashing his pack of cigarettes like a badge and saying "Speak Lark." This is well adapted to

Japanese thinking because his behavior caused him to be included in a group rather than excluded.

The difference can be a subtle one. In America, a famous catchphrase for cigarettes aggressively asserted "Us Tareyton smokers would rather fight than switch." In Japan an equally successful beer ad simply offered "Sapporo is your beer." An American car ad once asked about aspirations with the slogan "Wouldn't you really rather drive a Buick?" A Japanese car ad asked simply "How are you doing?" By identifying with the target or blending into the target's environment, the Japanese ad aims to gain "mind share" as a prerequisite to market share.

Interestingly, Honda's famous "You meet the nicest people on a Honda" campaign would have worked as well in Japan to create empathy for Honda as it did in America to disassociate the Hell's Angels biker image from motorcycles. Recently, Lawson's convenience store advertising in Japan used the same concept as Honda's. It showed the nice customers you meet at Lawson's, thereby gaining empathy and simultaneously disassociating Lawson's from the lonely, all-night convenience store image.

Careful attention should be paid to this point when considering adapting an ad produced in the West for use in Japan. It does not mean that the Japanese would not understand the ad made in the West, where one person (who uses the product) is shown as having an advantage over another because of his/her use of the product. Testing such an ad could show favorable results. This does not mean, however, that the ad would work in Japan.

NEED TO RISE ABOVE THE CLUTTER INFLUENCES AD EXECUTIONS

One valid reason for the esoteric nature of many Japanese ads (again whether print or TV) is the problem of clutter. Capturing the attention of the audience is paramount. This is especially true of magazine ads, considering the more than 2,500 weekly and monthly magazines available (some popular monthly women's magazines average 400 pages), full of ads for competing products and products in other categories. This is also the case in TV, where there are only five nationwide commercial networks and the majority of TV commercials are 15 seconds. The result is an average of over 4,000 TV commercials being aired each and every day.

Standing out from the clutter is vital. The first step is to grab attention visually. As every advertiser tries to do just that, some visuals have crossed the line between the esoteric and the bizarre. This mundane fact might disappoint the "experts" on Japanese image or mood advertising who have invented fancy theories on Japanese advertising, but it is a fact of life for Japanese advertisers and ad agencies when planning an ad.

At times, foreign celebrities are used as an attention-getting device. Examples range from bodybuilder Lisa Lyon and ex-bodybuilder/movie star Arnold Schwarzenegger to singer Madonna and director Woody Allen. Far more prevalent is the use of Japanese celebrities. Though not exotic, and therefore less useful as attention getters, Japanese celebrities have the advantage of being acceptable target-group surrogate members, and therefore can work to maintain the target's interest and trust. However, the increasing use of foreign celebrities in Japanese advertising since the 1970s deserves a separate chapter to examine it in detail (see Chapter 3).

Tactics to Gain Attention

Entertainment value is not the sole objective of Japanese TV commercials, but it is a critical component in holding viewer attention when the audience is capable of zapping the ad by remote control. Since the majority of spots in Japan are 15 seconds in length, advertisers cannot afford to lose the audience's attention. Song-and-dance numbers, and humor, that run throughout a TV commercial are common. Another tactic is the miniseries TV commercial, where the audience wonders what will happen in the next dramatic installment.

TV commercials commonly use humorous conflict-based slice-of-life situations, such as new employee versus old boss, wife versus husband, or child versus squabbling parents. By going against the cultural grain of harmony in a lighthearted manner, these ads involve the user at a gut level, creating the immediacy necessary to hold interest. Humor is used to balance and soften the conflict.

POOR RECEPTION OF HARD-SELL MESSAGES IN THE HOME

In every country, advertisers and their agencies are sensitive to producing the type of advertising that will be well received by their target. The same holds true in Japan. Many reasons have been put forward to explain the Japanese aversion to hard-sell advertising. All are valid to one extent or another. One basic reason, however, is far simpler, but often goes unnoticed. This is the lack of privacy and space at work.

The average Japanese works in an open-office environment, where aside from the very top management, the remainder of the employees, including middle management, do not have offices but instead sit together in one open-plan office. The average Japanese company office space is extremely cramped, with narrow aisles between rows of desks (which are usually side by side without cubicles). The average salaryman's desk size is 100–120 cm (width) x 70 cm (depth).[2]

More important is the home of the average Japanese, not that of a Japanese in top management, but of the average salaryman and his wife. After a day's work in the office environment described above, typically including overtime, and having fought the crowds on his or her long commute home (over one hour is the average in Tokyo), the average worker reaches home late at night. That home, though it might be a rabbit hutch (*usagi goya*) by Western standards, is the one place where he or she can have some measure of privacy. It is literally the only place.

Imagine this consumer finally relaxing in front of the TV. What do you think would be the reaction if a commercial came on that gave a hard sell? He or she would either change the channel or pay no attention to the commercial. Would there be a positive feeling toward the company giving the hard sell? Not very likely.

Advertisers must keep in mind that in Japan a commercial is entering the consumer's home. This is sacred territory. An ad must "knock on the door politely, ask if it is okay to come in, and then gently entertain the viewer." It must avoid being perceived as an uninvited intruder. This is probably the most important reason for the soft-sell, visual approach taken by most advertisers on TV. The last thing the audience is willing to do is listen to a hard sell, no matter how wonderful the product.

THE IMPORTANCE OF CORPORATE IMAGE

It has been argued that Japanese image advertising is a form of corporate branding. In image advertising, a direct selling message is not what is important; creating a positive image of the company selling the product is. "Corporate image advertising" would be a better description of these ads.

Japanese image advertising has several objectives not directly related to selling products. The first is that most image ads are aimed at the general public, since the successful establishment of relationships between consumer and corporation is key in Japan. The second, communicating to the trade, is also an important objective. TV commercials and print campaigns are seen as a means of encouraging the trade to handle the product, and of strengthening trade loyalty by demonstrating the company's support. A third objective of corporate image ads is strengthening employees' morale. By placing conspicuous ads, the company gives the employees "face" vis-à-vis their families, relatives, and friends who will see the ads.

Japanese companies spend heavily on both advertising and promotion to build their corporate image. This is particularly true, but not limited to, the consumer products industries. In the Japanese consumer's mind, a product's quality and reliability are directly associated with the image of the company producing it. A company's reputation and its history of stability often have more influence over a consumer's product selection than claims of product features, benefits, or customer service. A consumer's positive perception of a brand is directly connected to a high evaluation of the image of the company producing it. Thus in Japan, company identification and image acquire far more importance than in the West.

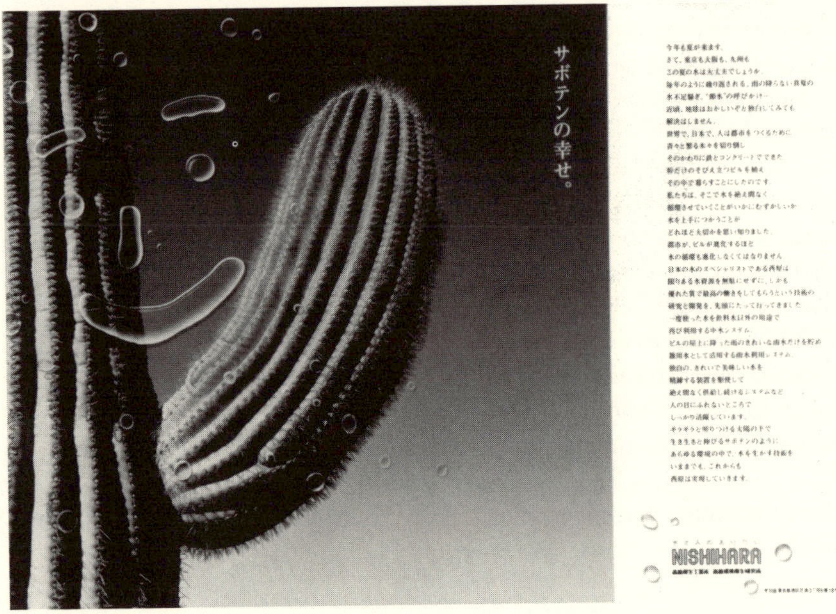

Plate 2.3
Nishihara
This corporate ad, one of a series, softens Nishihara Engineering Co.'s image by depicting an environmentally friendly image. The headline reads "The happiness of cactus." (*By permission of Dentsu Young & Rubicam, Inc., Tokyo)*

Most foreign marketers have no problem with their Japanese staff's insistence that their company must build a strong corporate image in Japan. It is when their Japanese marketing staff and ad agency begin discussing the inclusion of the company logo in a product commercial that the foreigner becomes confused. This confusion usually builds when they turn on the TV and notice that a majority of TV commercials in Japan include the company logo.

According to a study by Dentsu (*Japan 1996 Marketing and Advertising Yearbook*), over 80% of all TV commercials and magazine advertisements include the company logo. The company logo appears in both the opening and closing of 25% of commercials, only at the end of 57%, and only at the beginning of 17%. Since the majority of TV commercials are 15-second spots, the end is generally favored as the place to show the logo.

The reasons Japanese corporations include their company logo in TV commercials for their products are twofold. First is the consumer belief that if the company is large, old, or solid (or all three), the product must be good. Second, a strong corporate image allows Japanese companies constantly to introduce, and scrap if necessary, new products with a minimal investment in product branding.

In the West, advertising tends to concentrate on product advertising and product branding. In Japan, a company's standing on the social ladder and its participation in a group are more important. The corporation behind a product is as important as, and sometimes more important than, the product's attributes.

The necessity to adapt to Japanese norms of advertising is evidenced by the fact that Japan is the first country in which Procter & Gamble has included its corporate logo at the end of their TV commercials.

BRANDING, JAPANESE-STYLE

"Japan is different." Any foreign businessman dealing with the Japanese has heard this phrase innumerable times. Sometimes it is said with justification, sometimes as a convenient excuse. Superficially at least, it would seem that in Japan brands are different from anywhere else in the world. Only in Japan does the corporation assume such a prominent position ahead of the product brand.

Just watching a couple of prime-time commercial breaks any night of the week in Japan, the foreign marketer will notice that the vast majority of TV spots sign off with the name of the producer. The need for the corporate brand to be communicated so strongly is due to the nature of the Japanese market. With the myriad layers of distribution before the product gets into the hands of the consumer, one can readily understand the need for a sense of trust, reassurance, and reliability to be related first and foremost to the corporation behind the product.

At both the trade and the consumer levels, the corporate brand comes to represent a guarantee of trust and the basis of a long-term and consistent relationship. It cannot be summed up better than by the phrase that now circles the globe: "It's a Sony." But dig deeper, and you'll find that classic product brands, just as they are understood in other parts of the world, are strong, active, and alive in Japan, and are becoming increasingly important.

As competition has increased, so brands have proliferated. To bolster their chances of survival, there has been a dramatic growth in segmentation and the careful positioning of individual brands to respond to the needs of clusters of consumers. And segmenting to respond to the focused needs of a tight consumer group means giving each brand a clear, individual, and unique image and personality. The same basic premise that makes the brand and its values a crucial differentiator in consumer choice is now, thanks to changes in the patterns of retail distribution, beginning to apply in Japan.

In former times, when small local stores were the norm, it really was the company brand, and the relationship the company had with the store owner, that sold the product. But today, when faced with a choice between differing products in one of the growing number of large self-service supermarkets in Japan, how does Mrs. Tanaka make her choice among competing packages of noodles? Or how does Mr. Tanaka select his new VCR at the electrical goods superstore? Or how does Tanaka-san's daughter, a high-school student, select the package of instant noodles at a 24-hour convenience store? By price? By attractiveness of name and packaging? Or by a combination of these plus how they feel about the product on offer, the values of the brand?

Japan is different in many respects. But the role of brands in Japan is finally being recognized, and so is the role that brand-building advertising (and other forms of communication) plays in delivering the competitive advantage.

COMPARATIVE ADVERTISING

At the other end of the spectrum from mood or image advertising is comparative advertising. The very fact that any comparative advertisements have appeared in Japan runs contrary to what many experts, both foreign and Japanese, predicted. Their argument of Japanese reluctance to deviate from "social harmony" was proven wrong.

Comparative advertising became a hot topic in Japan when Japan's Fair Trade Commission (FTC) lifted the ban on comparative advertising by issuing a new set of guidelines in 1987. These stipulated that comparative ads could be run if the comparative claims were proven objectively, if the facts and figures were quoted accurately and fairly, and if the method of comparison itself was fair. Data used in comparisons should ideally come from independent sources, but this was not obligatory. Like should be compared with like as far as possible, and the overall impression given should not be misleading. Yet even with these new guidelines, the majority of Japanese companies, ad agencies, and media networks have been hesitant to run comparative ads.

Before the new 1987 guidelines were issued, most Japanese companies and their ad agencies had been reluctant to consider comparative ads. The media had hesitated to accept comparative advertisements, and industry associations discouraged their use. This reflected the spirit of the Japanese Advertising Code, which says, "Let us avoid slandering, defaming, and attacking others." The few times an ad showed a product being compared with another, the competitive product was usually not named. Another method of comparative advertising was to compare a product with another product from the same company. In 1983 Philips used this technique when it aired a commercial comparing its new shaver against an earlier Philips shaver, clearly demonstrating that their new shaver gave a better shave.

When the restrictions on comparative advertising were lifted, Japanese commentators often stated that since Japanese society was based on harmony, and confrontation was perceived as being in bad taste, it was unlikely that comparative advertising would take off in Japan. Yet a comparative campaign that ran counter to this argument had run just before the new guidelines on comparative advertising were made public in 1987. This was a campaign promoting All Nippon Airways' (ANA) wider seat spacing on their flights across the Pacific. The newspaper and television ads produced by Dentsu proclaimed, "We give you more space than the others," and showed ANA's seating configuration. ANA's competitor, Japan Airlines, also a Dentsu client, quickly responded by changing its seating plan to match ANA's.

Since the FTC's revision of the restrictions on comparative advertising, fewer than 50 such advertisements have been run. The ANA example is representative of the difficulty. Since no competitor was named, the comparison might not be considered "comparative advertising" by Western standards. The low number of comparative ads that have run in Japan is in contrast to the United States, where comparative advertising is more prevalent. It is hard to get an exact number, since some ads are considered comparative by some but not by others.

One of the more recent comparative ads run in Japan was launched by Akia Corp., a midsize Tokyo-based personal computer manufacturer. In June 1996, Akia ran comparative advertising in newspapers and magazines comparing its Tornado 513V notebook PC and the Latitude series introduced by Dell Computer KK. The advertisement compared the performance of the microprocessors and displays and the battery life of the two series. Akia had run similar comparative advertising against Sharp's Mebius Note earlier the same year.

Usually, Japanese companies tend to be more cautious when they run a comparative ad campaign. Instead of making direct comparisons using data, they prefer to present an image in the vague likeness of the rival product. In another watershed advertisement, Japan's largest personal computer maker, NEC, came out with a comparative ad when it began to lose its stranglehold on the PC market to upstarts like Dell and Compaq. To stem the tide, NEC ran an ad that showed how its PC with "Japanese roots" did a much better job of processing Japanese characters than a "foreign" computer.

In another case, Sony compared a new product with one of its earlier ones. Sony launched its new video camera in a television commercial that compared the new model with one of its old products. At the time, Sony clearly stated it had no plans to compare its products with those of competitors.

Benesse Corp., a preparatory school operator, ran what many considered a comparison ad, although it followed the precedent set by ANA. Benesse's ad claimed, "Our way beats the others." However, when questioned, Benesse insisted that "others" simply referred to "other study methods."

Foreign manufacturers have also been cautious, as can be see in the 1996 ad campaign run by Reynolds/M.C. Tobacco Co. The television commercial, produced by McCann-Erickson, directly compared Reynolds's Salem Pianissimo menthol cigarettes with a similar unnamed product, claiming that its product emitted less smoke. General Motors had no such qualms when it came out with an ad that compared its new Cadillac with a Nissan Infiniti. This would have been a non-event in America, but it raised eyebrows in Japan.

In January 1996, Japanese consumers, unaccustomed to comparative advertisements, were astonished by a newspaper advertisement for Ford Motor Co. that criticized Volkswagen's Golf. The ad questioned why the Golf was so expensive in Japan. It was believed that this provocation would spark an advertising war and force foreign automakers into a price war. Yet such aggressive campaigns do not easily take root in Japan, in contrast to the United States. Ford's ad opened with the question "Why are European world cars [cars produced for the mass market] more expensive than compact cars in Japan?" Ford then claimed that the pricing of the Golf "is a very strange phenomenon" because it cost more than Ford's Mondeo although it was a world car. Ford's model, on the other hand, was a compact car of higher ranking.

The advertisement compared the prices of Golf with those of the Mondeo, utilizing easy-to-understand, concrete data, and asked Japanese consumers to reconsider their choice of a European car. Volkswagen Audi (Japan) argued that it was unreasonable to differentiate among automobiles simply on the criteria of size and shape. They argued that the price of the Golf was justified by extras such as an air conditioner and automatic windows. Ford retorted that such extras would justify only a slight price difference.

As can be seen, since the change in guidelines, and during 1996 alone, several comparative ads have run in Japan. However, the comparative ad that created the most controversy in Japan was a PepsiCo TV commercial aired in the summer of 1991. Pepsi's ad featured rap singer MC Hammer and compared Pepsi with Coca-Cola. It was an attempt to go against the grain by taking advantage of the easing of the rules. In the commercial, MC Hammer was "rapping" at a concert when suddenly, to the dismay of the crowd, he was transformed into a schmaltzy crooner after sipping from a can of Coca-Cola. But after taking a drink of Pepsi, handed to him by a fan, Hammer was transformed back into a hard-hitting rapper.

Pepsi's commercial was suddenly pulled off the air by the five major television networks, under what PepsiCo claimed was pressure from Coca-Cola (Japan). PepsiCo immediately took its complaint against Coke to Japan's FTC. According to Pepsi's allegation, Coca-Cola, with its huge ad budget in Japan, had pressured the television networks to pull the commercial. The FTC ruled that PepsiCo's claim "could not be substantiated," although it also took the view that the commercial was not in violation of any laws regulating advertising. After the ruling, the networks allowed the commercial to be aired again, but with a cover concealing the name of Coca-Cola on the soft-drink can.

Still another example of a Japanese-style comparative ad, although run by a foreign company, is a print ad for Bose's AMS-1 stereo, which costs ¥98,800. The ad uses a hard-sell approach with the headline "We want you to compare it with the sound of a ¥300,000 stereo."

Leaving aside specific examples, a common assumption has been that comparative advertising goes against Japanese culture with its emphasis on harmony, and would cause consumer rejection. Reactions to the occasional comparative advertisements that have run have failed to prove or disprove these beliefs. Yet, regardless of the lifting of restrictions and the examples cited, comparative advertising in Japan remains rare. One good reason attributed to the relative lack of comparative advertising in Japan is the networks of closely knit industrial associations. Member companies refrain from sponsoring aggressive comparative advertisements for fear of upsetting each other. It has been argued that this interdependence among competitors belonging to the same trade association leads these companies to pay more heed to their rivals than to consumers.

Further explanation for the lack of comparative ads is that in Japan it is common for a single advertising agency to serve more than one client per product category. Of course, clients are well aware that their agency also handles a competitor's account. Under such conditions, it would be easy for a company to pull its account from an agency that produced a comparative ad for a competitor (who was also a client of the agency), in which its product was compared negatively with the competitor's. Thus, many Japanese agencies are deterred from planning comparative advertising campaigns that might pit two of their clients against one another.

Even though several Japanese companies have run comparative ads since the lifting of the ban, comparative ad campaigns in Japan are still considered to be mainly the domain of foreign-affiliated companies. Even so, to go as far as mentioning the name of a rival or its product, as Ford did, is extremely rare.

Regardless of the number of comparative ads that have run in Japan, they are still regarded with skepticism. Most Japanese agencies and advertisers strongly believe that comparative advertising is weaker than ads that leave the consumer with a positive image of the company advertised. Being perceived as self-glorifying or brash is the underlying risk in running comparative ads in Japan.

CONCLUSION

When one is advertising in Japan, the social pressure for conformity, and the need to balance image-building advertising with precise doses of product details, must always be kept in mind. When focusing on product benefits or promises, it is important to describe and/or demonstrate them in a way that is compatible with Japanese modes of expression and group dynamics. This is affected by product category and by demographics. With parity products, image is everything. On the other hand, the new Japanese consumers at the turn of the millennium are much more similar to consumers in the West, focusing on price and performance to a greater degree than did previous generations. Among them, "hard sell" is not always bad. Yet it still pays to remember that comparative advertising is a two-edged sword that should be wielded carefully.

NOTES

1. *Imēiji* is a loan-word often used in Japanese. It is the English word "image" (with Japanese pronunciation). *Kōkoku* is the Japanese word for "advertising." So *Imēiji Kōkoku* is "image advertising" (i.e., selling/promoting an image rather than a product). This ad technique is often used in Japan, where the image of a company—for example, a company that is modern, fun, caring—sometimes does more for selling the product than product features.

2. A section chief (i.e., middle manager) would get 120–140 cm x 80 cm. The average worker does not get a chair with armrests, which are first acquired when one reaches middle management. (In all other aspects, including the height of the back, the chair remains the same as the average worker's chair. The back of the chair gets higher as the person's rank goes beyond middle management.)

Chapter 3

Tarento
Foreigners and Celebrities in Japanese Advertising

Probably the strangest thing about Japanese advertising is the way it has attracted legions of Westerners. These are not expatriate personnel involved in the creation of the ads, but Western celebrities who are featured in the ads. The number of foreign celebrities peering out of print ads is staggering. They are even more noticeable in Japanese television commercials. Numerous Japanese and foreign companies use foreign celebrities in their advertising in Japan, and several companies use them consistently, year after year.

Among many other aspects of Japanese advertising, this chapter explores the industry's harnessing of *tarento* (talent) and the peculiarly Japanese phenomenon of using celebrities in advertising, particularly the "Hollywood element," and attempts to show how this fits with the Japanese psyche.

USE OF FOREIGN CELEBRITIES IN ADS

Without a doubt, Japan's use of celebrities in advertising far exceeds that of any other country. What most foreigners do not realize is that the majority of Japanese commercials feature Japanese celebrities, who almost certainly go unrecognized by foreigners. In total, every year almost 70% of Japanese commercials use celebrities, Japanese or Western. However, it is always the huge number of foreign celebrities that attracts the attention of foreign marketers new to Japan.

And it is not difficult to see why. These are not run-of-the-mill celebrities, but Hollywood-caliber stars. Over the years, major Hollywood celebrities have, one after another, graced Japanese TV screens. Action movie heroes are particularly popular, but all genres are covered. Paul Newman endorsed cars, then returned to endorse credit cards. Sean Connery promoted Japanese whiskey, and three later

Bond heroes—Roger Moore, Timothy Dalton, and Pierce Brosnan—appeared in commercials for Lark cigarettes.

Sylvester Stallone regularly appeared in Ito Hams commercials. Arnold Schwarzenegger pushed Nissin's instant noodles as well as vitamin drinks; promoted a new satellite TV channel, DirecTV; then appeared in a Suntory beer commercial. Brad Pitt has appeared in several commercials, notably for Honda and Edwin jeans. Bruce Willis appeared in commercials for mobile phones, cars, isotonic drinks, and jewelry. In a TV ad for Maki, a Japanese jewelry retail chain, while following Paulina Poritskova up a ladder his one line was "It's dream time!"

Mel Gibson and Antonio Banderas have appeared for Fuji Heavy Industries (maker of Subaru cars); Charlie Sheen endorsed Madras women's shoes, Parliament cigarettes, air conditioners, and Tokyo Gas; Quentin Tarantino promoted Rupert Murdoch's entry into Japanese satellite broadcasting, PerfecTV; and Michael J. Fox has appeared in a commercial for fishing equipment promoting Shimano (fishing reels and rods) in a series of the company's ads.

Japan's second largest agency, Hakuhodo, featured Harrison Ford in a series of commercials for Kirin beer. In the first commercial, he appeared in a sauna, stripped to the waist, a can of beer next to him. In another commercial, he appeared as a common salaryman (white-collar worker), out drinking with his colleagues. In the print ads, he was also featured as just one of the faces in the crowd. It is rumored that Ford earned over U.S.$1 million for the campaign.

Western musicians are also regularly featured in Japanese commercials. Jamiroquai has appeared in a series promoting Sony's MD. Michael Bolton sang "Georgia on My Mind" in a commercial for Georgia Coffee, the leading canned coffee in Japan.

Female Western celebrities are also popular. Jodie Foster has been a steady favorite, and Honda has had her appear in its Civic advertising; she has also promoted Mount Ranier café latté and Bristol Meyers' Keri lotion. Cindy Crawford appeared in a commercial for Suntory whiskey, and Winona Ryder has appeared in Subaru's commercial for Impreza cars.

In 1997, a Hakuhodo commercial for the Tokyo Beauty Center showed an ordinary-looking Japanese girl telling her disapproving parents that she was going to the beauty center. A short while later, Naomi Campbell walks into the house, to the astonishment of the parents, dramatizing the transformation powers of the beauty center.

Table 3.1 is a list of foreign celebrities who have appeared in Japanese ads.

Initial Appearances of Foreigners in Japanese Ads

Foreigners began appearing in Japanese ads during the 1960s, when the Japanese postwar economy really began to grow. At the time, they were exclusively in advertisements for prestigious and/or fashionable products associated with the

Table 3.1
Foreign Celebrities Who Have Appeared in Japanese Ads

Paula Abdul	Richard Gere	Jack Nicklaus
Muhammad Ali	Mel Gibson	Leonard Nimoy
Woody Allen	Whoopi Goldberg	David Niven
Seve Ballesteros	Gene Hackman	Hideo Nomo
Antonio Banderas	Arthur Haley	Greg Norman
Kathleen Battle	Stephen Hawking	Yoko Ono
Beavis and Butthead	Ernest Hemingway	Arnold Palmer
Michael Bolton	Dennis Hopper	Anthony Perkins
Lara Flynn Boyle	Michael Jackson	Scottie Pippen
Boys II Men	Jamiroquai	Brad Pitt
Charles Bronson	Billy Joel	Pizacatto 5
Pierce Brosnan	Ben Johnson	Paulina Poritskova
James Brown	Hank Jones	Tlya Prigogine
Naomi Campbell	Florence Griffith Joyner	Alain Prost
Mariah Carey	Patricia Kaas	Dick Reeves
Scott Carpenter	Konishiki	Jean Reno
Jackie Chan	Diane Lane	Mickey Rourke
Ray Charles	Tommy Lasorda	Winona Ryder
Eric Clapton	Cyndi Lauper	Arnold Schwarzenegger
Jimmy Cliff	Ralph Lauren	Steven Seagal
James Coburn	Ivan Lendl	Ayrton Senna
Jennifer Connelly	Sean Lennon	Charlie Sheen
Sean Connery	Carl Lewis	Brooke Shields
Cindy Crawford	Daniel Day Lewis	Sylvester Stallone
Timothy Dalton	John Lone	Ringo Starr
Miles Davis	Sophia Loren	Rod Stewart
Sammy Davis, Jr.	Rob Lowe	Sharon Stone
Alain Delon	George Lucas	Quentin Tarantino
Leonardo DiCaprio	Lisa Lyon	The Three Tenors
Kirk Douglas	Madonna	Alvin Toffler
Freeman Dyson	Gazz Mayall	Jean Claude Van Damme
Sheena Easton	John McEnroe	Lyall Watson
Peter Falk	Joe Montana	Sigourney Weaver
Farrah Fawcett	Demi Moore	Orson Welles
Peter Fonda	Roger Moore	Vanessa Williams
Harrison Ford	Meg Morgan	Bruce Willis
Jodie Foster	Eddie Murphy	Tiger Woods
Michael J. Fox	Youssou N'Dour	Chen-ning Yang
Andy Garcia	Paul Newman	Zico

West—typically cosmetics, European fashion goods, and foods—but today foreigners are found in advertisements for almost any product imaginable. Although for budgetary reasons they are sometimes limited to print campaigns, they are usually featured in combined television/print campaigns.

The first serious use of foreigners in Japanese advertising began in the late 1960s when Nissan produced a commercial for their Skyline model. Called "Ken & Mary's Skyline of Love," the commercial featured foreign models rather than celebrities. The models themselves were not famous and were specifically chosen for their average "American boy and girl next door" look.

The concept of this particular commercial was to show how buying a Skyline (i.e., ownership of a new car) would fulfill a dream. The use of foreign models was to emphasize that an aspect of the American middle-class lifestyle, a car, was within consumers' reach. The U.S. lifestyle was much admired at this stage of Japan's postwar reconstruction, and since television was in its infancy, lack of domestic programming meant that viewers were watching many U.S. programs (*My Three Sons*, *Bewitched*, etc.), which exposed them to American middle-class life. The Skyline campaign was a huge success both in terms of its popularity and in terms of the Skyline's positioning and sales. Nissan retained the campaign's catchphrase, "*Ai no* Skyline" (The Skyline of Love), long after the commercial stopped running.

The success of Nissan's Skyline commercial launched a boom in the use of foreign models. Since that time, the type of foreign models used in advertisements has gone through cycles. In the beginning, advertisers favored the blond all-American looks that had been popularized by Nissan's models. Gradually, a darker-haired "European" look began to be favored. Then, beginning in the mid to late 1970s, the "half" look (mixed Japanese/Western heritage models) was in vogue, which offered the perfect East/West mix, exotic yet familiar. In particular, firms interested in using foreign female models considered "half" girls "safe." They had the attractive features and the figures of Western models, yet also had an indefinable Japanese quality that evoked empathy. While still used today, "half" models are not nearly as prevalent as they were in the late 1970s and early 1980s.

As the "half" trend peaked, the never-ending search for a new formula, a new twist, continued with a shift to using dark-haired Latin-type girls who looked Eurasian. But since the late 1980s, all types of foreigners have been used without preference for one type or another. This is a result of the familiarity that today's Japanese consumer has with foreigners. This familiarity comes from a variety of sources. The strongest influence is the television broadcast of foreign movies and programs, followed by the use of local foreign celebrities who appear regularly on television talk and game shows. The large number of foreigners residing in Japan, and the multitude of Japanese traveling overseas, have added to the feeling of familiarity Japanese have for all types of foreigners.

Plate 3.1
Camus XO
The use of Westerners and English head copy that reads "Unforgettable nights with . . ." gives Camus XO a worldly cachet. *(By permission of Dentsu Young & Rubicam, Inc., Tokyo)*

Using foreign models in Japan need not be expensive. Besides the legions of professional models in Tokyo, many amateur models are available; these are generally scouted from among the foreigners working and living in Japan (Plate 3.1).

Foreign models remain a staple of Japanese advertising, but it is the widespread use of foreign celebrities that generates heated debate. This phenomenon was triggered by Charles Bronson's appearance in a Japanese TV commercial in the early 1970s. At the time, Yanagiya, an established Japanese toiletries firm, found its business foundering as its market share was threatened by the successful entry of foreign men's toiletry products.

Dentsu, Japan's leading ad agency, rescued Yanagiya in 1972 by producing an ad campaign for them that starred Charles Bronson. At the same time Dentsu persuaded Yanagiya to change its name to the more modern-sounding Mandom. The commercial featured Bronson splashing Mandom aftershave on his face in a macho kind of way, and ended with a close-up of his face as he said, "Mmmm, Mandom." The ad campaign was a smash success. Together with the change of name to Mandom, it reversed Yanagiya's downward spiral while creating a new genre in Japanese advertising. Building on the success of Bronson's appearance, in the following year Mandom's advertising featured David Niven.

After their successful use of Bronson for Mandom, Dentsu found it easy to persuade Japanese fashion house Renown to recruit Alain Delon to appear in its advertising. This proved so successful that Renown next featured Peter Fonda in its advertising. Hakuhodo, Japan's second-largest ad agency, reacted immediately to its rival's success. It persuaded Paul Newman, whose involvement in car racing was a top news story at the time, to appear in its campaign for Nissan's Skyline model. Newman's presence suggested that Nissan was making its mark in the global auto industry and that the Skyline could fulfill the Japanese consumers' car-owning dreams. In a sense, the concept was an extension of Nissan's earlier Ken and Mary campaign.

The successes of the advertisers who first used foreign celebrities in their ads led to a flurry of foreign celebrity appearances. Orson Welles appeared for Nikka whiskey, and Sammy Davis, Jr., for Suntory White. Honda called on Sophia Loren to push its motor scooters. Lux hired her to do the same for their luxury soaps, and Kanebo hired Anthony Perkins to appear in its advertising for men's toiletries.

Since those initial appearances, hundreds of foreign celebrities have been featured in Japanese advertisements. At times, those appearing may be lesser-known celebrities, such as the daughter of Yul Brynner. Yet the majority of the celebrities appearing in Japanese ads are of the stature of Mel Gibson, Sean Connery, Alain Delon, Arnold Schwarzenegger, or Sylvester Stallone. The trend is still strong, and shows few signs of weakening.

Foreign Celebrities in Japanese Ad Campaigns

Inevitably, Japanese ad agencies (and their clients) have often been accused of falling back on the use of a foreign celebrity when they are short on new advertising ideas. While this is true in some cases, many advertisers and agencies in Japan believe that using foreign stars can help break through the advertising clutter very dramatically and get their products noticed in the process.

It is often believed that the high cost of hiring foreign celebrities limits their use to those few advertisers with huge ad budgets, yet the truth is quite the opposite. Despite the high cost of hiring foreign celebrities, their appearance can capture higher GRPs (gross rating points). When the cost of hiring a celebrity is compared with the cost of buying more ad exposures to gain the same number of GRPs, recruiting the right celebrity is usually the cheaper option. Japan's major ad agencies figured this out in the early 1970s and have taken advantage of it ever since.

Because of competition and confidentiality, facts regarding the efficiency of using foreign stars in commercials are hard to come by. Information on ad budgets is highly sensitive and closely guarded. To further complicate matters, foreign stars usually have contracts that expressly forbid agencies or clients from disclosing any information about their involvement to third parties. This particularly pertains to how much the star is paid for appearing in the ad. The contracts usually also forbid releasing the advertising materials in which the foreign celebrity appears outside Japan, which is why such commercials never surface outside Japan.

Considering the potential results, it comes as no surprise that Japanese advertising agencies are extremely secretive concerning their experiences and future plans to use foreign celebrities in campaigns. Yet the evidence that these commercials achieve results is irrefutable.

Besides the foreign celebrities' power to break through the competition and gain cost efficiencies, there are several other valid reasons for using a foreign celebrity. Two schools of thought defend the use of foreign celebrities in Japanese ads. One argues that foreigners convey a feeling of uniqueness while standing out among all the Japanese faces in advertising. The other school of thought argues that in this day and age, foreign movie stars, singers, and other celebrities are not so foreign to the Japanese consumer. They concede that foreigners were originally used to make ads stand out and convey uniqueness. Yet foreign musicians and movie stars are now so familiar to Japanese consumers that they are an integral part of Japanese culture. By their reasoning, what's so strange about featuring a star with whom the target associates?

The obvious next question would be "Why use a foreign celebrity rather than a Japanese celebrity?" The argument put forth is that if consumers see a Japanese star, they will start thinking about what they know about that star's life and won't pay attention to the product. However, if they see a foreign star they know only from movies, they will not know enough about that star's personal life to distract them from the message of the commercial. This is not to say that using Japanese celebrities is not helpful. As already mentioned, Japanese celebrities are used more frequently than their Western counterparts.

Another important reason for using foreign celebrities is that it allows for a type of testimonial ad where the celebrities appear as themselves. This is generally not possible when a commercial features a Japanese celebrity, since the Japanese celebrity usually plays the role of a member of the target audience's group (boss, husband, wife, coworker, etc.) in order to build horizontal identification (personal empathy) between the audience and the product. Furthermore, the appearance of a foreign celebrity in an ad campaign in Japan allows many otherwise barely distinguishable brands to easily set themselves apart.

Not only foreign celebrities can create an impact for a brand. Dentsu has built a high-class image for Nescafé Gold instant coffee by airing commercials featuring Japanese celebrities. Ajinomoto General Foods' instant coffees chose the "traditional" method of having foreign celebrities, such as Arthur Haley and Scott Carpenter, appear in its ads, to give its coffee an "international" flair.

Foreign stars appearing in Japanese commercials are often required only to flash a smile and maybe say a word or two. Sometimes they literally just appear. No smile necessary. The appeal of their fame and Japan's interest in things foreign are considered enough to do the trick.

In 1982, Woody Allen appeared in a television and print campaign for Seibu, one of Japan's leading department stores. Allen simply stood still, holding up a sign that said *oishii seikatsu* (delicious life).

While some foreign celebrities appearing in TV commercials may speak a few lines in Japanese, the majority who have lines usually give them in English. This has given rise to an ongoing debate on whether average consumers understand what is being said, but it is commonly agreed that whether they do or not is irrelevant. This line of reasoning argues that the debate is academic, since Japanese viewers are not concerned with what is being said in English. In most cases the lines are very short and consist of only very basic English, and the Japanese audiences can usually grasp the meaning of the words. On the other hand, when the dialogue is lengthy and/or uses complicated English, the English is simply considered to add atmosphere to the commercial.

It is also pointed out that the associations of certain foreign celebrities with certain products may sometimes be quite clear, and at other times may appear quite odd, if not far-fetched. In Japan, eating meat is considered to give one strength. So Ito Ham featured muscular Hollywood star Sylvester Stallone in its TV commercial. Stallone munched on some ham and said, *"Oishii desu!"* (Tasty!) to express this concept. Other advertisers use humor to link their featured foreign star to their product. An example of this was the use of Ringo Starr in an ad for apple juice. *Ringo* means apple in Japanese.

Regardless of whether the connections between the star and the product are clear or not, the correct use of a Hollywood movie star in Japanese advertising can produce dramatic results. An example of such a success was Dentsu's use of the innovative *Star Wars* director George Lucas. Lucas's appearance in Matsushita Electric's advertising helped transform the company's dull image to one of a company capable of creating new ideas.

In the early 1990s, movie superstar Schwarzenegger's comic antics (weightlifting with iron kettles) gave a strong boost to Nissin's Cup o' Noodle brand's popularity and sales. Sillier still was a commercial for Tsumura Bathclean (bath products) that featured Dennis Hopper taking a bubble bath while playing with a yellow rubber duck.

Hollywood sex symbol Mickey Rourke's appearance in Suntory commercials added a touch of worldliness to the Suntory (whiskey) label, which has to compete with world-class scotches. Rourke's appearance boosted Suntory Reserve's attractiveness among Japanese drinkers, particularly among young women who were fans of Rourke and his movies, such as *9 1/2 Weeks* and *Wild Orchid*. Suntory, a large user of foreign movie stars in advertisements, claims to have had very positive results with the use of Rourke. Since whiskey, brandy, bourbon, and wine are originally foreign products, the international touch foreign celebrities can bring to a brand is believed to give it an added feeling of authenticity.

Actors are one thing, but the sophisticated use of modern musicians in advertising is quite another. An example of this was the use of Madonna by Mitsubishi Electric in its 1987 advertising to launch a new video recorder. While the objective in featuring her was to push the new product, Mitsubishi was astonished to find that her appearance did more than just that. Overnight, she virtually erased the company's image of being "safe but bland." After the Madonna ad campaign, researchers found that most Japanese no longer considered Mitsubishi Electric a conservative company. Madonna's appearance also doubled Mitsubishi's share of the domestic VCR market to 13%.

The success of Mitsubishi Electric's Madonna campaign led to a rush by Japanese agencies and advertisers to feature musicians in advertising, again invigorating the overall interest in using foreign celebrities in advertising. Clients demanded that their agencies produce campaigns featuring foreign musicians that would accomplish the same dramatic results for them that Mitsubishi Electric achieved with Madonna.

Mitsubishi's success with Madonna showed Japanese advertisers the impact that the use of foreign musicians in commercials could have. Since that time, many foreign musicians have appeared in Japanese TV commercials. TDK's audiotape campaign was representative of this new advertising genre. The series of commercials featured musicians such as Jimmy Cliff, the late Miles Davis, Patricia Kaas, and Youssou N'Dour discussing what music meant to them. The message of the commercials was that TDK was a company that really cared about music; thus its tapes were of the highest quality.

Madonna returned to Japanese TV in a commercial for Jun, a Japanese rice liquor. Dressed in a samurai outfit, she battled a dragon. Having defeated it, Madonna intoned, "I'm pure," which was a play on words. (*Jun* means "pure" in Japanese.)

One problem that often arises when using foreign musicians in Japanese commercials is that they are not as widely recognizable as foreign movie stars. For this reason many Japanese commercials featuring foreign musicians have a small credit in the corner giving the musician's name.

A Japanese ad campaign featuring a foreign musician or singer offers advantages not only for the advertiser but also for the musician. The star's appearance helps build a positive image and boost awareness of the product and/or corporation in whose ad he or she appears. In addition, a foreign singer's appearance in a Japanese commercial can give a great boost to his or her popularity in Japan. Kathleen Battle, the black soprano recruited by Dentsu Young & Rubicam to appear in a Super Nikka (domestic whiskey) commercial, experienced this phenomenon. Battle's performance in the commercial sent sales of Super Nikka skyrocketing. A virtual unknown in Japan before appearing in the Nikka campaign, she saw her popularity—and, more important, sales of her recordings—soar. Eventually Battle was invited to return to Japan for several concert performances.

To capture a greater share of the youth market, some advertisers have turned to using young, up-and-coming stars to hawk their products. An obvious reason is that up-and-coming talents cost much less than established entertainers. Another is that the advertisers hope to capture their audience's attention through an empathic feeling for the struggling star. This is based on the knowledge that the Japanese audience appreciates an advertiser with the foresight to spot a rising star. The flip side of this argument is the risk involved if the chosen star's success turns out to be a flash in the pan or if his or her career develops too slowly.

Interestingly, some of the foreign stars featured in Japanese commercials are more popular in Japan than in the West. Although the movie careers of Diane Lane and Jennifer Connelly have slumped, they are highly popular in Japan, where they grace many commercials. Their images as icons is what is important to the Japanese audience.

The most noticeable trend in the mid-1990s concerning the number of foreign celebrities was the growing number of foreign celebrities from outside the entertainment industry. Today, only about half of the foreign talents featured in advertisements are entertainers, down from over 60% in 1988. Many of the new faces are male and female athletes, and the remainder have reputations in other fields.

The original purpose of using foreign entertainers was to stand out from the general advertising competition. The overwhelming growth of this trend subsequently forced agencies to find a way to break through the clutter of ads featuring foreign entertainers. A further reason for the swing away from hiring only foreign entertainers is that the cost of featuring famous movie stars or musicians in commercials has become extremely expensive.

These higher costs have forced both advertisers and their agencies to think carefully about the cost performance of using foreign entertainers. The search for an alternative solution led them to an untapped pool of foreign talent that would serve their purposes while also reflecting the changing values of society brought about by the bursting of Japan's bubble economy. Many companies began using foreign personalities to communicate fairly serious corporate messages. Entertainers were not always the best choice for delivering those solemn messages.

In 1990, Nippon Telegraph and Telephone Corp. (NTT), Japan's leading telephone service, launched its data communications business with a campaign featuring the slogan "The future will soon be here." The campaign's commercials featured four physicists: Stephen Hawking, Tlya Prigogine, Chen-ning Yang, and Freeman Dyson. The commercial featuring Hawking had him speaking in English through his voice synthesizer. A voice-over in Japanese said, "The professor says human beings want to know all they possibly can about space. He believes it is conceivable."

Joining the "companies with a serious message" bandwagon, Nissan hired *Future Shock* and *Power Shift* author Alvin Toffler to appear in its 1991 corporate image commercial. Toffler's English dialogue was "Uniformity was yesterday, diversity is tomorrow. Survival in the Power Shift era may require another kind of shift as well as a mind shift." This was a departure from Nissan's previous campaign, which contained two commercials composed of montages of old film footage and still shots. One featured Ernest Hemingway and the other featured Muhammad Ali. While Nissan was taking a highbrow approach with Toffler, Toyota took a much more traditional approach by featuring comedian Eddie Murphy in a commercial for its Celica model.

In Japan's immediate postbubble mood, many advertisers were following the conservative advertising style of NTT and Nissan. Foreign celebrities were more commonly being used to give seriousness to a commercial's message. Nippon Steel Corporation used Sigourney Weaver to add depth to its image, and Kokusai Denshin Denwa Co., Ltd. (KDD), the international telephone service provider, had Yoko Ono discussing her life and her communications with her son.

Foreign companies advertising in Japan were not exempt from this trend. In the mid-1990s, AT&T ran an ad campaign featuring Nobel Prize winners from Bell Labs. The campaign was effective in positioning AT&T as a technical innovator. The downside to all this "intelligent" advertising was that there were obvious limits to the appeal of intelligent actresses and concerned environmentalists. As a result, this trend was short-lived.

Foreign sports figures of world renown are often featured in Japanese advertisements. However, the hiring of world-renowned athletes is not limited to Japanese sports equipment manufacturers; they commonly appear in ads for a wide range of products. A recent Konica campaign featured Mark McGwire of the St. Louis Cardinals, and Merrill Lynch used Chicago Cub Sammy Sosa to raise consumer awareness. Earlier, when Hideo Nomo made a hit playing baseball in the U.S., his visage was almost immediately used for an ad campaign for Wonda canned coffee.

However, commercial use of sports figures is not limited to athletes, as can be seen in the case of Los Angeles Dodgers manager Tommy Lasorda, who was hired to appear in a coffee ad because he coached Japanese pitcher Hideo Nomo.

Inevitably, whenever an international sports event is held in Japan, the agents of foreign athletes schedule time to visit Japanese ad agencies.

However, home-grown foreign sports celebrities are not ignored. Zico, a Brazilian who played for a Japanese J-League soccer team, the Kashima Antlers, has also appeared in several TV commercials.

More recently, the heaviest sumo wrestler in the sport's history, the 270-kilo, Hawaiian-born Salevaa Atisanoe, known as Konishiki, began appearing in a series of Suntory whiskey commercials produced by Dentsu in 1998, after his midyear retirement. The commercials focused on the resemblance of his rounded body (dressed in black) to the Suntory Old whiskey bottle, and had him singing a ditty. During the campaign, sales jumped 50% over the same period one year prior.

When it comes to sports in Japan, golf is king. For years, a long list of world-class golf champions has steadily raked in a small fortune from appearing in Japanese commercials. Jack Nicklaus has been reaping profits from Japanese ad appearances for over 15 years. He has appeared in commercials for the American Express green card, Sanyo, Pentax, Asahi Kasei, Nissan, and Melbo, to name a few. Nicklaus's longtime rival, Arnold Palmer, also has long been a favorite on the Japanese ad scene over the years. In addition, other golfers, such as Australia's Greg Norman, have been appearing in Japanese commercials off and on over the years. Tiger Woods's recent ascension in the golf world was immediately followed by contracts to appear in commercials for Asahi's canned coffee brand, Wonda, and American Express. Although sports celebrities like Greg Norman and Arnold Palmer may make less money per commercial than the Hollywood stars, they are less vulnerable to shifts in popularity and appear year after year, promoting one product or another.

The Price of Using Foreign Celebrities

The fees paid to top foreign celebrities to appear in Japanese ad campaigns are a closely guarded secret. However, in 1992 *Nikkei Entertainment* obtained details of the amounts paid to several celebrities, and agency sources claim that these figures remain an accurate guide to market prices. What is not a secret is that foreign celebrities appearing in Japanese ads are paid a lot of money. Just how large their fees are is closely guarded by contracts that rule out any mention of the figures as well as any exposure of the ads outside of Japan.

Top Japanese stars can fetch U.S. $500,000 to U.S. $1 million for a one-year contract, and foreign stars can count on as much or more. Talent fees for foreign stars range from ¥40–60 million to over ¥100 million for a megastar. Considering the small amount of time involved in shooting a commercial, the fees paid to Hollywood stars for appearing in an ad in Japan compare well with what they get for appearing in run-of-the-mill movies. During the boom years of Japan's bubble economy, prices increased rapidly. This began with annual increases of 10% during the latter half of the 1980s, and peaked at 20% increases in 1990 and 1991.

A top Hollywood star can command a fee of a million dollars for appearing in a Japanese ad campaign. In 1990, Mickey Rourke and Arnold Schwarzenegger were both rumored to have collected checks for that much. Starring roles in megahit movies as well as commercials for Nissin instant noodles have made Schwarzenegger a household name in Japan, where he has earned the nickname "Schwa-chan."

According to the *Mainichi Shimbun*, the highest-paid performer was Eddie Murphy, who supposedly received $3 million for appearing in Hakuhodo's Toyota Celica campaign over 1989 and 1990. Since the bursting of the bubble economy, the costs of hiring a foreign celebrity to appear in an ad campaign have stabilized. Fees have basically remained at the levels set during the early 1990s, and there are now fewer million-dollar contracts being offered. Of course, not every Western celebrity is paid a fortune to appear in an ad campaign. The majority accept offers of a few hundred thousand dollars.

The amounts paid to foreign stars are almost inevitably in U.S. dollars, whereas the Japanese ad budgets are in yen. Thus, whenever the yen is strong, the possibilities of featuring foreign stars in ads increase, since they become more affordable and are more likely to be tempted by the high fees offered. The strength of the yen between 1985 and 1995 enabled foreign stars to demand higher dollar rates while not affecting the yen budgets dramatically.

One way of using a foreign celebrity but holding costs down is to use only the foreigner's visage. If the celebrity does not speak any lines, the cost is less, although not by a substantial amount. Having the star say even a few words costs more. Those few stars who utter a few words in Japanese enjoy increased popularity, as opposed to those who just appear, or appear but speak only in English.

Most of the highest-paid foreigners appearing in Japanese commercials are Hollywood stars. However, top singers and musicians like Madonna and Michael Jackson can also earn in the range of a million dollars per campaign, as did the late Formula-1 ace Ayrton Senna. Though the majority of foreign celebrities featured in Japanese ad campaigns are Westerners, Jackie Chan, whose kung-fu movies enjoy great popularity in Japan, and John Lone, who rose to fame in the movie *The Last Emperor*, have both received substantial paychecks for appearing in Japanese commercials.

Celebrities appearing in Japanese ad campaigns must lead exemplary lives. Scandal, in the form of drug abuse or unethical behavior, can bring commercial appearances to a screeching halt. For instance, Kyodo Oil immediately pulled its commercial featuring Olympic runner Ben Johnson when he tested positive for performance-enhancing drugs.

When a scandal hits a celebrity featured in a Japanese ad campaign, it is usually the agency that suffers, since the major agencies will always ensure that their client suffers no financial loss. When Rob Lowe's sex antics became public on video, Hakuhodo sued the actor for breach of contract.

Most Western celebrities who appear in Japanese commercials do not make commercial appearances anywhere else in the world. Since the idiosyncrasies of Japanese advertising are apt to be misconstrued outside of Japan, most foreign movie stars demand strict contracts with clauses that prevent the showing of the commercials outside Japan. George Lucas's contract for his appearance in Matsushita's campaign stipulated that neither the ad agency nor the client was even allowed to respond to questions about his commercial. When a Japanese commercial featuring a Western celebrity airs outside of Japan, a lawsuit ensues without fail.

Most Hollywood stars appear in Japanese advertising because it is lucrative, but they do their utmost to hide their appearances from their fans back home. This is mainly to protect their image and their career from charges of political incorrectness in their home country. For example, some do cigarette ads (Charlie Sheen, Parliament Lights) or hard liquor ads (Mickey Rourke and Cindy Crawford), and do not want that publicized. Others do not want speculation on the amounts they earn for appearing in a Japanese ad to spur accusations of selling out to big bucks.

But money is not the sole motivation for appearing in an ad in Japan. Some suggest there is a key cultural difference. In the West, a star's appearance in a commercial is perceived as signifying that his or her career has peaked. In Japan, a star's failure to appear in commercials is thought to indicate that his or her career is on a downswing.

Recession's Effects on the Use of Foreign Celebrities

After spending up a storm in the 1980s, Japan in the 1990s faced the bursting of the bubble economy. The continued economic downturn, as well as attitudinal shifts, reshaped the ad market and recast the commercial use of foreign celebrities. Whereas in the late 1980s Japan was buying everything, in the 1990s there was pressure to be much more strategic with advertising budgets. That meant carefully choosing the foreign celebrity whose appearance would give the greatest possible boost to the product advertised.

This led to a decline in the use of foreign stars in Japanese commercials, although it is barely noticeable. Another result has been that when Japanese agencies and clients decide to use a foreign celebrity today, they tend to go for either a big star or someone who has not yet appeared in Japanese commercials. Hot U.S. *tarento* (talent) has included Brad Pitt (Honda) and Mariah Carey (Kose cosmetics), and veterans like Harrison Ford and Jodie Foster. Paul Newman is one of the few Hollywood legends who has steadily been invited back. One of his most recent appearances was in a commercial for Evance, a chain of watch stores dealing exclusively in Rolex.

Despite a general cutback in the use of foreign stars, Hollywood actors have hardly disappeared from Japanese commercials. Spend enough time in front of a TV, and out will pop Andy Garcia and Sean Connery (cars), or Sharon Stone and Lara Flynn Boyle (cosmetics). However, there is a marked difference in how Western celebrities are being portrayed, for which Sylvester Stallone in the Ito

Ham commercials proved a perfect example. The trend is moving away from the foreign star as an untouchable icon and toward the star-as-neighbor. They now tend to be used in a more natural way. That is why Harrison Ford appeared in a Kirin beer ad as an ordinary salaryman out with his colleagues.

Despite the recession, Japanese cultural pride, and an aging population, work for foreign stars in Japan will probably never dry up completely. For one thing, foreign celebrities equal quality, and quality means increased sales. Second, the Japanese view foreign stars more as images than as people, a dissociation that helps move products off shelves.

JAPANESE CELEBRITIES IN ADVERTISING

The overwhelming use of foreign celebrities in commercials does not mean use of Japanese stars is uncommon. Commercial appearances by Japanese celebrities are far more numerous than those of Western celebrities.

Today, there is a trend to reduce the cost of making TV commercials, from production costs to costs for hiring talent. This gives Japanese talent an edge, since they tend to be less expensive than foreign talent. What's more, generations of Japanese consumers have grown up watching foreign movies and now take overseas travel for granted. At the time of the 1964 Tokyo Olympics, the number of Japanese who traveled abroad annually was 125,000. Today, about 17 million Japanese, out of a population of 125 million, travel overseas every year. Subsequently, they are much less impressed with foreign celebrities as unique creatures. When comparing a U.S. star with a Japanese star, Japanese teenagers today don't perceive as great a difference in their stature as their parents' generation might have done.

Nearly 70% of Japanese ads use celebrities, the majority of them local. Of the foreign stars, the most popular are noodle pitchman Arnold Schwarzenegger and whiskey ad man Steven Spielberg. In general, the Japanese celebrities used are from the entertainment industry. These entertainers are not just celebrities in the Western sense. They could also be considered part of the family or of a peer group. The average Japanese is very familiar with the private lives of Japanese celebrities. They see them every day. They are, in a sense, friends. Ask average Japanese citizens about celebrities, not necessarily ones you would expect a person of their age, background, and/or interest to know about, and you would be surprised at how familiar they are with the most intimate details of the celebrities' lives. They watch them every week on their favorite variety shows, which feature the same set of celebrities week after week. In between the programs, consumers see the same celebrities in commercials.

Many of the most popular Japanese stars are comedians or singers with their own TV shows. In their commercials, they behave much as the average consumer would in everyday situations. A long-running Dentsu campaign for Sanyo Electric featuring popular comedian George Tokoro encapsulated this idiom. The campaign advertised a cordless phone that can be used hands-free. Tokoro was cast as a young husband grappling with household chores. His hands are full of babies, or diapers, or cooking. Clearly he doesn't know what to do next, and needs a hands-free phone in order to get instructions from his wife. We never see the wife, who is presumably at work, earning the family income.

As noted earlier, there is a major difference in attitudes between Western and Japanese entertainers with regard to appearances in ad campaigns. In the West, major stars are often reluctant to appear in commercials, while in Japan it is quite the opposite. For an established Japanese celebrity, being selected to appear in a commercial is a barometer of popularity. For the up-and-coming Japanese celebrity, appearing in a commercial is a step up on the ladder to success. Another difference is that in the West aspiring models are just that, aspiring models, but in Japan full-time models are often aspiring celebrities. If they are lucky, they will be propelled to fame through appearing in an ad campaign. Suddenly they have contracts to appear on TV dramas, game shows, variety shows, and so on.

In a rather different approach than in the West, Japanese celebrities in advertising do not usually present testimonials. They don't appear as themselves to say how much they like a product. In the West, celebrities in ads often appear as themselves in a testimonial ad. Less commonly they play a plumber, shop owner, or other working person. In Japan, celebrities usually portray everyday people, and much less commonly appear as themselves. This is due to the Japanese group culture.

Since consensus-building is a part of Japanese society, ads in Japan must build consensus. Desire for a product/service is created through personal trust and empathy. The mechanics of the group take over here. Rather than having an authority figure sell a product (a dentist or an actress selling toothpaste), we see an everyday person saying how much he or she likes the product. The difference is that the everyday person might be played by a Japanese celebrity.

While their usefulness as attention getters is high, the success of using Japanese celebrities to break through the advertising clutter is less than that of foreign celebrities.

There is no racial prejudice when it comes to star appeal. Top Japanese talent can receive checks ranging from ¥40 million to over ¥100 million. Though big fees command the headlines, the way for a star to make money from commercials is seldom to charge the highest possible price. Rather, the goal is to appear in as many commercials as possible. In the U.S. or Europe, it would be hard for a star to appear in so many ads, but in Japan the lack of exclusivity is seldom a problem. If a star(let) captures the mood of the times, there is almost no limit to the range of products he or she can endorse.

CONCLUSION

Without doubt, the most common reason for putting celebrities in commercials in Japan remains the idea that their recognition value can help products stand out from the competition. This is especially true for foreign movie stars and musicians. Yet, with television viewers inundated with a dozen or more commercials between peak-time programs, advertisers obviously need something more than just a recognizable face to grab viewers' attention. So, while more advertisers and agencies are using celebrities more for their relevance to the product/service being promoted, the norm is still to arbitrarily attach the product/service to the star of the moment. Does it work? To a certain extent, yes. The star's popularity is of primary concern. Whether the star is foreign or Japanese is not the primary concern.

Chapter 4

Kopī
Japanese Copy

Can strong ad copy be written in a language where sentences often don't have a subject, and sometimes omit an object? If the language is Japanese, the answer is yes.

An ongoing headache facing all foreign companies advertising in Japan is whether what their ads say in Japanese is what the advertisers have agreed they want to say in English. Unless everybody involved with the advertising (both in Japan and in the head office) is completely fluent in Japanese, this problem will never disappear. Yet an understanding of several basic points can help make the process less frustrating for both the foreign and the Japanese personnel involved with the advertising.

Although you may prefer to skip, for the time being, some of the following sections, a basic knowledge of the Japanese language—its pronunciation, writing system, and alphabets, and how it uses and adapts vocabulary borrowed from English—is essential to an understanding of the problems and differences in producing ad copy in Japanese.

THE JAPANESE LANGUAGE

Unless they are fluent in Japanese, foreign advertisers' contact with Japanese copy (or voice-overs, in the case of TV commercials) is limited to translations. Most foreigners grappling with the Japanese language will agree that there is a good reason why the Portuguese missionaries to Japan during the sixteenth century called Japanese "the devil's tongue."

Non-Japanese marketers would do well to be aware of two basics regarding the language of their ads in Japan. First, it is worth taking the time to learn a bit about the structure of the language, even if learning the language itself is impractical. In Japanese, verbs appear at the end of a sentence. Thus, the audience does not know where the narration of a commercial is heading until the end. This quirk of grammar can lead to a buildup of anticipation similar to the anticipation of a punchline in English. Unfortunately, this minidrama does not survive translation into English. Thus, the English translation of a commercial narration that the Japanese staff think is great can come across as very flat and unexciting. Mercedes-Benz ran a successful print ad showing a man in his underwear looking at a Mercedes. However, the English translation of the Japanese headline would sound uninspiring: "I don't want to buy unnecessary things anymore."

Second, non-speakers of Japanese need to understand that the Japanese language contains a verbal status system. The choice of words used and the grammar that rules them clearly define the status of the speaker and of the listener. The Japanese language is structured in such a way that there is always a tendency for the speaker to be either above or below the listener in a hierarchical sense. In order to compensate for this and to achieve a level of parity between speaker and listener, the language used in ads, whether print copy or commercial narration, must be handled very carefully. Unfortunately, when translated into English, this social ranking disappears, and foreign marketers are usually unaware of the subtle nuances in the Japanese wording of their ads.

One campaign for an English school that targeted children and their mothers featured a popular cartoon character bantering in a childlike language with other child characters. To the Japanese, the language used would evoke a heartwarming, nostalgic sense through the choice of words. Yet the copy, when faithfully back-translated into English, came across to the foreign client as trivial, nonsensical, and idiotic. Quite the opposite effect! Another example is Brother's ad for a home fax machine aimed at housewives. The English translation of the headline (*Okasan ni kantan fakusu*), "Mother's easy fax," can only be described as sounding bland. Yet in Japanese it comes across as warm and inviting.

When looking at a translation, there are a few more things to be aware of. First, there are some Japanese words that do not have English equivalents. Thus, you'll be looking at an English rendering that was the closest the translator could get to the original Japanese meaning.

To take an example, the word *egao* in Japanese would literally be translated into English as "smiling face," which is what it in fact means. However, it would usually be translated as "smile" (as in "She has a nice smile"). Yet *egao* is not just a smile. In English, you could say someone's "smile is not sincere." Yet you could not say that about a person's *egao* in Japanese. An *egao* is a sincere smiling face that people show when they are happy. While you can "smile for the camera," you would never say (in Japanese), "put on an *egao* for the camera." It is these subtle nuances that are often lost when Japanese copy is translated into English.

Once foreigners learn that verbs come at the end of Japanese sentences, they then discover the disconcerting fact that many Japanese sentences omit verbs, objects, or even subjects.

When they are used, Japanese verbs do not indicate person or number. The dictionary form of all verbs ends with the vowel "u." The dictionary form of verbs in English conventionally is the infinitive. For instance, *nomu* could be translated as "to drink," although it could also mean "drink," "drinks," or "will drink." At the same time, the negative form, *nomanai*, could mean "do/does not drink" or "won't drink."

Thus, the Japanese copy on your ad may say "*i ite ki ta*," which basically means "went." However, the English translation would have to include a subject. Thus, the translation may say "I went." Or, if the intended meaning is clear in Japanese (which is not always the case), the English translation may say "They went" or "She went." If the meaning is not clear, the translator has to arbitrarily guess which pronoun to use (I, he, she, we, they, or it).

Japanese sentence construction differs greatly from English. While an English sentence requires a subject and a verb, neither is necessarily required in Japanese. When both are contained in a sentence, a typical Japanese sentence follows the pattern of subject-object-verb. Thus in Japanese, the sentence "I'll buy a book" (*Watakushi ga hon o kau*) would literally be translated as "I-book-buy." More commonly, this would be said in Japanese without the subject "I": *hon o kau* (book buy).

Since the word order of Japanese sentences is very different from English, some translations may sound jerky on account of the translator's having to reorder the words in English. The headline for Allergen's Concept F contact lens cleanser ("*H_2O no chikarade moto kuria ni*"), literally translated from Japanese, would read "H_2O's power by more clear." Obviously, the words in this translation would have to be reordered to read "More clear with the power of H_2O."

Japanese nouns have neither number (singular or plural) nor gender. The Japanese copy might say *tori ga imashita*. This could mean either "There was a bird" or "There were birds."

Whereas in English, and most other languages, the form of the verb is changed to indicate the switch from present to past tense, in Japanese it is sometimes necessary to change the adjective. For instance, in English we say "I am happy" and "I was happy." But the Japanese equivalents are *ureshii desu* and *ureshikata desu,* where *ureshii* means "happy" and *desu* is the verb. (There is no subject, "I".) Confused?

Another thing to be aware of is that the Japanese language has many literary and conversational styles. Several factors determine the style of language used in Japanese:

1. Demographic—Is the speaker (in the ad) male or female, older or younger, than the audience?

2. Social status and relationship—Is the speaker in a more prestigious occupation than the audience? Within the organization, is the speaker high-ranking or low-ranking?
3. Social and personal relationship—Is the speaker addressing his or her peers or someone from outside his or her usual group?
4. The setting—Is the venue formal (an official situation) or a private conversation?
5. The topic of conversation—This also helps determine the style of language.

The basic forms of language are casual, neutral, and formal (known as *keigo*). The different levels of politeness in spoken and written Japanese change the verb form, or even require that a different word altogether be chosen.

In the example cited, the form *i tte ki ta* was used. This is a casual form. The copy could have said *i tte ki mashita*, which is a more polite form. Or an even more formal form, *mai ri mashita*, could have been used. Regardless of the form used, the foreign advertiser would see only the English translation, "I/he/she/they went," without knowing the tone of voice it was written in. Thus the translation loses a lot of the context and tone of the original Japanese language.

In addition to casual and formal forms (and variations in between), there are male and female styles, young and old styles, and various levels of politeness. (Table 4.1 gives examples of all these variations.)

The way copy or narration is developed depends on the audience being addressed (elderly persons, young persons, etc.) as well as on how the advertiser wants to be perceived: casual, friendly, authoritative. Nissan's ad for its Silvia

Table 4.1
Different Ways of Saying "Let's Go" in Japanese

	Politeness Level	Gender	Age
Ukagaimashō	Very polite	Both	Adult
Ukagaimashōne	Very polite	Female	Adult
Ittemairimashō	Polite	Both	Adult
Ittemairimashōne	Polite	Female	Adult
Mairimashō	Polite	Both	Adult
Mairimashōyo	Polite	Female	Adult
Ikimashō	Standard	Both	All
Ikimashōne	Standard	Female	All
Ikōyo	Friendly	Female	Youth, children
Rettsu go (let's go)	Friendly	Both	Youth
Ikō	Friendly	Both	All
Ikōze	Rough	Male	Youth

model says "*Doraibu shiyō.*" Translated into English, this means, "Let's drive." What's lost in the translation is the fact that the wording is very casual and young. If the ad were aimed at an older, more formal audience it would say "*Doraibu wo shimashō.*" (However, the English translation would remain the same.) Add to this the various inflections or "accents" of the many regional dialects of Japanese, which can give an image ranging from "sophisticated cosmopolitan" to "country-bumpkin" to the language used.

Maybe now the description of Japanese as "the devil's tongue" begins to make sense!

ADVERTISER CAN CHANGE PRONUNCIATION OF BRAND OR CORPORATE NAME

Another aspect of the language hurdle facing foreign advertisers in Japan is pronunciation. On the surface pronunciation might appear to be a relatively easy problem to overcome, since Japanese is pronounced phonetically. There are long vowels and short vowels, and few accents. Furthermore, all Japanese words, without exception, end with a vowel or "n" sound.

Yet a simple example will illustrate the difficulties pronunciation can cause. How a foreign company's name, and/or its product's name, is pronounced in Japanese is important. This should not pose a problem, right? Wrong.

Interesting things happen to English words when they are pronounced in Japanese. When pronouncing foreign words, the Japanese use their Japanese phonetic style, referred to by some foreigners as "Japanized English" or "Katakana English." The Japanese use the nearest-sounding syllables to their own tongue when pronouncing foreign loanwords. Thus hotel becomes *hoteru*, and grape becomes *gurēpu*. Regardless of the fact that Japanese is pronounced phonetically, deciding how a company name should be pronounced/read in Japanese is not always straightforward. For example, Toys 'R' Us in Japan is pronounced *Toi Za Rasu* (although logically it could just as easily have been pronounced *Toizu Aru Asu*, which would be closer to the original English pronunciation).

Should General Foods be pronounced *Je-ne-ra-ru Fu-do-zu* (which, although closer to the original English pronunciation, sounds harsh and stilted to the Japanese ear), or (as was decided) *Je-ne-ra-ru Fu-zu*? Usually the deciding factor is how the pronunciation sounds to the Japanese ear rather than the pronunciation closest to the original English.

Thus, a popular coffee shop in Tokyo whose name is written in roman letters, "Almond," is pronounced *A-ma-n-do* rather than a pronunciation closer to the original (which would be *A-ru-mo-n-do*). To the Japanese ear, in the cases mentioned the Japanese pronunciations decided upon are the best. They are considered easier on the ear and easier to pronounce. Obviously, the easier to read and pronounce, the better.

This seemingly arbitrary change of pronunciation is not limited to loanwords from the Western languages. When counting bottles in Japanese, one bottle is *ippon*, two bottles are *ni-hon*, and three are *san-bon*. Four bottles are *yon-hon*, and five bottles are *go-hon*. But six bottles are *rokk-pon*. Although the pronunciation is different for the last word (*hon*, *bon*, or *pon*), which defines "bottles" in this case, the *kanji* (Chinese ideogram) remains the same. In other words, the spelling of *hon* remains the same although the pronunciation changes. How do the Japanese know when to change the pronunciation? They can tell by the preceding *kanji*, in this case the *i* (pronounced *ichi* when unaccompanied by any other *kanji*), *ni*, *san*, and so on.

To complicate matters, long, thin objects (such as bottles or bananas) are counted using *hon* (or its derivatives), but round objects are counted using *ko*. *Ik-ko* is one, *ni-ko* is two, and so on. (These all remain *ko*, regardless of the number counted.) However, if you are counting something flat (tickets, paper), you count them as *ichi-mai*, *ni-mai*, *san-mai*.

Japanese pronunciation of non-Japanese products should be carefully considered, since it may have certain connotations in Japanese that it does not have in English. For example, the English word "glass" can mean either the material a drinking glass is made of or the drinking glass itself. In Japanese the word *gurasu* means only "drinking glass," whereas the word *garasu* means only the material out of which the drinking glass is made. Both *gurasu* and *garasu* are loanwords derived from the English word "glass." If the Acme Glass company called itself *Akumi Gurasu*, it would mean it was a company selling drinking glasses. If it called itself *Akumi Garasu*, it would be a glass manufacturer.

Care must also be taken with the pronunciation of non-Japanese family names when they are part of a company's name. A person with the family name Jordan should avoid having his name pronounced *jōdan* (which means "joke" in Japanese). In this case, it might be wiser to choose the pronunciation that is a bit harsher-sounding to the Japanese ear, *Jorudan*, which, by the way, does not have any specific meaning in Japanese.

Although it is a rare occurrence, some foreign names can pose particular problems: the family names Barlow and Barker sound like the Japanese words for "idiot." If you have a family name like mine, Mooney, you are out of luck. No matter how you try to pronounce it in Japanese, it sounds exactly like the name of one of the leading brands of baby diapers, Mū-ni!

THE WRITING SYSTEM

The Japanese writing system uses a combination of three alphabets. The base of the writing system is the Chinese characters (*kanji*), which are modified with *hiragana* and combined with *katakana* for loan words.

Kanji are used to express the meaning of most words (from which the pronunciation can be inferred). *Hiragana* are used to write inflectional endings, grammatical particles, and certain native Japanese words for which *kanji* do not exist. *Katakana* are used for loanwords from other languages, and sometimes for emphasis. All three alphabets are used together in writing. The two simpler alphabets (*hiragana* and *katakana*) are called *kana*, and are based on phonetic syllables.

Kanji

Kanji (the Chinese ideograms) each represent a word or part of a word. It is said that a minimum of almost 2,000 *kanji* must be learned in order to be able to read a Japanese newspaper.

There are 1,945 Chinese characters in the *jōyō kanji*, the list approved by the government in 1981 for use in publications for the general public and for writing names (however, large dictionaries may have 40,000 or more *kanji*). Before 1981, there was a list of 1,850 *kanji* selected in 1946 by the Ministry of Education for general use, *tōyō kanji*. An additional 284 characters were approved for writing names alone. The *jōyō kanji* are learned by the end of the ninth grade.

Practically every *kanji* corresponds to a word. Combining *kanji* allows other words to be formed. For example, "electricity" combined with "car" makes the word "train." *Kanji* are used for verbs, adjectives, and nouns.

Most *kanji* have more than one pronunciation or reading. There are two basic types of readings. *On yomi* are the pronunciations used when characters are used to write Chinese loanwords. These reflect an original Chinese pronunciation but as pronounced in Japanese. Some characters have more than one possible *on yomi* reading, reflecting loanwords that were imported from different parts of China, or during different historical periods. For most reading purposes, over 5,500 *on yomi* readings for Chinese characters must be understood.

Then there are the *kun yomi*, which are native Japanese words that have the same meaning as the character. They are, in effect, the Japanese words that the characters stand for (rather than represent). In addition to *on yomi*, most *kanji* have several *kun yomi* readings. For most reading purposes, you would have to understand over 6,000 *kun yomi* readings for Chinese characters. There are almost 70,000 combinations of Chinese characters to form Japanese words.

These readings/pronunciations are determined by the preceding or following *kanji*. If a *kanji* is used alone, or in combination with other *kanji*, the general rule says the reading is *on yomi*. If the *kanji* is used in combination with *hiragana*, the reading is usually *kun yomi*.

An example of the difference between *on yomi* and *kun yomi* is the single *kanji* for "mountain." When this *kanji* is preceded by the *kanji* for "Fuji," the two are read "*Fuji san*," which means "Mount Fuji." The "*san*" pronunciation is *on yomi*.

When the *kanji* for "mountain" is written by itself, it is pronounced "*yama,*" which is the Japanese word for "mountain." "*Yama*" is *kun yomi*. The two *kanji* for "Mount Fuji" would never be pronounced "*Fuji yama,*" only "*Fuji san.*"

Kanji have certain connotations that are not seen by the foreign advertiser when they are translated into English. A cosmetic ad might have the word "makeup" written in *katakana* as *meiku-appu* or the accepted abbreviated form *meiku* (make). But if the Japanese word *keshō* is used, the connotation is different although the meaning is the same. In both cases (*meiku-appu, keshō*), the foreign advertiser would see just the English translation "makeup." If the Japanese word *keshō* had been used, it would be written in *kanji*. The *kanji* is made up of two characters. The first is the character for *ke*, which means "transform," "disguise," "bewitching," or "to deceive." The second character, *shō*, means "powder" or "adornment." Thus, the literal translation of *keshō* is "bewitching powder" or "disguising powder." Obviously, the connotation is quite different from *meiku*, which is foreign-based and trendy.

In another example, an ad's copy, translated into English, might contain the word "wife." In the original Japanese the word used for wife could have been *oku-san* (written in *hiragana*), which originally came from the fact that during the Edo (1603–1867) period, nobles' houses were divided into the outer sanctum, which was for the husband (lord), and the inner sanctum, which was for the wife. Inner is *oku*, so wives were called *okugata* (literally "inner people"). This eventually changed to *oku-sama*.

On the other hand, the Japanese word used for wife could have been *nyōbō*, which is written in *kanji*. The *kanji* for *nyōbō* is made up of two characters. The first character, *nyō*, is read "woman" or "lady." The second character, *bō*, is read as "room." In the Heian (794–1185) period, court ladies had their own rooms, or *nyōbō*. In due course, *nyōbō* came to refer to the court ladies themselves. After a while the use of *nyōbō* spread downward to the other classes, and eventually came to be applied to housewives.

To further point out the difficulties, there is yet another Japanese word for "wife." This is *kami-san* (or, in a more formal context, *o-kami-san*), written in *hiragana*. It is usually used to mean "wife" only in the Tokyo area. In the Osaka area, *kami-san* refers to the female owner of tearooms, coffee shops, small snack restaurants, and, more commonly, bars.

These examples illustrate how difficult it is for English translation of Japanese ad copy to present the connotations behind the Japanese words used.

Kana: *Hiragana* and *Katakana*

The two *kana* alphabets are *hiragana* and *katakana*. Both were originally derived from *kanji* but were greatly simplified over the centuries. Each begins with a, i, u, e, and o. The remaining "letters" consist of these vowels combined with a consonant (ka, ki, ku, ke, ko, for example). The only exception is the *kana* n, which stands alone without a vowel.

Hiragana is a phonetic alphabet consisting of 46 syllables plus 25 sound variants called sonants and half-sonants. It is a cursive form commonly used for native Japanese words and any words of Chinese origin not to be written in *kanji*. *Hiragana* is usually used for grammatical endings of verbs, nouns, and adjectives, as well as for particles and several words of Japanese origin for which *kanji* do not exist.

Katakana, the other phonetic alphabet, consists of 46 syllables to represent the 72 distinct sounds within the Japanese language that are pronounced in the same manner as *hiragana* characters. The syllables were derived by writing various *kanji* in rigid block-form format; hence they have been called "square syllabary." *Katakana* is a noncursive (angular) form, and is most typically used for *gai-rai-go* (foreign loanwords), for Western names, for onomatopoeic expressions, to serve as a phonetic script in the pronunciation of *kanji*, for geographical place-names that

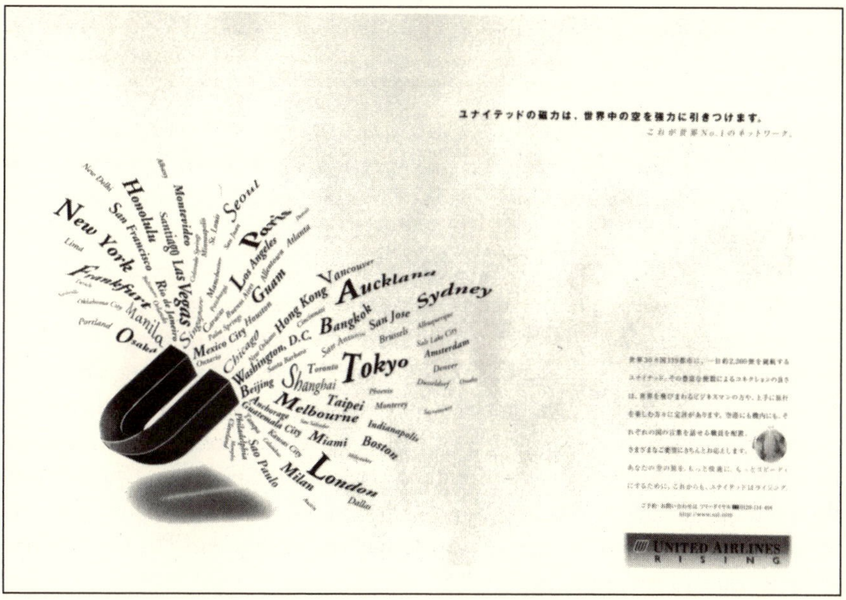

Plate 4.1
United Airlines
Japanese flair for using everyday objects to symbolize a brand's values is portrayed in this ad for United Airlines. Note the destination names are all in English. *(By permission of Dentsu Young & Rubicam, Inc., Tokyo)*

are not written in *kanji*, and/or for emphasis. The syllables of both *kana* scripts are used to express sounds rather than the meaning of individual words.

Rōma-ji

There is one more alphabet often used in Japanese in a supplementary manner, especially in advertising. This is *rōma-ji* (Roman letters). *Rōma-ji* is used for foreign words, often English, that appear in all aspects of marketing communications. Thus, *rōma-ji* is found throughout the nation on packaging, in ads, on signs, and so on (see Plate 4.1).

"JAPLISH" AND LOANWORDS IN JAPANESE ADS

It would be impossible to calculate the number of, and catalog the origins of, all the loanwords used in Japanese. Some words have been part of the Japanese vocabulary for so long that they are now considered Japanese words. Others, which may be in vogue now, will soon disappear and be replaced by other short-lived expressions. At any rate, a decade or so ago, researchers decided that more than 10% of the currently popular Japanese vocabulary consisted of loanwords. And the percentage is still growing. No one would dare to predict what colloquial Japanese will sound like in 10 or 20 years.

While the Japanese have borrowed words from a variety of languages (including French, German, Dutch, Portuguese, and Italian), the vast majority come from English. For naming new inventions like television or the internet, the Japanese often do not create new words in Japanese but use loanwords. Most loanwords are written in *katakana.*

It is beyond dispute that the mass media are the leading source of new loanwords. News programs, documentaries, game and quiz shows, sports, even dramas add more and more foreign words and phrases to the Japanese language. But their contributions pale beside the additions stemming from the eye-catching slogans in print advertising and TV commercials. An example of a loanword that made the transition from ads to common language years ago can be seen in Kose's lipstick ad, which says, "*kuchibiru, happi?*," which translates as "lips, happy?" "Happy" is also used in the Japanese context in an ad for the Walker Hill Casino in Seoul, aimed at young Japanese women, which says, "*Rakki ga happi ni.*" The literal translation is "Lucky becomes happy."

Sometimes the word retains its original meaning. More often than not, however, it takes on a new or limited meaning when adopted into Japanese. In Japanese, the loanword *abeku*, from the French word *avec* (with), refers to a couple in love. In the process of being borrowed, changes are often made in structure and pronunciation. In baseball, for example, a strike is called a *sutoraiku.* But a union strike at a factory is called a *sutoraiki* (usually abbreviated to *suto*). Handkerchiefs have become *hankachi*; building has become *biru*; department store, *depāto*; and personal computers, *pasokon*. Even in the ad industry, words have been created by shortening the original English words. Examples include *rokehan* (location hunt), *masukomi* (mass communication), *tesuto* (test), and *gera* (guarantee, or fee paid to a model).

While some words are abbreviated, for others the meaning is changed. Thus, a *kūra* (cooler) in Japanese is an air conditioner (also called *ea-kon*). When something is *sābisu* (service), it means it is free of charge. *Sutando-purē* (grandstand play) is "grandstanding." *Se-biro* (Saville Row) is a word for a business suit. *Pantsu* (pants) is restricted to references to underwear.

There has been much ado about the inclusion of English words and phrases in Japanese ads. It is commonly pointed out that English is too difficult for the average Japanese to understand and is, more often than not, grammatically incorrect. This is undoubtedly true of many of the phrases found in many ads. A perfect example is Alba's ad for its new wristwatch. The headline, in English, says, "New Face Spoon." Other examples of strange use of English in Japanese ads include Rover's MG ad with the headline "Air." And cigarette ads by Japan Tobacco tend to use strange English, such as the ad for its Zephyr brand, which says, "Make your story," and the ad for their Valiant brand, which says, "Men's soul. Men's Hard Menthol."

What is usually not commented upon is the huge use of loanwords in ads. This usually goes unnoticed by foreigners because the loanwords are written in *katakana*. Some estimates say that as much as 80% of all Japanese advertising contains at least one loanword.

When used in Japanese and written in *katakana*, some loanwords have only one meaning or usage. For example, *akusesari* (accessory) refers only to artificial or costume jewelry. Hats, ties, scarves, and other such objects that are included in the English definition of the word have other terms in Japanese.

Loanwords often become "Japanized" by shortening, limiting, combining, or extending the original foreign words to the extent that they are incomprehensible to native speakers. It would take a special imagination to link *mai-kon* with the English "microcomputer." *Ame-futo* is a long way from "American football." In English "ice" refers to a frozen substance. But in Japanese the term *aisu* is restricted to ice cream, iced tea, and/or iced coffee.

The Japanese also create new Japanized English words. Famous examples are "walkman" and "salaryman," a Japanese word for a typical company worker. Japanized English words are commonly used in ads, such as Mazda's ad for its Roadster, which says *"Opun ka to kuraso,"* "Let's live with open car." In Japan, convertibles are called *opun ka* (open cars).

In many cases, loanwords are only used in combinations. *On-za-rokku* fills in for scotch "on the rocks."

Most loanwords are nouns in their original language. But in Japan they are often used as verbs by adding a verb ending or verb. Others merely add *suru* to make a verb. *Dabingu suru* for "dubbing" or "to dub" comes to mind.

Loanwords are frequently blended with *kanji* or other loanwords to make a new word. *Denwa fakkusu* is a telephone/fax machine; *doa-tsu-doa* means from one place to another.

Although the pronunciation of loanwords usually resembles the pronunciation in the original language, adjustments have to be made to conform to the Japanese phonetic system. And when these words are written in *katakana*, even the most skillful nonnative speakers of Japanese are often hard-pressed to come up with the original spelling of the word.

The Japanese pronunciation of those loanwords can be rather different from the original pronunciation: for example, curtain = *kāten*, elevator = *erebētā*, girl = *gāru*.

Adding to the confusion are the frequent cases of loanwords being abbreviated or combined with Japanese words or other loanwords. These loanwords have no resemblance to their original source, such as *sūpā* = supermarket, *kiro* = kilometer and kilogram, *depāto* = department store, *wā-puro* = word processor.

Finally, the rules of grammar that applied to the loanword in its original language are often disregarded when it is used in Japanese. Prepositions become nouns, nouns become verbs, and conjunctions and suffixes just disappear. All in all, for the foreigner, confusion abounds.

ENGLISH IN JAPAN

The average Japanese receives six years of mandatory English-language education, and most can understand basic English words and sentences. Overall, though, reading ability is stronger than speaking ability and comprehension. The Japanese basically learn only English grammar in school, rather than conversation or comprehension. As a result, although they can understand rudimentary English, their overall English-speaking ability is generally poor to nonexistent.

Foreign tourists to Japan are sometimes surprised that although the Japanese they encounter cannot converse with them even in simple English, if the tourists write out their English sentences, the Japanese understand them more completely.

Foreign words in ads are considered a tool for capturing viewer attention. Of course, the words used are usually related to the product or service in some way. An example is Wrangler's ad for its khaki jeans, which says, "Real. Comfortable. Pants." More to the point is Nestlé's ad for its Excella instant coffee. The headline in English reads "Wake up!" Foreign words are also considered to add authenticity to the product's appeal or message (Plate 4.2).

Then again, sometimes the inclusion of foreign words in a Japanese ad is just a design element that the audience does not necessarily have to understand. This

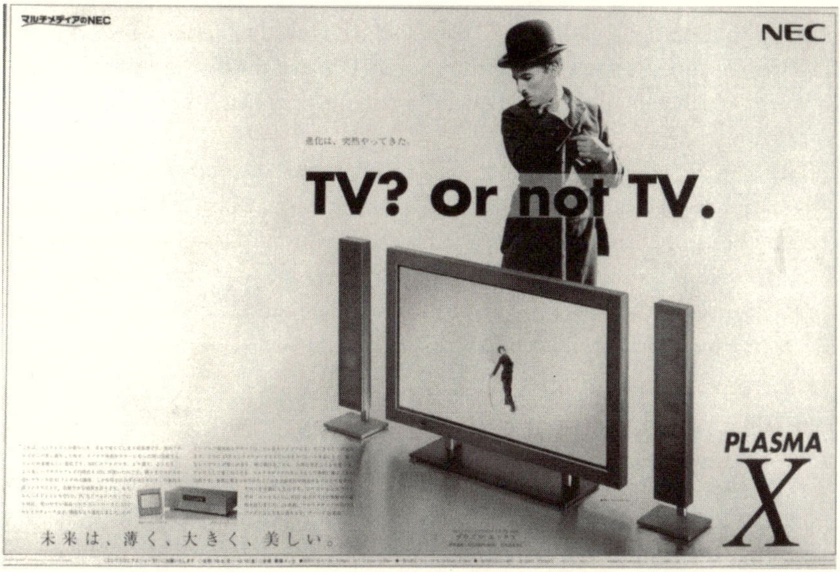

Plate 4.2
NEC Plasma X
This example of Japanese creativity utilizes simple English head copy to assert a powerful message. Visually, the contrast between the Charlie Chaplin look-alike and the modern design of the monitor seizes the audience's attention. *(By permission of Dentsu Young & Rubicam, Inc., Tokyo)*

fact worked in favor of Virginia Slims cigarettes. When the Philip Morris brand came on the market over ten years ago, the brand's U.S. tag line, "You've come a long way, baby," was retained for the Japanese market. The message was not understood, and did not have much relevance to Japanese women. But, due to the overall impression of the ad, women responded positively. Another example of this use of English as a design element is the ad for Yamazaki whiskey, which says in English, "A tree with a century life."

On the other hand, English is often used in a manner that, while understandable to the Japanese consumer, can sound odd to a native English-speaker. One of the most famous examples of Japlish in Japanese advertising for a foreign brand is Coca-Cola's tag line "I Feel Coke." Kanebo, one of Japan's leading cosmetic firms, for years has used the tag line "For Beautiful Human Life." English tag lines are common, such as Nestlé's "Good food, good life"; Panasonic's "What's new Panasonic"; and Mazda's "That's Mazda," which are included in all ads.

Years ago, when Seven-Up tried to translate its slogan "Wet and Wild," tests showed it was unsuitable for Japan. In Japanese the English term "wet" (pronounced *wetto*) is used to describe a person with an emotional personality, as opposed to the English term "dry" (*dorai*), which is used to define a person with a frank personality. As a result of testing, Seven-Up used the line "Fresh and Sharp" in Japan, which had all the same qualities and nuances that "Wet and Wild" had in English.

This all makes sense to the Japanese consumer, who knows that if he or she says "American" in a restaurant in any part of Japan, he or she will receive a cup of weak coffee. The same consumer has no qualms about putting "Creap" in his or her coffee. After all, it's a milk substitute that is a major brand. If the consumer is at home, chances are he or she will go to the refrigerator and take out a can of Calpis or Pocari Sweat to quench his or her thirst on a hot day!

THE WRITTEN LANGUAGE OF COPYWRITERS

With three alphabets available, plus *rōma-ji*, Japanese copywriters have much more leeway than their Western counterparts. This is especially true since Japanese can be written vertically (top to bottom), horizontally (left to right), and even diagonally. Technically, Japanese can also be written from right to left, although this practice has fallen out of use.

English words in Japanese copy can be written in either *rōma-ji* or *katakana*. In advertising and packaging, *rōma-ji* is liberally used. However, it is not always used as copy. Often the inclusion of *rōma-ji* in an ad is considered a design element rather than copy. It is there for the look it gives the ad, not for its meaning.

For some reason, copywriters believe that foreign words add class or mystique to their copy. It makes no difference that the average reader doesn't understand the message. That is not required. What does matter is that the text evokes an image and attaches prestige value to the product being advertised (Plate 4.3).

Japanese copy is usually written to appeal to the emotions rather than to be direct, logical, and informative. There is a strong tendency toward copy that tends to be poetic rather than to spell out the functions of a product. Japanese consumers dislike garrulous sales messages, and respond better to advertising copy that is presented in a short, indirect manner. An easy-to-understand example is Coca-Cola's copy that says "I feel Coke," in English.

Japanese copy is unique in that each *kanji* and/or *kana*, no matter how complex or simple, takes up one unit of space. Thus, the Japanese copywriter can accurately write for a given space. And with the exception of headlines, Japanese copy can be broken anywhere. Hyphens are not used.

One result of each character/syllable taking up one unit of space, rather than being proportionally spaced, is that the resulting block of copy can often look splotchy. (The simplest single-stroke *kanji* is given the same space as the most complicated 23-stroke character!)

Plate 4.3
Cross
Japanese use of a visual to convey subtle nuances of history and elegance is highlighted in this ad for Cross pens. The headline whimsically asks, "When you want to send a lasting message, what do you hold in your hand?" *(By permission of Dentsu Young & Rubicam, Inc., Tokyo)*

Japanese copywriters usually still use copy sheets to write the copy by hand. The sheets are like graph paper in that they are printed with lined squares on them. Copywriters write one *kanji*, *hiragana*, or *katakana* per square. They later type up the finalized copy on a computer. The copy sheets are calculated for 200 or 400 spaces. There is general agreement as to what copy lengths are ideal. For example, a double-page spread would normally require one 200-space copy sheet. Phrases should usually be shorter than two lines of copy sheet.

There are several regulatory agencies restraining excesses in copy. Any copy for drugs/medicines must be checked by the Medical Department of the Ministry of Public Welfare. Any contest or prize promotion must abide by rules set by the Fair Trade Commission. In addition, many industries, such as banking and photographic, electronic, and automotive products, have self-regulatory standards on copy. Most major media vehicles also have copy standards that are enforced. The aim of all these rules and regulations is to avoid excessive and misleading claims.

JAPANESE TYPEFACES

The wide variety of typefaces available in the West is not available to the Japanese typographer because the number of the characters required for a single font would be over 2,000!

Basically, there are two fonts available. All others are variations of these two popularly used families of Japanese typeface, *Mincho* and *Gochiku*.

Mincho is roughly comparable with the Times Roman family of typefaces in the West. It has thick and thin strokes and spurs that can be compared with serifs. It is the most Chinese-looking typeface, and thus the most traditional (because its characters resemble calligraphic brush strokes). It is most commonly used for body copy because of its legibility.

Gochiku, the other major typeface family commonly used in Japan, is roughly comparable with Western Gothics (Helvetica, Arial, and others) and is used mainly in headlines. Its characters are simplified so that there are no variations in the width of the strokes. Generally speaking, *Gochiku* gives a modern, bolder, heavier feeling to copy, whereas *Mincho* gives a traditional or softer feeling to the copy.

Occasionally, when a traditional effect is required, calligraphy or hand-brush lettering is used in copy. This is usually limited to headlines only, unless the product is something like a traditional green tea.

CONCLUSION

Unless foreign advertisers have a strong understanding of Japanese, they will be reviewing English translations of copy (for print advertising) or narration (for TV and radio commercials) that are one or several steps removed from the original nuance and meaning of the original Japanese copy. That translation will never sound like copy in English.

However, there are several things foreign advertisers can do to make the copy review process easier. First, they must make sure they have a clear understanding of the purpose of the copy/narration. Is it declaring something? Or is it trying to persuade the audience of something?

Next, they must ask what tone the copy/translation is written in. Is it appropriate for the purpose the ad/commercial is trying to accomplish? Is it appropriate for the target audience? If there are differing opinions, Japanese colleagues whose opinions are respected should be asked. If confusion still reigns, those Japanese who represent the target audience should be queried.

If the ad contains any English, it must be clear whether it is supposed to get a message across through its original English meaning or its Japanese meaning or if it is there to give the ad a certain "feel."

In any case, it is not impossible to get a complete understanding of what a Japanese ad is saying, and how it is saying it. It just entails a bit more time and effort. When it comes to the subtle nuances, foreign advertisers will have to depend on the opinions of Japanese colleagues whose opinions they respect and trust.

Chapter 5

◆◆◆

Kōkoku Dairi-ten
Advertising Agencies in Japan

Can companies that produce movies, television programs, and cartoon shows be called ad agencies? In the case of Japan's major ad agencies (*kōkoku dairi-ten* in Japanese), the answer is often yes. While Japan's ad industry is dominated by Japanese agencies, most of the major multinational agencies are present in Japan. Though they have their share of expatriates, the vast majority of their staff are Japanese. Thus, the basic question facing the foreign advertiser is, "What's the difference between the multinationals and the Japanese ad agencies?"

THE ORIGINS OF AD AGENCIES IN JAPAN

As the world's second largest advertising market, it comes as no surprise that Japan boasts a huge number of ad agencies, from one-man operations to those employing thousands.

According to the Ministry of Trade and Industry, as of December 1996 there were 4,705 ad agencies in Japan employing 91,041 people. Tokyo led the pack with 1,069 agencies employing 40,132 people, followed by Osaka with 620 agencies employing 13,430 people. Only about 130 agencies belong to the official Advertising Agency Association.

Japan's leading agencies are roughly a century old and have reigned supreme for decades. Both Dentsu and Hakuhodo began primarily as media space brokers. Dentsu, which traces its roots back to 1901, is the largest ad agency in Japan. About 95% of its business is domestic, and it accounts for around 25% of all advertising expenditure. Second-ranked Hakuhodo, founded in 1895, controls 10% of Japan's total advertising billings.

All told, the top ten agencies in Japan account for just over 50% of all advertising, whereas the top ten in the U.S. hold an aggregate 16% share of national advertising expenditure. Many of the major Japanese advertising agencies are members of one of Japan's large commercial groups, a pattern that is found in other industries. Dai-ichi Kikaku belongs to the Mitsubishi group of companies; Tokyu Agency and I&S are members of the Tokyu and Saison retailing groups, respectively. Daiko, Yomiuri, Asahi, and Nihon Keizaisha are each linked with a leading newspaper—the *Mainichi Shimbun*, the *Yomiuri Shimbun*, the *Asahi Shimbun*, and the *Nihon Keizai Shimbun*, respectively. Group membership is an entrenched feature of the business scene in Japan in all industries, and seldom has much bearing on the selection of an advertising agency. Table 5.1 lists the top 20 advertising agencies in Japan in 1997. However, Dentsu and Hakuhodo, the two largest agencies, are both independent of Japan's commercial groups and, like all agencies except Asatsu, are privately held.

Table 5.1
Top 20 Advertising Agencies in Japan, 1997

Ranking	Agency	Billings (¥ million)
1	Dentsu	1,335,054
2	Hakuhodo	709,782
3	Asatsu (Asahi Tsushin)	200,274
4	Tokyu Agency	198,250
5	Daiko	170,115
6	Yomiuri (Yomiko)	127,771
7	Dai-ichi Kikaku	113,789
8	I & S	107,057
9	JR East Japan Advertising	83,993
10	McCann-Erickson	78,099
11	Asahi Advertising	71,752
12	Nihon Keizaisha	53,246
13	Sogei	48,821
14	Orikomi	47,721
15	Dentsu Young & Rubicam	44,498
16	Nippo	42,247
17	J. Walter Thompson	42,081
18	Chuo Senko Advertising	41,371
19	Nihon Keizai Kokokusha	40,032
20	Mannensha	39,732

Source: Senden Kaigi (January 1999).

Most of the multinational ad agencies have established operations in Japan in some form, either as wholly owned operations, joint ventures, or affiliations. Of the major multinational agencies, J. Walter Thompson has the longest history, having established an office in Japan in 1956. McCann-Erickson opened its offices as a joint venture with Hakuhodo in 1960. Grey formed a joint venture with Daiko in 1963, and Dailey & Associates (the forerunner of Kenyon & Eckhard, now known as Bozell) formed a business affiliation with Meiji Tsūshin-sha (the present Meitsu) in 1968. This later became Meitsu BJK&E in 1986, Bozell Meitsu in 1989, and finally Bozell Worldwide in 1994, when Bozell took over 100% of the operation.

In 1976 Leo Burnett formed Leo Burnett-Kyodo, a joint venture with Kyodo Advertising, and in 1981 Young & Rubicam merged its wholly owned subsidiary with JIMA Dentsu, creating Dentsu Young & Rubicam. Orikomi Bates, established in 1981 as a joint venture, became Bates Japan in 1994 when Bates acquired majority equity. Ogilvy & Mather opened a Japanese office in affiliation with Tokyu Agency International in 1983. A wholly owned subsidiary followed but was soon closed. O&M opened its third agency in 1995.

Regardless of their size globally, the operations of most foreign agencies in Japan are quite small.

MEDIA SPACE-SELLING VERSUS SPACE-BUYING

Though media-buying companies have flourished in the U.S. and in European markets, Japan was the first country to introduce media-buying over a century ago. Japanese agencies started business that way and are now the most formidable buyers in the world. The advertising industry in Japan is based on space-buying ability. This emphasis goes back to the roots of the nation's ad industry.

An ad agency's ability to buy media space is of the utmost importance in Japan, and it varies greatly from agency to agency.

Japanese ad agencies evolved similarly to their counterparts in the West. As Japanese newspapers developed as a medium over a century ago, independent agencies were established to solicit advertisements on their behalf. Once the agencies had won a commitment, they forwarded the copy (ads consisted only of copy text at the time) to the newspapers. The agencies then received a commission on the value of the space they sold. The agencies sold space in as many newspapers as they could.

The key to understanding Japanese agencies' relationship with the media lies in the fact that the media are perceived as clients. The agency is selling the media "client's" space, for which service the media pay the agency a share of the gross proceeds. This attitude remains deeply ingrained in Japanese ad agencies. The influx of Western advertising norms since the end of World War II has introduced the concept of the advertiser as "client." Today, when a client places an ad, the agency acts on behalf of both the client and the media vehicle. The booking of ad space is not only a space-buying transaction (on the client's behalf) but also a space-selling transaction on the media vehicle's behalf.

American ad agencies also got their beginnings by selling space in newspapers. However, from the beginning they charged the client a commission on the net space cost. They were not paid by the media. Another difference is that Japanese ad agencies began buying the ad space first (initially in newspapers, later in magazines, then time on radio, and television) and then selling it. Again, the media, not the clients, paid the agencies a commission on the net space cost. This practice of prebuying still exists. Dentsu and Hakuhodo, Japan's largest agencies, began primarily as media space brokers.

At about the same time some agencies were selling space in a variety of media vehicles, other agencies appeared that had exclusive links with particular newspapers. These agencies, which were specifically established by those newspapers to sell their space, include Asahi Advertising (for the *Asahi Shimbun*) and Yomiuri Advertising (for the *Yomiuri Shimbun*). Realizing the advantages of having an agency that would concentrate solely on ensuring the best space-buys, certain corporate groups established their own house agencies. Tokyu Agency (for the Tokyu Group) and Dai-ichi Kikaku (for the Mitsubishi Group) are two examples.

Inevitably, some agencies began to buy large volumes of space in advance and then sell it piecemeal. Publishers encouraged this practice because the agencies were financing them by prebuying the space, as well as saving them an enormous amount of work. The agencies could take advantage of the substantial discounts offered by publishers on volume purchases of space. This meant that the agencies not only provided good space for their clients but also offered it at competitive rates. The agencies could also make a tidy profit by selling the space to smaller agencies, who could not buy space directly, at a considerable profit. The smaller agencies benefited by being able to buy the space at a lower rate than the newspapers' card rates, a practice that continues today. For obvious reasons this type of prior space-buying is mainly limited to the biggest agencies. "Prior" buying tactics are not limited to newspapers; they also apply to TV airtime and magazine space.

Another method of obtaining newspaper space during the establishment of the advertising industry in Japan was the barter of news for ad space. Agencies that practiced this specialized in the communications and wire services (*tsūshin* in Japanese) that were similar to UPI today. Though this practice no longer exists, traces of it can be found in the names of some of the present Japanese ad agencies. Dentsu's name is actually short for *dempo tsūshin*. Some other examples are Asatsu (which stands for *Asahi tsūshin-sha*) and Standard Advertising (whose Japanese name is *Standard tsūshin-sha*).

The initial media space-buying function of Japanese ad agencies is responsible for the present major agencies that are strong in media-buying, and thus able to handle competing accounts. A select few of the very largest agencies continue to buy space in advance, and worry later about selling it to clients. They thereby continue to finance the media by paying in advance and are also financing clients in that the clients do not have to pay up front.

Although the advertising media often have their own sales divisions to sell ad space, such divisions usually depend heavily on the sales of the major ad agencies who deal with clients directly. Ad space is often periodically sold or contracted to the major agencies to be sold to their clients or to secondary agencies. In Japan, ad agencies consider both advertisers and media to be their clients.

THE REQUIREMENT FOR *KŌZA*: BUYING MEDIA SPACE

An ad agency in Japan that wants to buy ad space in mass media must first have an account (*kōza* in Japanese) with the media vehicle in question. A media vehicle will not sell space directly to a client or to an ad agency with which it has not had prior dealings. Rather, it will introduce the client to an agency that has an account with that media vehicle. In addition to the largest ad agencies, many of the middle-sized agencies have accounts with certain vehicles that they frequently use. Thus they can buy directly from these vehicles; if a client asks the agency to buy ad space in a vehicle with which the agency does not have an account, the agency has to buy through another agency that does.

However, just because an agency has an account with a vehicle and/or steadily places a high volume of ads in the vehicle does not mean it can get space whenever it wants to. Media vehicles try to ensure all agencies having an account with them have access to space in proportion to their regularly placed volume. When an agency wins a new account and that client wants space in a certain magazine, the agency may find it difficult to acquire the space because it has already used up its allocation for other clients.

Ad space is at a premium in Japan because neither magazines nor newspapers add pages on an issue-to-issue basis to allow more advertising. Newspapers are limited in the number of pages they can print by the cost charged to them by their distributors. Additionally, to take advantage of lower taxes on distribution costs, they are required to keep the advertising-to-article ratio below 50%. Most popular magazines are already so thick, and correspondingly heavy, that adding pages is not practical. Television and radio broadcast 24 hours a day. Television is restricted in its advertising-to-program ratio and already airs as many commercials as legally permitted.

Media vehicles limit the number of agencies that can have an account with them. Thus, accounts are exclusive and not easily acquired. Some of the major magazines allow fewer than ten agencies to buy space directly. *Katei Gaho*, a popular mature-woman's magazine, is one of these. *Kodansha*, a major magazine publisher, has allowed only about 40 agencies to open accounts with it. Newspapers are no exception. The *Asahi Shimbun* has allowed only around 50 agencies to open accounts with it.

To deal with a media vehicle directly, an agency has to negotiate to open an account. If the vehicle is a popular one, its owner may decide that it already has all its space sold each year to the agencies that have accounts with it. Allowing another agency to open an account means that the vehicle owner will have to decrease the number of ad pages that agencies with existing accounts can access. The vehicle may decide against doing this.

If, however, the media vehicle is amenable to the agency's opening an account, it will check the reliability of the agency. In particular, close scrutiny is given to whether the agency has the ability to undertake financial risk. The existence of positive interpersonal relations is also taken into account. Often, even if the opening of an account is approved, the agency is required to pay in advance, or even to deposit substantial guarantee money with the media vehicle.

Unsurprisingly, the vast majority of the roughly 4,500 ad agencies in Japan cannot buy media space. Even among the agencies that can buy space, some find themselves being asked at times to buy space in a media vehicle with which they do not have an account. In these cases, the agency has to buy through another ad agency that has an account with the media vehicle in question. Rarely is the client informed of this.

When a client's agency buys space through another agency, there is the problem of commission to be settled between the agencies. Whether the client (unwittingly or knowingly) pays double commission (full commission to each agency) or the agencies split the regular commission is negotiated on a case-by-case basis by the agencies. Most Japanese clients do not require their agencies to attach copies of third-party invoices to the agency invoice, so the client has no way of knowing the real costs. In the case of print media, the commission paid to the agency by the media vehicle is sometimes more than the traditional 15% of gross cost. A rule of thumb is that a combination of low circulation and a large proportion of circulation outside the major metropolitan areas of Tokyo and Osaka usually means higher commissions. As some Western clients have become aware of the situation, they have insisted that their agency split the commission (based on 15% of gross cost). Otherwise, they limit their agency to handling only the creative work, assigning media space-buying to another agency.

As can be seen, it is the ability to buy media space that determines the major players among Japanese ad agencies. Of course, among the agencies that can buy space, the stars are those that, due to their volume of buying, can access the best positions and timings. A result of this focus on media-buying ability is that many of the leaders of Japanese agencies worked their way up from the media department. Conversely, in the West, the leaders of agencies traditionally come from the account and creative ranks. Unsurprisingly, the agencies with media-buying capabilities are the ones ranked at the top in Japan.

Interestingly, in 1996 the total billings handled by foreign agencies in Japan was about ¥300 billion. Half of that amount was media space-buying handled for the foreign agencies by Dentsu and Hakuhodo.

With so much media-buying concentration, advertisers new to Japan are sometimes worried whether any but the few top Japanese agencies have enough clout to negotiate and buy media competitively. This is not a problem. Aside from a number of Japanese agencies, McCann-Erickson and J. Walter Thompson are among the top buyers in some categories of media. However, advertisers who wish to implement or change plans at short notice may find it hard to get good media space or airtime regardless of who their agency is. Those who planned ahead will have gotten there first. Some major advertisers, like Kao and Nestlé, have been making certain buys for over a decade. As a result, certain space is totally locked up.

AGENCY–CLIENT RELATIONSHIPS

Relationships between the major Japanese agencies and their Japanese clients tend to be permanent. The leading advertisers each use a number of agencies, and although assignments may move around, and billings may fluctuate, the ties are more enduring than is the norm elsewhere in the world.

In other countries, Western clients very often have contracts with their agencies, and switch agencies from time to time. In Japan, major account moves are still rarer than elsewhere.

Usually, the bonds between Japanese agencies and advertisers are based on custom and precedent, not on a written contract. When problems arise, both sides try to resolve them in the context of the relationship. It is unheard of for Japan's trade press to announce a major advertiser's decision to stop advertising through one agency and to start a new relationship with another. A rare exception was the announcement that Nissan was removing Dentsu from its agency roster and consolidating its advertising in its three remaining agencies (Hakuhodo, Standard, and Nippo) in the early 1990s.

HOW JAPANESE AGENCIES HANDLE CONFLICTING ACCOUNTS

In Japan, a Japanese client rarely assigns its entire account to one agency, as is common practice everywhere else in the world. Japanese clients usually appoint a group of designated agencies. These agencies may be assigned parts of specific brands, launching campaigns, buying media, handling sales promotions, and so on. One agency might handle creative print work (and its media placement), another handles TV creative work (and its placement), and yet another handles radio commercials (and their placement).

Yet, no designated agency's account is protected. Each is constantly pitching for other parts of the business in order to enlarge its share of the pie. In addition, outside agencies can come in and pitch their ideas whenever the client allows.

Often the agencies must repitch for their business, and pieces of the other work business, every several months. So the agency that handles the print creative work and space-buying today might lose that business but win the TV creative work and placement. Again the variations are endless. This results in a project-by-project mentality among the agencies and, among clients, makes many projects one-shot deals. This occurs when an agency that is not on a client's roster comes up with an idea and sells it to the client, the most common practice among agencies to get their foot in the door and generate new business. It is hoped that the client will be so pleased with the result of the project, and that close interpersonal relationships will have been built during the project, that the agency can pitch for more business.

In working with their agencies, Japanese clients often separate media and creative assignments for a particular product. Sometimes one agency will be used to buy magazine space, another to buy national newspaper space, a third for spot TV, and so on. This pattern reflects the historical role of the agencies as media brokers. Sometimes a campaign includes creative work from two or more agencies, and several handling specific media assignments. In 1988 Suntory's campaign for its dry beer featured posters with Mike Tyson, by Dentsu, and with the Australian Rules football player, Jacko, by Hakuhodo.

This means that at some point during the year, one of the designated agencies may be in charge of TV space-buying and creating TV commercials. Later in the year, it may lose that business to another agency. However, it may gain the below-the-line and PR activities for a different brand under the client's umbrella. During this entire time, two other agencies could be handling magazine and newspaper advertising, respectively. There are endless variations.

Usually the designated agencies enjoy a long-term relationship with the client. It is rare that an agency is taken off the roster. Although its piece of the account may be constantly changing, the relationship with the client remains. Clients believe this system gives them access to more fresh ideas and keeps the agencies on their toes to do a good job.

One advantage for clients who allow several agencies to handle their account is that, either by playing agencies off each other or by threatening to do so, they can easily know if each agency is giving them the best media buy and passing on any discounts negotiated with the media. Each agency is kept guessing as to what the other is offering the client.

This system of assigning agencies gives rise to business practices unique to Japanese agencies. First, Japanese agencies have a "damn the minimum billings" attitude and will take on any job they can get. The theory is that even if you lose money on a small job, you will make it up on the big job that will come your way if you do a good job. The potential for growth is more important than immediate billings. Second, since agencies do not have an entire account, they have no qualms about pitching for the account of a competitor of their present client. They can often convince the competitor client that they already have experience in its industry.

The concentration of clients in major agencies in Japan is possible because Japanese clients allow their agencies to handle conflicting accounts. If they did not, it would have been impossible for the top Japanese agencies to become the size they are today.

Agencies in Japan handle competing clients with impunity. Most agencies have more than one client per industry. Japanese clients are relatively tolerant of their agency's handling of a competing client's account, so long as it is not handled by the same account group.

Nowhere is this more clearly demonstrated than at Dentsu. Toyota, Honda, and Subaru are all clients. So, too, are the brewers Kirin, Asahi, Sapporo, and Suntory. Matsushita, Hitachi, Toshiba, Sanyo, Sharp, and Sony are among Dentsu's electronics clients, and Kao, Unicharm, Lion, and P&G all give Dentsu assignments in the personal care markets.

Agency size makes it easy to separate and handle competing accounts. In Tokyo, Dentsu has 31 account service divisions, six creative divisions, and several buildings.

While clients accept sharing their agency with their competitors as the price of having an agency that can buy media directly, it tends to inhibit them from allowing the agency to become too deeply involved in their marketing plans. The reasoning behind this decision is that it is considered too risky to entrust market planning to an agency that handles competing accounts, regardless of how much the agency insists that the teams on the competing accounts will be kept completely separate.

Thus, Japanese companies on the whole tend to keep most marketing functions within the company rather than relying on ad agencies to provide these services. They tend to depend on their ad agency mostly for mass-media advertising (creative and media-buying) and sales promotions. Much of the sales promotion work is farmed out by the ad agency to sales promotion companies.

In-channel promotions, aimed at wholesalers and retailers, remain very much the domain of the client, although the ad agency may be called upon for assistance from time to time.

As a result, the marketing service provided by Japanese agencies is not nearly as comprehensive as that of foreign ad agencies, and therefore the many foreign ad agencies in Japan find it difficult to recruit staff with the necessary marketing capabilities/experience demanded by their foreign clients. This basically explains why, although many of the major ad agencies in Japan offer full marketing services, their marketing service lags far behind that of ad agencies in the West.

Since the bursting of Japan's bubble economy, the nation's prolonged recession, abetted by the high yen, has cut corporate profits and prompted an examination of agency–client relationships.

Accountability, cost-effectiveness, improved efficiency, and performance are the watchwords for advertisers today, and have become a key part of the new vocabulary in Japan's advertising industry. During the past few years, most major advertisers have been quietly reducing their roster of agencies. Toshiba, for example, which used to split its ¥24 billion budget among almost 30 agencies, now uses fewer than a dozen, with most of the money going through Dentsu, Hakuhodo, and Asatsu.

DIFFERENCES IN AGENCY STRUCTURE

While they may share the same titles, the people working in Japanese ad agencies have different responsibilities than do their counterparts in the West. It should be noted that the English titles on business cards do not always match the Japanese titles on the other side. The Japanese titles show the person's real standing within his or her company.

While Japanese ad agencies provide their employees with the same titles as Western ad agencies, the similarity ends there. In Japanese agencies there is commonly no job description attached to a title. Employees are valued for their ability to work as members of the organization, and to do things that have to be done without being told, whether or not those things are within their day-to-day realm of activities.

Traditionally, major full-service ad agencies in Japan have been involved in a wider range of activities than their counterparts in the West. These can range from new product packaging to product naming, trade shows, expositions, receptions, sales promotions, PR, and many other activities.

One of the first differences between Japanese agencies and non-Japanese agencies that is usually noticed by foreigners is that the account service departments of Japanese agencies seem huge, while the creative departments seem tiny. The ratio of 90:10 for account executives to creative personnel is often used to describe Japanese agencies in general.

Several reasons can be given for the account service department in a Japanese agency being larger than that usually found in the West. The most obvious is that the Japanese business culture still requires frequent face-to-face meetings for matters that in the West could be handled by a phone call, fax, or E-mail. In Japan, there is much more emphasis on verbal communication than on communication through the use of paper/electronics. (A parallel to this can be seen in the open office plans in Japan, where the whole group can constantly hear what's being discussed by any member of the group.) The large size of account service departments in Japanese agencies is also justified by the fact that Japanese clients expect higher levels of service and greater frequency of meetings (including socializing) than are usually demanded by non-Japanese clients.

The Japanese word for account executives is *eigyō*, which actually means "sales." This gives a good indication of their function in the agency. The vast majority of AEs in Japan are males. Among the many reasons that have been suggested for this is the traditional belief that women will leave the agency after marriage or childbirth, and thus do not justify the agency's time and effort in developing their skills, and that (male) clients would not feel as comfortable being entertained after hours by a woman. In regard to utilizing females as AEs, Japanese ad agencies are woefully behind Western agencies. A vast pool of talent is being underutilized.

For a long time, creativity was not a major concern of Japanese agencies, since they were primarily media space suppliers. The mentality that "creativity can be bought" still remains. Most agencies make heavy use of freelancers, not just for the execution/production of an ad but even for idea generation.

The reason for this ties in with the proportionally smaller creative division in a Japanese agency. This is a result of the seniority system. If an agency has to give a creative director pay raises as he gets older, even if his creativity falls off, an agency could lose money. On the other hand, if a creative director (CD) does excellent work, why should his salary be limited by the company seniority system, whereby his salary is pegged to the person next to him who has worked for the same number of years at the agency, is the same age, but does inferior work? It would make more sense for the CD to branch out (freelance) and sell his services to his present employer for more than he would receive in salary.

The other reason for the creative department in a Japanese agency being smaller than its counterpart in the West is more pragmatic. First, a smaller creative department is possible because Japanese agencies have the ability to obtain creative work from freelancers. This is advantageous in that it keeps personnel costs down. (It is also beneficial in that the agency does not have to choose between firing a creative person whose ideas have become bland, and keeping him or her on the payroll.) An additional explanation for the smaller size of Japanese agencies' creative departments is that most of the best creative personnel opt to become independent, which allows them to make more money than they would in an agency, where seniority and other factors play a large role in determining their salary, as opposed to the salary being based solely on achievement.

This accounts for the small size of creative departments in Japanese agencies, and why the account department in a Japanese agency usually vastly outnumbers the creative department. The account department has frequent business meetings with clients. It also frequently wines and dines clients after work hours, and has a company-approved expense account for it. It is fairly safe to say that the account person is in a much stronger position vis-à-vis the creative person.

Japanese agencies are also staff-heavy because they have to provide a wider range of services than their counterparts in the West. As was said earlier, major agencies in Japan aim to provide a total service that includes not only advertising, public relations, research, and direct marketing but also cultural events, sports sponsorships, production of feature films, design, urban redevelopment, and the piloting of new media. Elsewhere these wider-ranging services would be provided by specialist companies.

It should be noted here that most client–agency relationships in Japan are still on a commission basis, as opposed to the fee basis that has become prevalent in the West. While many foreign clients in Japan are insisting that their agency in Japan charge them a fee, which is usually based on "time spent on the account," Japanese companies have not followed this practice for the simple reason that it would cost them more money. Japanese clients tend to ask their agencies for a lot of "extra" work that tends to be time-consuming. This work is not charged for by the agency because it is considered *sābisu* (service), which means "free of charge." Japanese clients also insist on frequent face-to-face meetings with the agency, often several times a day. If the agency were to charge based on time spent, the clients would see their charges balloon out of control.

The vast majority of business relationships between Japanese clients and Japanese agencies are not based on a contract. In fact, it is rare for a client to ask an agency to draw up a contract. Since the relationship is considered to be based on trust, asking for a contract is the same as saying that one party does not trust the other. Not a good way to begin a relationship!

Contact reports, a standard feature of agency–client relationships in the West, are rarely provided by a Japanese agency to a Japanese client after a meeting. Both sides have an aversion to putting things down in writing because it leaves no room to negotiate later. It is understood that both parties will do their best to implement whatever is decided at a meeting, but that things might not go exactly as discussed.

It is still true that most of the smaller foreign agencies in Japan work mainly for Western clients. The larger multinationals, on the other hand, handle a balanced mix of Japanese and foreign clients, and the smaller Japanese agencies work mainly for Japanese clients. The major Japanese agencies all have significant assignments from Western clients.

DIFFERENCES IN THE WAY ADVERTISING IS DEVELOPED

One of the major differences between Japanese and foreign agencies is their approaches to developing advertising. Some foreigners believe that Japanese agencies have no concept of an account planner who is dedicated to solving questions of strategy and positioning based on analysis of the characteristics of target groups.

However, this is certainly not the case. Many Japanese agencies have people in planning positions, although they might have a title other than Account Planner on their business card. Although some Japanese agencies have their planners in the marketing division, planning is most often the responsibility of the AEs.

Similarly, media-planning in Japanese agencies is not always located in the media division. Most agencies have their media-planning done by their AEs or, if they have them, by the planners in the marketing division. Media plans put together by either AEs or marketing planners commonly clash with the needs of the media departments of Japanese agencies, which often maintain their own inventories of media space and time. The media department is under pressure because it is obligated (through precedent) to buy a certain amount of space from each media vehicle with which the agency has an account.

Most, but not all, foreign agencies in Japan usually do not carry media inventories. This is because they cannot prebuy space and time, and because most do not deal directly with the media. They will try to convince foreign clients that, in contrast to Japanese agencies, they focus on buying the most efficient media plan rather than trying to sell from a media stockpile. Yet, in fact, even most of these agencies are allocated a certain amount of space in the media vehicles they usually use, regardless of whether they buy directly or through a Japanese agency. If they want to maintain good relations with the media vehicles and continue to be able to gain access to this space and to good positions, they must continuously buy the space allocated to them. In this sense, the foreign agencies' account and media staff face the same pressures as those in the Japanese agencies.

With advertising standards in Japan gradually moving closer to those of the West, multinational agencies in Japan have become more competitive with Japanese agencies. The multinational agencies have begun to convince foreign advertisers that they (the agencies) can call upon years of strategic creative development and media-planning techniques that are not yet developed to Western standards in many Japanese agencies. This gives the foreign agencies an advantage that offsets the fact that most are still small and must buy media space through a Japanese agency.

For years, foreign ad agencies have claimed that Western disciplines of planning and strategy can build business in Japan for Japanese and Western clients alike. A few long-timers try to use the fact that, numerically, close to half of their clients are Japanese companies as a demonstration of this. Yet, as seen earlier, these numerically large clients are usually small bits and pieces of business.

Japan remains a difficult market for foreign ad agencies. The major Japanese agencies control so much of the market that the environment is always a difficult one for both foreign newcomers and the smaller foreign agencies. One of the constant challenges is that some Japanese agencies with strong media ties can offer steep discounts on media. These discounts are passed on to them by the media, and foreign agencies and smaller Japanese agencies cannot match them.

DIFFERENCES IN MEDIA PLANNING

Although Japan is the world's second largest advertising market, it has grown without parallel development in the media-planning techniques that are now widely used in the U.S., Europe, and Asia.

Media-planning as it is known in the West does not exist in Japan. Media data are very limited, and the research is very restricted. Much of it is not national, and what exists tends to cover only certain periods of the year. Lack of accurate media data has frustrated attempts at better media-planning in Japan. For example, most of Japan's 4,000 consumer magazines do not provide audited circulation data. And, until recently, TV audience measurements relied entirely on a monthly diary recording individual viewership plus a meter to record household ratings (GRPs). This service, provided by Nielsen and its larger rival, Video Research (owned by Dentsu, Hakuhodo, and the broadcasters), had not changed substantially since its introduction in the 1960s.

The deficiencies of the diary and household ratings system became evident to Japan's major advertisers in the early 1980s, when they began to develop new products for smaller consumer segments rather than monolithic brands for the whole family. In 1986, the Japan Advertisers' Association (JAA) announced that it felt the time had come to explore ways to improve TV audience measurement. Advertisers needed more specific and better information about who was viewing commercials and when, if they were to plan their marketing effectively. The people meter technology used in Europe and the U.S. looked interesting.

Yet, the status quo remained in place until November 1994, when Nielsen Japan introduced its Advanced People Meter (APM) measurement service in the Tokyo area. The APM allows individuals to record their viewership via a button on a remote control unit. Every 15 minutes a sensor counts the number of viewers and sounds an alarm if the counts do not tally. The APM measures ratings every 60 seconds and provides a more realistic picture of viewing than the household GRP measurements that Nielsen and Video Research had provided.

Though welcomed by advertisers, the APM was shunned by television broadcasters. The broadcasters feared that the new system would encourage advertisers to use the demographic data to target specific audiences, and that this could lead to decisions not to place advertising on certain programs or in certain time slots. They felt this would reduce their ad revenues or lead to pressure on the networks' programming policies. Even today, the broadcasters will not allow APM data to be used in space-buying negotiations, and insist that the only valid audience measurements are household GRPs.

APM data have changed the TV planning landscape in Japan. The one area where agencies in Japan can make the most use of modern media-planning skills and show improvements in efficiency is television. This is also where the major international advertisers tend to concentrate a large portion of their ad budgets. For TV, agencies now have the data to apply modern concepts such as communication goals, reach, and frequency.

Now that accurate viewer data are available, agencies and advertisers are taking a fresh look at television. Until the advent of the APM, lack of data held back the development of the quantitative aspects of television media-planning in Japan. For example, there had been little study of the relationship between advertising frequency and communication effectiveness in Japan. The advent of the APM changed that. More advertisers are showing an interest in cost-efficiency based on individual viewership data. Finally, the concept of the target audience rating point (TARP), and its value against the more general household GRPs, is becoming understood.

While Japanese advertisers took the lead in pressing for better television audience data, it was the foreign advertisers and agencies that introduced the media-planning techniques that use that data. P&G, Mars, and Coca-Cola, three of the largest foreign spenders, were among the leaders.

With the development of more precise television viewing data, both advertisers and agencies are able to fine-tune their brands' positions and to use media more effectively and strategically. It makes media a more effective tool in correctly positioning products and targeting audience. The planning tools readily available in the West, and their use, are still in the development stages in Japan. They are not as sophisticated, but are slowly moving in that direction.

Despite these beginnings, it may be some time before media planning in Japan becomes as refined as in the U.S. or Europe. One hurdle is the lack of clarity about media-pricing in Japan. It is not uncommon for advertisers to be shielded from the details of how their money is spent. And when they do know, efficiency is not always the most important criterion. Even if an advertiser knows that another agency can buy or negotiate lower media space rates, it usually decides to stick with its present agency out of loyalty and to avoid upsetting the client–agency relationship.

Apart from TV, there has been little progress in improving the flow of media data. Other media remain very limited either in terms of the data available or how the data can be manipulated to achieve media objectives.

The media industry in Japan is finally becoming more oriented toward the quality of data that the advertiser needs.

DIFFERENCES IN ADVERTISING (WET VS. DRY)

The most striking contrast between advertising agencies in Japan and in Western countries lies in the different views the Japanese agencies have about how advertising operates and the way those beliefs are reflected in their creative work.

Western advertising is often characterized as being "hard sell," focused on a product's benefits and those benefits' relevance to people's lives. In other words—dry. The Japanese approach to advertising is more indirect, more of a "soft sell"—often called "wet." In Japan, as elsewhere, advertising works on both rational and emotional levels, but in Japan the emotional dimension is relatively more important than in many other countries. Of course there are examples of Japanese advertising that is very benefit-oriented, just as there are many Western campaigns that are strong on emotional elements. The differences are those of nuance and degree rather than of absolutes.

The frame of reference for creating advertising in Japan is, of course, the Japanese language and culture, so the manifestations of the rational and the emotional may be very different from those in a Western culture. This, too, is an argument for choosing an agency on the basis of its advertising and marketing skills, and not simply because key members are good at English. It is also a further reason for working with an agency that appreciates your own corporate culture and therefore can help to make this a part of Japanese life.

DIFFERENCES IN PRESENTATIONS

Since the account person in Japan spends an inordinate amount of time with the client, he or she gains a great understanding of the client's intentions. Through continual contact (both in and out of the office), the account person and the client build a consensus regarding what the advertising should do. Thus agency presentations often have a feeling of "going through the motions." In fact, there are often "prepresentations" where the account person shows his or her counterpart on the client side exactly what will be included in the presentation, and asks for input and approval. Modifications are made accordingly. Thus, more often than not, the final presentation to the client's decision makers is extremely bland, since basic consensus has already been reached.

A typical presentation begins with an exchange of business cards among those (on both the client and agency sides) who are meeting for the first time. On the agency side, the tendency is for quite a large number of people to attend. Everyone who had anything to do with putting the presentation together, as well as a few senior personnel, are included. This is to show the agency's commitment. (It is also used as a forum to train young AEs by exposing them to a presentation, or as a reward for their helping put the presentation together.)

Usually the only agency people to speak at the presentation are the senior person, the account person in charge (who is usually the presenter), and one person from the creative department, who will present the creative work. The rest of the agency attendees remain silent. Many non-Japanese experiencing a typical Japanese presentation are quite unnerved at facing all these silent faces for the duration of the presentation!

After the exchange of business cards (a uniquely Japanese custom), everyone is seated. Seating is determined by the person's rank. Then there is a formal *aisatsu* (greetings/opening comments) from the senior person on the agency side, followed by distribution of the presentation document. Usually this document is quite thick, the bulk consisting of reams of data relating to the client's product, competitors' products, market shares, and so on. Almost without fail, the vast majority of the data is openly available. Much of it has been provided by the client. In other words, the client either already possesses it, or has better data. The purpose here is for the agency to show how much homework it has done. There is a noticeable (to the non-Japanese) lack of analysis of the data presented.

Besides the data, the remainder of the document consists of the agency's proposal. Typically, this consists of many pages of impressive schematics: boxes, circles, and triangles of various sizes and thickness. Connecting all of these are arrows going in all directions. Once the document has been handed out, the agency presenter proceeds to read it. Only quite recently have many Japanese agencies begun making full use of overhead projections, slides, and computers in their presentations. Even so, the volume of information presented is enormous.

The presentation is quite formal by non-Japanese standards. There is no "song-and-dance" or overt enthusiasm (raised voices, large grins), since many Japanese agencies believe the client would interpret these as "not serious" and inappropriate. As a result, it is probably understandable why so many Japanese clients fall asleep/doze off at presentations!

An interesting, if confusing, feature of Japanese presentations is that many creative ideas are presented visually. What amazes foreigners who are subjected to these typically "Japanese" presentations is that the creative ideas are not based on one strategy the agency strongly believes in. Instead, they are based on several different strategies, and the client is basically asked to pick and choose. This is a uniquely Japanese approach, and most agencies familiar with Western clients will not take this approach, since those clients would accuse the agency of asking the client to do the agency's work (i.e., choosing the best strategy for the client's problem).

Thus strategy is less important to the presentation, which becomes more a process of selecting among a broad variety of proposed creatives (of which there are many).

Japanese clients in general never pay an agency for the costs of a pitch.

CONCLUSION

Japanese agencies are different from agencies in other countries, yet their differences are not necessarily bad. However, with many agencies working on one brand, or "one-shot" campaigns, cohesive branding is not the norm, and tends to be a weak spot for Japanese agencies.

Furthermore, with many Japanese agencies handling competing clients, do not expect them to rock the boat with aggressive ads. Agencies tend to follow Japanese advertisers' thoughts, in that the role of advertising is to raise interest, seduce, attract, and/or accelerate purchase decision/brand choice. Selling is the salesman's job (manufacturers have good control of retail distribution). Thus, creative executions are seldom relevant to product. People are the center of interest, not the product.

Finally, since Japanese agencies perceive both clients and media to be the agency's clients, aggressive media-planning is not the norm.

Chapter 6

◆◆◆

Terebi
Advertising on Television

Imagine how expensive, yet effective, television advertising in the U.S. would be if there were only five nationwide networks. That describes television advertising in Japan.

Although the most surprising aspect of television in Japan is the small number of channels available, with the growth of satellite television and local UHF stations in recent years, this situation is expected to change. Unfortunately, at the time of this writing, neither the existing satellite system nor UHF stations have been overwhelming successes.

HISTORY OF JAPANESE TELEVISION

In 1925, Japanese television broadcasting took its earliest steps with both the first local transmission of an electronic image and the development of a directional antenna. The latter, developed by Hidetsugu Yagi, served as the prototype for the television antennae found on household roofs throughout the world today.

In the years preceding World War II, further research into television broadcasting was conducted by the Technical Research Center of the government-run NHK (Nippon Hōsō Kyokai, Japan Public Broadcasting Corporation), culminating in Japan's first television signal transmission in 1937. The government at the time hoped to host the 1945 Olympic Games in Tokyo and telecast the event for the first time in history. With the outbreak of World War II, however, plans for the Olympic Games were canceled and experimental television broadcasting was discontinued.

In the immediate postwar years, Japan found itself struggling to survive. Reviving the development of television was of low priority and thus was postponed for several years. Then, in 1950, the new Broadcasting Law (*Hōsō Hō* 1950) reorganized NHK as a strictly public-service organization. The law also made provision for a commercial broadcast sector, resulting in preliminary licenses being issued for 16 broadcast stations in the early 1950s. The first license, granted to Nippon Television Network (NTV) in July 1952, marked the inception of commercial television broadcasting in Japan.

The first actual television broadcast in Japan, however, was not made until 1 February 1953, when NHK's Tokyo station began broadcasting. On 28 August of the same year, Nippon Television went on the air. However, the broadcast areas of the two stations were limited to Tokyo and its suburbs, and the number of TV sets nationwide at the time numbered only 866. At the time, the cost of a television set imported from the U.S. (about ¥250,000) equaled the annual salary of an urban middle-class white-collar worker.

NTV's launch was spearheaded by its president, Matsutaro Shoriki, president of the *Yomiuri Shimbun* (Japan's largest-circulation newspaper). Shoriki ordered large TV sets from the U.S. and had them placed at 42 strategic outdoor locations in Tokyo and surrounding areas: at busy street corners, parks, railway terminals, and other locations with heavy pedestrian traffic. Nicknamed "street television," they were a huge success. A newspaper article on 27 October 1953 estimated that a crowd of 20,000 had gathered to watch several of Shoriki's sets during the airing of a boxing match (Shirai vs. Allen).

Sales of domestically produced TV sets slowly grew through purchases by service establishments such as coffee shops, restaurants, bars, and barber shops. When sports shows or other popular programs were aired, these establishments charged their clientele a surcharge to watch. Of the 16,000 TV sets nationwide in March 1954, the majority were owned by commercial establishments.

By the late 1950s the number of television sets in use had increased dramatically due to lower production costs. By this time, NHK had added an educational channel, and other commercial broadcasting stations besides NTV had taken to the air, further stimulating interest in television.

The televised wedding of Prince Akihito and Michiko Shoda (the present emperor and empress) at the end of the 1950s gave a huge boost to television ownership. The announcement of the royal wedding was made almost six months before the event was held on 10 April 1959. Television manufacturers mounted intensive campaigns to persuade the nation to watch the wedding parade on television, and television broadcasters announced that the entire parade would be broadcast live. Within a single year, 2 million TV sets were sold.

Scarcely one month after the royal wedding, in May 1959, the International Olympic Committee's announcement of its decision to hold the 1964 Olympics in Tokyo created tremendous excitement throughout the nation.

During the five years leading up to the Olympics, the Japanese public was bombarded with Olympics-related news and stories. Electronics manufacturers aggressively promoted sales of TV sets with advertisements that promised the "best seat to see the games." When the Olympic Games were finally held in Tokyo (10–24 October 1964), the opening ceremony was watched by an estimated 65 million people in Japan, about 85% of the population.

TELEVISION IN JAPAN TODAY

By 1975, television had overtaken newspapers as Japan's prime medium for advertising, a position it maintains to this day.

Today, television in Japan can be divided into three sectors: ground (or terrestrial) broadcast, cable, and satellite. Ground broadcast is the sector of major significance to advertisers.

Ground Broadcast

The ground broadcasting system in Japan is divided into the public sector and the commercial sector. The public sector is represented by NHK, which broadcasts on two public VHF channels: NHK 1 (general programs and news) and NHK 3 (more educational programming). Neither channel accepts any advertising. NHK is the original pay-TV in Japan, with 98% of revenues coming from viewing fees. It collects those fees from households that have reception contracts with NHK. These contracts are mandatory for all households that own a TV set.

The commercial sector of ground broadcast consists of the five nationwide commercial TV networks, each of which operates as a cooperative led by a key station based in Tokyo. Japan's five nationwide networks are Japan News Network (JNN) with 28 stations, led by key station Tokyo Broadcasting System (TBS); Nippon News Network (NNN) with 30 stations, led by Nippon Television Network (NTV); All Nippon Network (ANN) with 26 stations, led by Asahi National Broadcasting (ANB); Fuji Network System (FNS) with 28 stations, led by Fuji Television Network (CX); and TX Network (TXN), with six stations, which is led by Television Tokyo (TX).

The national TV networks are basically organizations for the distribution of programs by the key stations, which, in addition to broadcasting, produce their own programs. These programs are provided to the network affiliates.

The local television stations, which are members of a network, broadcast the programs that originate from their key station. They are paid for keeping their schedule clear to air these nationwide programs, and do not keep revenues generated by network advertising (they go to the key station, which produces or buys the program in question). However, the local stations are allowed to set aside certain advertising time during network program slots for their own use. The majority (roughly 80%) of programs aired on local stations are provided by the key stations. Of course, the local stations generate advertising revenues from the airing of their own locally produced programs.

Although almost all of the TV stations in Japan belong to at least one of the five nationwide commercial networks, there are a few unaffiliated, independent stations. Usually these are based in the major cities. In the U.S., by contrast, roughly half of the 1,100 TV stations are independent.

Beginning with the *Yomiuri Shimbun*'s involvement in the launch of NTV, each television network's key station has close ties to a major daily national newspaper.

Nippon Television (NTV, channel 4) is affiliated with the *Yomiuri Shimbun* (Japan's largest nationwide daily); Tokyo Broadcasting (TBS, channel 6) is affiliated with the *Mainichi Shimbun*; Fuji Television (CX, channel 8) is affiliated with the *Sankei Shimbun*; and Asahi National Broadcasting (ANB, channel 10) is affiliated with the *Asahi Shimbun*. The fifth key station, Television Tokyo (TX, channel 12), is affiliated with the *Nihon Keizai Shimbun* (Japan's leading financial newspaper).

The connection between the major television stations and the major nationwide newspapers enables them to share news facilities. Inevitably, it sometimes influences the programming of each station.

Cable TV

Cable television (CATV) traces its beginnings in Japan to 1954. Originally it was developed to provide television to areas that had difficulty receiving regular ground broadcasts (in many cases, communities ringed by mountains that blocked TV reception).

The Japanese cable industry is underdeveloped compared with the U.S., with a penetration rate of 35% versus 67% for the U.S. The notable lack of attractive programs has limited consumer demand, since cable television is still perceived as expensive and unappealing.

There are three basic types of cable facilities in Japan: small-scale cable, community cable, and urban cable.

Small-scale cable is used to provide good reception in areas where normal reception is difficult. Most of these facilities provide VHF, UHF, and NHK satellite channels.

Community cable generally provides the same channels as small-scale cable, with the addition of some local programming (community access).

Urban cable is defined as a cable system that has 10,000 subscribers or more, and provides five or more of its own private broadcast channels. Of the 662 areas designated as cities in Japan, 136 have urban cable. Cities with populations of 100,000 or over are more likely to have urban cable than smaller cities. Table 6.1 shows the number of cable stations in Japan.

Table 6.1
Total Number of CATV Stations and Subscribers

	1997	1998
Number of stations	66,272	68,234
Number of subscribers	12,629,438	14,482,000

Sources: 1997, Ministry of Posts and Telecommunications; 1998, Dentsu, *A Research for Information and Media Society.*

For the foreign marketer, use of cable television is not usually a major consideration due to the low number of subscribers (12.6 million in 1997, according to the Ministry of Posts and Telecommunications), compared with the viewership of the nationwide ground broadcast networks. The largest urban cable company, Japan Network Services, serves little more than 100,000 households. Due to the forces of supply and demand, airing commercials on cable channels is very inexpensive in comparison with ground television.

Satellite Television

Japan's first experimental use of satellite communication for a regular television broadcast was on 23 November 1963. A live broadcast from the U.S. to Japan was planned, during which a personal message would be delivered by President John F. Kennedy. Instead of seeing the U.S. president deliver his message of greeting, the Japanese public watched the shocking news that he had been assassinated that day in Texas.

In 1968 NHK began experiments in direct satellite broadcasting (BS) as a means of reaching small communities whose reception of regular TV was blocked by mountains. BS signals can be received by homes equipped with a small dish antenna.

A novelty item in its early days, NHK picked up the pace of development in the 1980s by launching two NHK-operated BS analog television channels in July 1987. Within a year, over 1.25 million households were receiving the satellite transmissions. NHK's BS-1 channel airs news and informational programming, and BS-2 features more culturally oriented material, such as musicals, movies, and operas. Neither channel accepts advertising. NHK's BS satellite channels are the only ones Japanese viewers can receive without use of a descrambling device. These channels now have viewers numbering in the millions (in 1997 there were 8.5 million households with a BS tuner).

Japan's 24% penetration rate for satellite television (in 1998) is quite high compared to the 8% in the U.S.

Japan's first commercial BS satellite TV station was inaugurated by Japan Satellite Broadcasting (JSB) in 1991. The station, called WOWOW, is a pay-TV system; subscribers rent a decoder to unscramble the transmission and pay a monthly subscription fee. By early 1993, 1.2 million households were watching WOWOW. This figure grew to 2 million subscribers by January 1996.

Although none of the current BS channels accepts advertising in principle, WOWOW has occasionally sold a very limited amount of ad time between programs on an ad hoc basis.

By 1998, there were 2.4 million subscribers, according to Japan Satellite Broadcasting. Table 6.2 shows the number of BS satellite contracts between 1990 and 1998.

Communication satellite (CS) broadcasts are digital, as opposed to BS broadcasts, which are analog. The difference between communications satellites and broadcast satellites is important, because the digital capabilities of CS allow many more channels to be broadcast. Receiving CS broadcasts requires a different dish antenna than BS, further alienating consumers who have invested in one system or the other.

Japan's first commercial CS service, Japan Digital Broadcasting Service (known as PerfecTV), offered 60 channels of digital broadcasting upon its launch in October 1996. Subscribers must invest ¥50,000 for a decoder box and satellite

Table 6.2
Number of BS Satellite Contracts, 1990–98

	NHK	WOWOW
Apr. 1990	2,356,000	—
Apr. 1991	4,050,000	341,346
Apr. 1992	5,430,000	833,722
Apr. 1993	7,010,000	1,276,676
Apr. 1994	8,100,000	1,511,396
Apr. 1995	9,010,000	1,760,900
Apr. 1996	10,000,000	2,077,291
Apr. 1997	10,120,000	2,277,682
Apr. 1998	13,300,000	2,405,147
Nov. 1998	14,000,000	2,454,576

Source: Dentsu, *Introduction of Satellite TV* (November 1998).

Table 6.3
Number of CS Satellite Contracts, 1990–98

	Digital		
	PerfecTV	DirecTV	Skyport TV
	(JSkyB)		
1990 Apr.	—	—	—
1991 Apr.	—	—	—
1992 Apr.	—	—	0
1993 Apr.	—	—	18,051
1994 Apr.	—	—	31,131
1995 Apr.	—	—	51,180
1996 Apr.	—	—	76,948
1997 Apr.	168,079	—	NA
1998 Mar.	407,952	7,000	*
1998 Nov.	875,000	181,000	*

*Out of service
Source: Dentsu, *Introduction of Satellite TV* (November 1998).

dish to receive PerfecTV's signal. For a monthly fee of about ¥2,900, subscribers receive 61 channels (due to increase to 100) of television and 103 channels of radio. PerfecTV had attracted 670,000 subscribers by April 1998. In mid-1998, less than one month after its debut, JSkyB, another CS service, merged with PerfecTV on an equal basis. The new venture offers 200 channels, and is called SkyPerfecTV.

SkyPerfecTV's competitor, DirecTV Japan, began CS digital broadcasting in December 1997, offering 63 channels. Subscribers to DirecTV must invest ¥54,000 in a receiver set, television tuner, and antenna, and pay an initial subscription fee of ¥3,000. Both new CS channels accept advertising. By the end of November 1998, DirecTV had attracted slightly more than 180,000 subscribers.

The overall slow growth of commercial satellite television has been largely attributed to its high cost to the consumer. Aggravating the high cost of satellite reception for the consumer is the fact that subscribers wishing to view both DirecTV and SkyPerfecTV must buy two different CS decoders. Table 6.3 shows the number of CS contracts from 1990 to 1998.

In addition to SkyPerfecTV and DirecTV, new BS channels are expected to be introduced by major ground broadcast TV stations beginning in 2000.

DISTINCTIVE FEATURES OF JAPAN'S TELEVISION

In Japan, television is the medium that provides the greatest degree of contact with consumers. Color television has penetrated almost all Japanese homes. Since 1991, there have been an average of 2.13 TV sets per household, and people spend an average of three and a half hours each day watching television.

Due to the wide dissemination of TV sets and the high rate of TV viewing among all age groups, the use of television makes it possible for an advertiser to reach a great many viewers simultaneously. Furthermore, since TV viewership is constantly being measured, it is possible to monitor advertising effectiveness.

TELEVISION SCHEDULES AND AIRTIME

In Japan, the television program schedule is divided into two six-month segments. The first begins in April and the second in October. These segments reflect the Japanese professional baseball season, which runs from April through September; the TV stations broadcast the night games (*naitā* in Japanese).

For advertising purposes, television's twelve-month year (from April through March of the following year) is divided into four three-month periods. Each quarter is called a *kūru*. Thus, for example, a six-month TV program is said to run for two *kūru*.

Round-the-clock broadcasting was initiated by TBS and Fuji TV (October 1987), followed by Nippon TV and TV Asahi (October 1988). Today, most ground channels broadcast for close to 24 hours per day.

Most TV stations divide their daily airtime into four segments, ranging from the most expensive segment A, through Special B and B, to the least expensive segment C. Each segment has published card rates.

Segment A is considered the best because it covers prime time (19:00-23:00 on weekdays and 18:00–23:00 on the weekend). (The very best period within prime time, called "golden time," is 19:00–22:00.) The next segment is Special B, covering the next highest peak viewing times on weekdays (12:00–14:00, 18:00–19:00, and 23:00–24:00), with more extended periods on Saturdays and particularly Sundays. The charge for Special B is around 70% of that for A. Segment B covers the less popular viewing times during the rest of the day (07:00–10:00 and 14:00–18:00 on weekdays) and costs about 40% of A. Weekend viewing times differ. Finally, time segment C covers early mornings and late nights, when most people are asleep or busy (05:00–07:00, 10:00–12:00, and midnight onward), with slight modifications on weekends. The cost is around 30% of that for A. (See Figure 6.1.)

The exception to the time segmentation method employed by the majority of TV stations (NTV, TBS, Asahi, and TX all use the system based on A, B, Special

Figure 6.1
Airtime Rankings

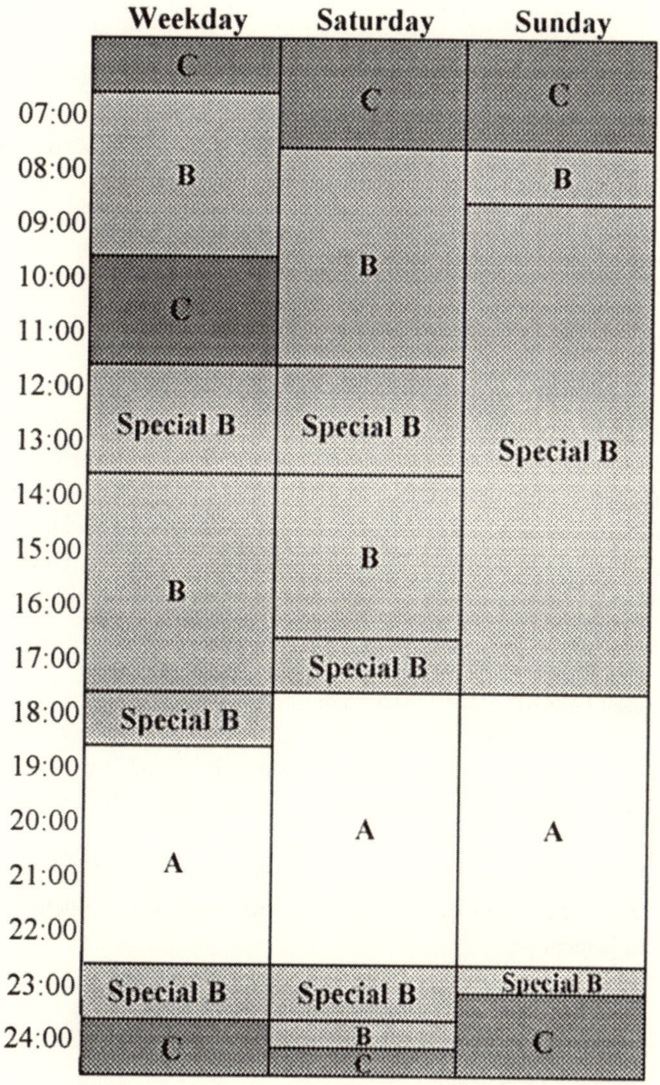

B, and C) is Fuji TV, which divides airtime into three categories: P, S, and D. For every six P spots, a client will get two S spots and one D spot.

Since the five major commercial TV stations average 22.6 hours of programming per day, with six minutes of advertising per hour, they can carry about 678 minutes of commercials per day (more than two hours each).

On average, a single station can broadcast about 850 commercials per day. Thus, the five key stations together broadcast about 4,250 commercials per day. Close to 70% of TV commercials are spots; the remainder are program sponsorship commercials.

The cost of airing TV commercials in Japan is high, and competition for airtime is intense. This is due to the inherent limitations caused by supply and demand (only five major nationwide TV networks, and many advertisers). Partly because of high airtime costs, and partly because of TV stations' desire to give as many advertisers as possible a chance to air their commercials, the majority of commercials are 15 seconds.

PROGRAM SPONSORSHIP COMMERCIALS

According to the *Nihon Minkan Hōsō Renmei* Law 135, TV commercials are divided into three types: program sponsorship commercials, participating spots, and station break spots. Figure 6.2 gives an example of CM insertion style.

Program sponsorship commercials (called "time" CMs), are commercials for a program's sponsor that are shown during the program in an agreed upon, limited number. Listing in the program's sponsorship credits is included. Usually, a contract for program sponsorship is for a minimum of six months (two quarters). In rare cases, a one-quarter (three-month) sponsorship may become available. Programs can be sponsored nationwide or in selected local areas. Contract cancellations must be made at least 60 days in advance.

There are several types of program sponsorships. The most basic is the network program sponsorships. Network "time" CMs are inserted in nationwide network programs. (The number of stations differs by network and by program.)

Commercials are placed in programs that are broadcast once a week on the same day and in the same time slot. Sponsorship announcement before and after the program is included.

Sales unit: 30-second minimum
Time rate: broadcast rate + production cost + network fees
Contract period: usually six months

Local program sponsorships are also available. Like network program sponsorships, commercials are broadcast during a network program, but only in a selected local station's broadcast area (for example, in the Tokyo area). These are also called "local time" program sponsorships.

Another type of sponsorship is the belt program sponsorship. Its commercials (CMs) are aired during regular programs broadcast at the same time daily,

Figure 6.2
Example of CM Insertion Style

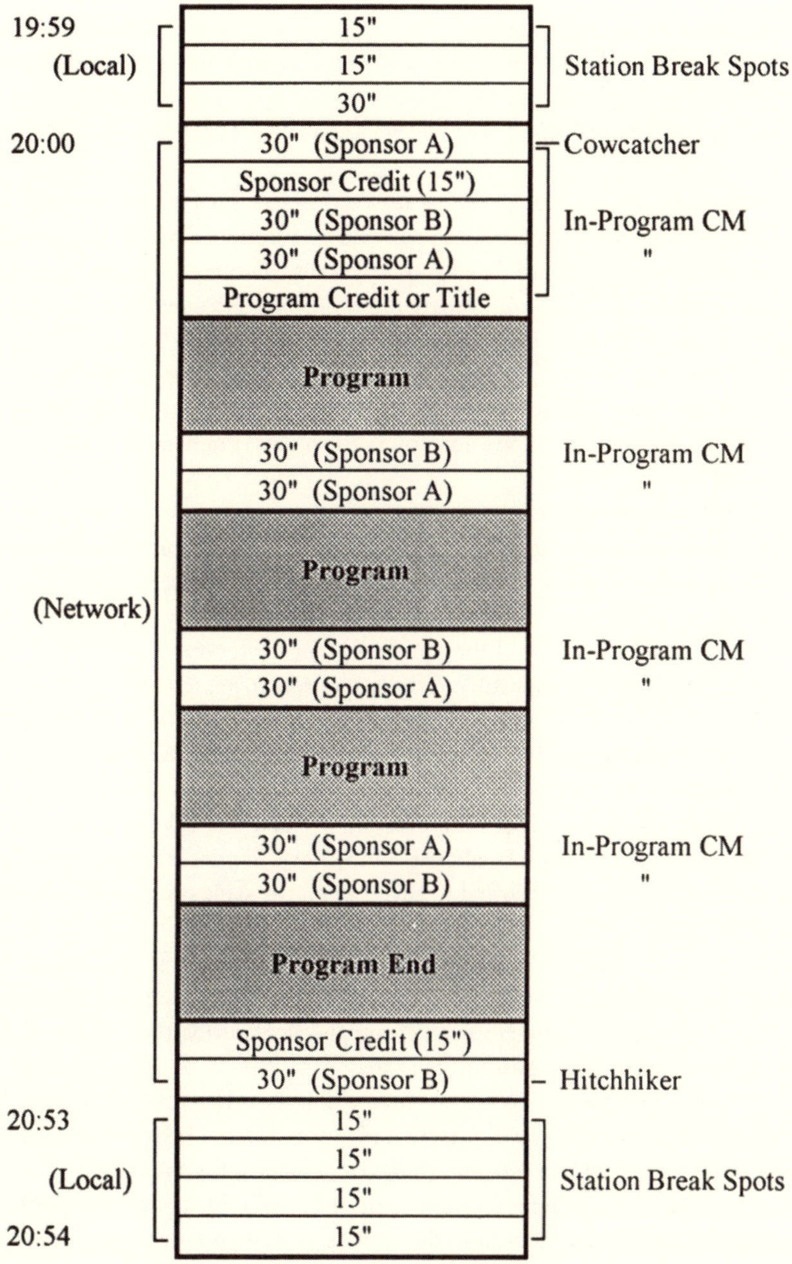

Source: Asahi Advertising, Inc., *Media Fact Book in Japan* (July 1996).

throughout the week (Monday to Sunday or Monday to Friday). There are two basic variants of belt program sponsorships:

1. *Tereko* sponsorship—sponsorship of daily belt programs with CM insertion on an every-other-day basis. (Monday/Wednesday/Friday, or Tuesday/Thursday, or a combination of these)
2. Specified day sponsorship—sponsorship of belt programs only on specified days

Finally, *hako bangumi* sponsorships are also offered. This is a sponsorship of a program that is broadcast only once per week, on the same day, at the same time.

The only way to guarantee that TV commercials will run at the same time every day is to sponsor a TV program. Program sponsorship is frequently used by advertisers in Japan to project a stable, respectable corporate or brand image.

Aside from the types of program sponsorships mentioned, some advertisers occasionally sponsor grand-scale special programs to enhance total corporate image. This kind of sponsorship allows advertisers to present commercials of 60 seconds or more.

Program cosponsorships are also possible. In these cases network program sponsorship commercials are run during national network TV programs on a long-term basis. Generally, several advertisers sponsor the same program jointly.

Popular programs with high ratings are often "presented" by a group of regular sponsors who have sponsored the same program for several years. Unless such sponsors withdraw, it is impossible for new sponsors to get airtime.

When a program is cosponsored (sometimes by ten or more sponsors), sponsors' commercials are rotated so that each has a chance of having its commercial aired first.

Obviously, an important principle in the TV stations' selection of program cosponsors is to avoid sponsors who are competitors. In principle, advertisers from the same industry are not allowed to advertise on the same program broadcast to the same areas.

Program sponsorship CMs are typically 30 seconds long. In the case of sole sponsorship of a program, it is possible to broadcast CMs that are 60 seconds long. For long special feature programs, which are prevalent during the New Year's season, 120-second CMs are possible, but rare.

In situations where an advertiser wants to aim for sole sponsorship instead of cosponsorship, the station will present a plan for a special program that will air only once, as opposed to a program (series) that is aired for two quarters (i.e., six months). The station retains editorial control but will discuss its plans with the sponsor at least six months prior to the air date. It is important to understand beforehand that the sponsorship rates for a special program include a sizable production cost in addition to the basic broadcast cost.

In addition to these specials, which can be produced for an advertiser who wants to be the sole sponsor, there are *tanpatsu bangumi*, which are concentrated around April, October, and New Year's.

Tanpatsu bangumi is sponsorship of an existing nationwide program for a short period of time and/or in one specific geographical area. As mentioned, program sponsorships are usually available only for at least two quarters. A *tanpatsu bangumi* sponsorship occurs when, for a six-month program, a sponsorship opening covering a short period becomes available. In this case, an advertiser can request to sponsor the program for the time available (five weeks, for example) in all areas where the program is broadcast, or to sponsor that program for a few weeks in one broadcast area.

From the mid-1950s (when TV broadcasting began) until the mid-1960s, most one-hour programs were sponsored by a single company. Due to high cost and demand for space by advertisers, since the mid-1960s cosponsorship has become most common. While there are still some sole sponsorships of hour-long programs, most sole sponsorships are of *mini-waku* (five-minute) programs.

A one-hour program is usually divided into 54 minutes of program time (including six minutes of commercials), followed by one minute of spot commercials, and then a five-minute miniprogram (*mini-waku*), usually created and inserted by the local stations. The *mini-waku* includes one minute of spot commercials.

Since the networks generally replace failing programs at the start of each six-month programming season (beginning in April and October), an ad agency's media division will be able to guess (by low ratings) which programs will be replaced, ahead of the stations' announcements.

For the new TV season beginning in April, ad agencies begin submitting lists of clients who wish to sponsor a program to the station in January. In the interests of safety, the agencies usually list several programs for each client (in descending order of preference). Usually it is mid-February before the TV stations officially release preliminary information regarding what programming changes will be made, and what openings are likely to become available. This sets off another round of negotiations (between client and agency as well as between agency and TV station). It is at this stage that the relationship between the media buyer (on the agency side) and the media representative (on the TV side) comes into play. Also taken into consideration is the total amount of airtime booked by the agency and by the client, the agency's clout (i.e., what other prestigious clients it has whose TV spending it could influence), and the client's prestige.

Sponsoring a popular program can be difficult. An existing sponsor would have to step down, and thus provide an opening. It is also very difficult to sponsor the highest-rated programs. Maneuvering and deal-making for time slots begin about two months before the season for program adjustments (in April and October), when it becomes clear that sponsorships will be available. In addition to the usual negotiating that occurs when requirements don't match up, adjustments must be made by the TV station in question, with regard to balancing advertisers' needs due to the limited sponsorship slots available.

When a sponsor informs a TV station (through its agency) that it is planning to pull out of a program's sponsorship, the station informs ad agencies of the opening. Obviously, the agency whose client is pulling out has prior knowledge of the plan, and usually tries to find a replacement client. Then, when it informs the TV station of the original client's intention to leave, it can also inform the station that it has found a replacement. However, since Japanese companies tend to use several ad agencies at the same time, the agencies other than the one handling the TV space-buying will usually hear of the client's plans through their day-to-day contacts with the client on their portion of the account, and will also try to find a replacement sponsor before the opening is made public.

Certain agencies have managed to buy up certain program sponsorship times and have held on to them for decades. This is known as *kaikiri* (to buy up forever). In such cases, the agency has a lock on the space based on precedent. Some agencies have done this by selling the station an idea for a program (and subsequently producing it), thus acquiring the right to handle all sponsorships for the program. Unless the agency indicates to the TV station that it (the agency) will give up the time (unheard of), the time will never become available for other agencies to buy for their clients.

There are a few specialized companies that buy up all the sponsorship time on certain programs and then sell it (at a markup) to ad agencies. Usually these brokers specialize in a certain type of TV program (sports, for example). In these cases, the ad agency has no contact with the TV station; all negotiations (on price, time allocation, etc.) and money matters are between the broker and the ad agency.

Program sponsorship time is sold in a minimum of 30-second units. This can be broken into two 15-second commercials. If the sponsor has only one version of a 15-second commercial, it is sometimes run back-to-back.

Network program sponsorship covers multiple areas. It is important to exercise caution because there are area differences by program or arising from circumstances at network stations. Local area sponsorships are also available—for example, sponsorship of a program in the Kanto area only.

Costs of TV program sponsorship vary widely, depending on the popularity of the program, the time the program is run, whether the sponsor's name is listed in the program credits, and so on. Rates for program sponsorship consist of a time charge, a network fee, and production cost. The network fee is the cost of networking a program. The production cost covers the expenses incurred in the production of a program.

Program sponsorship rates are normally quoted in monthly amounts. For example, using any of the affiliates of Nihon TV, Tokyo Broadcasting, and Fuji TV, and sponsoring a nationwide, full-network program during golden time with one 30-second CM will cost something in the range of ¥5 million (Spring 1996 rate). However, as mentioned before, that rate can rise or fall, depending on viewership rates, supply and demand, and other factors. If the same program was sponsored during a daytime slot, correspondingly lower rates for a less expensive time slot would be charged.

Booking for program sponsorships should be made two to three months in advance. Confirmation from the station usually comes one month in advance of air date.

Material (one-inch VHS videotape) must be given to the station airing the program one week in advance of airing. If it is a nationwide program, one tape to the key station will suffice. The key station will send the CF to the local stations.

When a program is sponsored, a sponsorship announcement is made at the start and at the end of the program. The program sponsorship announcement is handled according to the length of the commercial(s). Obviously, the more sponsorship time bought, the more the station will say about the program sponsor in the announcements.

Typical program sponsorship announcements are as follows:

30 seconds: Narration says "This program is brought to you by the following sponsors," as the list of sponsor credits is shown on the screen.

60 seconds: Narration says "This program is brought to you by [sponsor's name (and product name)]."

90 seconds: Narration says "This program is brought to you by [sponsor's name and product name with simple catchphrase]."

SPOT COMMERCIALS

Spot CMs, usually just called "spots," are not related to program sponsorship. Spots are the mainstays of every local station's ad inserts. The majority of spot commercials are 15 seconds, and the remainder are 30 seconds. Spot commercials run during station breaks between programs, and can be aired nationwide or in selected local areas. Intensive spot campaigns are often used in a concentrated period to raise brand awareness or to launch a new product.

Spot CMs are divided into two categories:

1. Participating spot commercials. These commercials (commonly called PT) are broadcast at specified times during a program, although the advertiser is not sponsoring the program. Participating spots include "cowcatchers," shown just before the beginning credits of the program, and "hitchhikers," which are aired after the program's closing credits.
2. Station break spot commercials. These commercials are run between programs (during the station break). They are commonly referred to as SB, or *sutē-bure*.

Figure 6.3
TV Spot-Buying Patterns

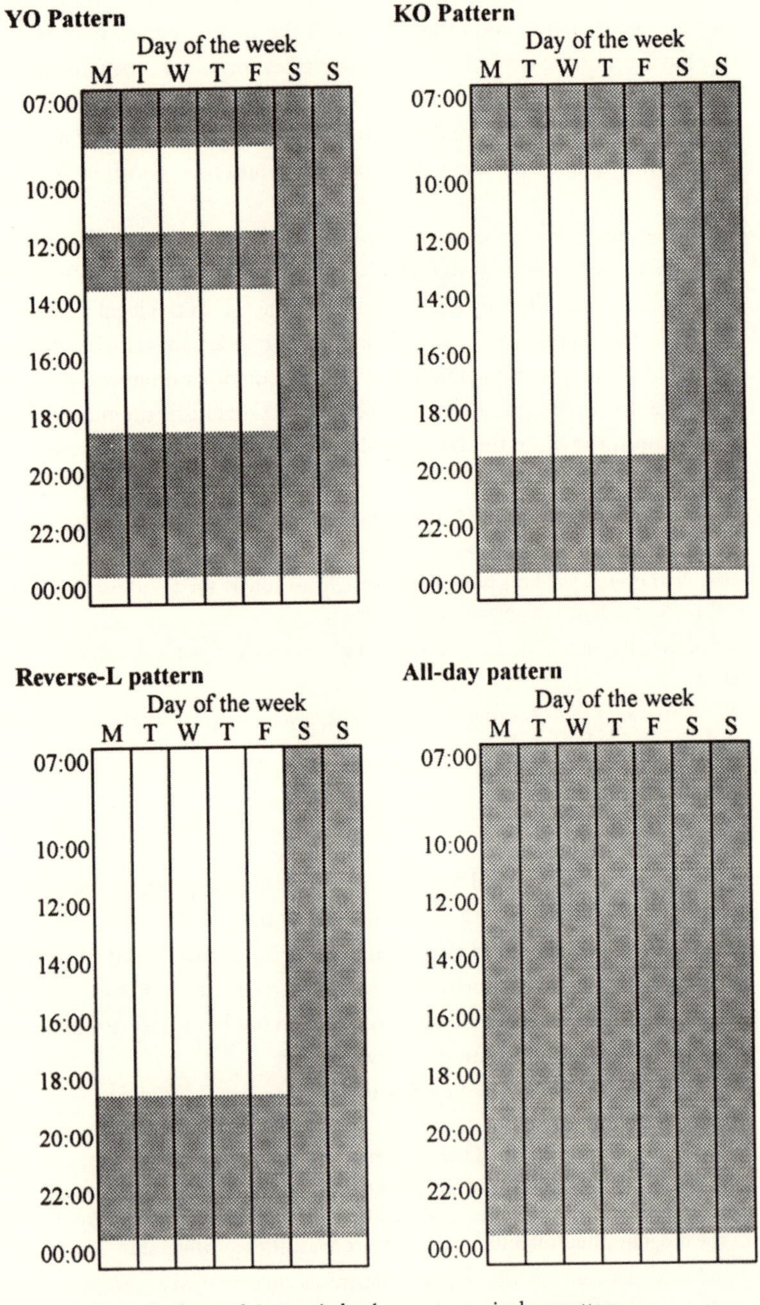

Gray areas indicate the days and time periods when spots are aired per pattern.

Spot buys are made in sets that are usually a mix of airings during prime and nonprime times. The basic sales unit is 15 seconds, although 30-second units are also available. The contract period can be set to match the advertiser's campaign period.

When booking spots, obviously the earlier the TV station is contacted, the better the chances are of obtaining the placements desired. After placing the booking order, the CM materials must be delivered to the station four days before the air date at the very latest.

Spot airtime is sold in sets of the stations' time segments. In other words, it is not possible to buy only prime-time segments. TV stations sell spot time by GRP. For example, when an agency requests a spot time of 3,000 GRP within one month, the station puts together (usually within one week) a set of spot times consisting of a mixture of A, Special B, B, and C time segments that will add up to 3,000 GRP. The advertiser could end up with spots at 7:30 P.M. on Monday, 4:15 A.M. on Tuesday, 12:45 P.M. on Wednesday, 3:00 A.M. on Thursday, 10:00 A.M. on Friday, and so on. The agency can then negotiate with the station if it feels a better combination of segments can be put together. It is customary to purchase a set that includes all types of time segments. These sets are referred to as "patterns." The four basic patterns are *yo*, *ko*, "reverse-L," and "all-day" (see Figure 6.3).

Media rates for spots are not calculated by the number of commercials aired, but are based on the number of GRP (gross rating points) the advertiser is aiming for. For example, if an advertiser wished to run 1,000 GRP worth of commercials on one of the nationwide networks (1,000 GRP equals a cumulative viewership total of 1000% for your commercial), at a rate of ¥48,000 per GRP, it would cost about ¥48 million. Thus, 100% of households have been exposed to the commercial ten times.

Since spots are run locally, spot space is bought from each local station separately. It is possible to buy 30-second spot airtimes, but in reality TV stations first try to sell 15-second airtimes. Only after they have sold the bulk of their airtime in 15-second allotments will they make any effort to sell the remainder as 30-second airtimes.

Each station has its own spot card rates, based on area, time, and demand. Rates fluctuate according to the balance between supply and demand, and are influenced by the total volume of spot buying by the advertiser during the previous years.

Costs for spot commercials consist of a time charge only. Standard card rates for TV advertising are determined primarily by the time segments the spots are placed in and the number of households (population) in the broadcast area.

Rates fluctuate widely due to the forces of supply and demand, as well as viewership ratings. During periods when there are many spot deals, ad rates go up. This is especially true when the economy is prospering and during periods of

Table 6.4
Monthly Differences in Spot Rates

Jan.	Feb.	Mar.	Apr.	May	June	July	Aug.	Sep.	Oct.	Nov.	Dec.
66	77	101	107	107	115	110	72	95	115	125	110

Note: All patterns and stations averaged; base = 100.

intense marketing activity (usually March to July and October to December). Conversely, rates usually fall during periods when there are fewer spot deals being made, during recessions, and during quiet marketing periods (typically August to September and January to February).

While a combination of factors influences the rate charged for spots, the month in which the spots are aired is one of the most basic factors. Table 6.4 gives an indication of the monthly rate difference, averaging all patterns and stations. (Note: February and August are traditionally low television advertising months [referred to as *nippachi*].)

Space bookings should be made two to three months in advance, depending on the season you want the spots to air. Even two months' prior booking for space in October could be difficult, whereas space in August might be bought on short notice. There is no minimum airtime period that must be booked.

If a spot booking is canceled less than one month prior to the air date, the station usually holds the agency responsible for full payment (or for finding a replacement client).

Agency commission is 15% of gross (on average) on TV spots, and 11% of gross on program sponsorships.

TELEVISION COMMERCIAL MATERIALS

These days, videotape is the most commonly used medium for commercials. If a commercial is going to be aired in only one region covered by one station, only a single one-inch videotape needs to be submitted to that station. But, if the commercial is going to be aired on a network in an area covered by 12 of the network's affiliates, a one-inch videotape of the commercial must be provided for each station.

The deadline for submitting the videotapes to the stations is one week in advance of air date (but this can be compressed to four working days). The station has to check the commercial to make sure it does not break any of the station's self-imposed regulatory rules, and this will take time. The check usually takes one week. Most agencies submit the storyboard to be checked before shooting the commercial, so that in the rare case that the station does not accept it, the commercial does not have to be reshot. Most checks for regular products and services are not that stringent. However, checks for real estate and loan companies are more severe. No station will air a commercial that has not been approved.

AD REVENUE VERSUS PROGRAM CONTENT

As in any country, the commercial ground broadcasting companies in Japan rely on advertising revenue. Thus, sponsors are very sensitive to the audience ratings, a sensitivity that encourages the Japanese television broadcasters to focus on programs which deliver the highest possible ratings. As in most countries, this is often at the expense of the program content. In Japan, any program with a rating above 20% is considered a success, giving the program a good chance of being carried over to the next season. Conversely, a rating below 15% raises major doubts of a program's ongoing viability.

THE RATING OF TV PROGRAMS

Television ratings in Japan are calculated by two market research companies, Video Research Co. (VRC) and A. C. Nielsen. VRC is the leader, with an estimated 90% share of the television audience measurement industry.

Since 1962, when television ratings began to be compiled in Japan, ratings have been measured on a household basis. Household ratings are a measure of the percentage of households with sets tuned to any one program at a particular time of day. The system monitors whether the TV set is on, not who is sitting in front of it. Household ratings are presented as GRP (gross rating points). A GRP represents 1% of a particular viewing market being measured. (If 20% of all households in Tokyo are tuned in to one particular program, that program is said to have a GRP of 20.)

As a consequence of this dependence on what is considered an antiquated rating system, media-modeling and the planning techniques used in the U.S. and U.K., where more sophisticated media research data are available, are not commonly used in Japan.

The household rating system was adequate when households owned only one TV set, and the entire family watched TV together. However, since the 1980s, Japanese households have owned more than one TV set, and advertisers and ad agencies began requesting an individual rating system similar to those used in the West. The television networks resisted the new system for fear it would result in a drop in ratings and revenues.

At the end of 1994, A.C. Nielsen began selling mechanically obtained individual audience rating data (Nielsen's People Meter) in Japan. This system provides individual TV viewership data by narrow time segments, in contrast to the broad household viewing data available until then. The National Association of Commercial Broadcasters in Japan made numerous requests to have the service withdrawn. An agreement was arbitrated by the Japan Advertisers' Association. It was agreed that the individual ratings information would be sold as marketing data, and would not be used in media transactions.

Nielsen's new service, called the Advanced People Meter System (APMS), was launched in November 1994 with a panel of 300 homes in the Tokyo region. Until then, the only viewer measurement data available were total household ratings, supplemented by a monthly diary providing limited information about the viewing habits of individuals. Close on Neilsen's heels, VRC introduced its own People Meter System.

While most media-planning in Japan still focuses on GRP, the newer individual rating systems offer target audience rating points (TARP).

Today's audience ratings use mechanical means to measure household ratings, while relying on diary techniques for individual ratings. Technically, mechanical surveys break down into three methods, involving the use of a push-button People Meter developed in the U.S. in 1987, an improved People Meter with a headcount sensor attached, or a Full Passive Meter that automatically detects the number of viewers.

It should be noted that neither of the two leading rating services in Japan measures ratings for cable and satellite TV shows. Their overall viewership is considered too small to be captured accurately.

CONCLUSION

Television airtime in Japan remains a sellers' market, and will continue to be so for the foreseeable future. However, while it will never be inexpensive, proper GRP and TARP analysis will allow most advertisers to use television as a strong medium to reach a broad base of consumers.

Chapter 7

Shimbun
Advertising in Newspapers

In most countries, newspaper advertising is mainly considered a means of reaching a specific target in a particular geographic region. Similar use of newspaper advertising is possible in Japan. In addition, Japan's major dailies, with their huge circulations and nationwide reach, offer advertising opportunities not found elsewhere.

Ad space rates in the major Japanese dailies are extremely high at first glance, yet their nationwide coverage and extremely high circulations result in lower CPM (cost per thousand) than magazine advertisements.

Japan has 121 daily newspapers registered as members of Japan Newspaper Publishers and Editors Association (JNPEA). All the major daily newspapers print both morning and evening editions, which are often subscribed to as a set. Total daily circulation is 72 million (morning and evening issues counted separately): 48 morning and evening "set" papers, 57 morning-only newspapers, and 16 evening-only newspapers. This translates into 545 newspapers sold for every 1,000 people. If morning and evening editions are counted as one "set," rather than separately, then there are about 53 million copies per day.

Depending on which circulation figures are used ("set" figures, or morning and evening editions counted separately), the combined circulation of the three major national daily newspapers covers between one-quarter and one-third of the entire population. This "reach" is one reason for the extremely high cost of newspaper ad space.

HISTORY

Japan's first modern newspaper was the *Nagasaki Shipping List and Advertiser*, an English-language paper published twice a week beginning in 1861. The following year, the *Kampan Batabiya Shimbun*, a translated and reedited edition of *Javasche*

Courant, the organ of the Dutch government in Indonesia, was published by the Tokugawa shogunate. Both of these newspapers contained only foreign news.

Newspapers covering domestic news were first established in Edo (now Tokyo), Osaka, Kyoto, and Nagasaki in 1868. These newspapers, known as *ōshimbun*, were subsidized by political parties and focused on political stories that stressed their backers' views. As a result of strong government pressure and lack of revenues, the *ōshimbun* soon failed. This assisted the establishment of *koshimbun*, popular general-interest newspapers that featured unbiased local news, human interest stories, and light fiction. The *koshimbun* used advertising as a means of financial support, enabling them to maintain editorial independence.

At first, newspapers were sold on consignment to bookstores, but in the early 1900s a home-delivery system based on exclusive dealerships was developed. The dealers were responsible for delivery and also acted as subscription salesmen. This system is the mainstay of the newspaper industry today.

The Japanese press was under constant regulation and periodic suppression from the time of the Press Ordinance of 1875 through the militaristic regime of the 1930s. By the late 1930s the newspaper industry had come under the strict control of the military government. Under that government's policies, the 1,200 dailies published in 1937 dwindled to 104 in 1940, and a mere 54 by 1942. During World War II the government forced many papers to merge. American air raids destroyed or crippled many of those remaining.

During and immediately after the war, there was a severe shortage of newsprint in Japan. Some newspapers published a four-page paper, or even a single broadsheet. During the postwar occupation, the Supreme Commander, Allied Powers (SCAP), saw the press as an ideal tool for democratizing Japan, and allowed the surviving newspapers to continue publication after purging their executives. Prewar censorship laws were repealed, and the Japanese press came under the protection of article 21 of the 1947 Constitution, which guarantees "freedom of assembly and association as well as speech, press and all other forms of expression," and prohibits censorship.

In a further effort to promote democracy, SCAP encouraged the founding of new newspapers to avoid monopolies. However, shortages of materials and newsprint prevented Japan's press revival from really taking off until the 1950s. In May 1951, all controls on newsprint were lifted, and in October of the same year, all the major national dailies began to publish morning and evening editions.

NEWSPAPER CATEGORIES

Newspapers in Japan can be divided into two categories: general and specialized. Table 7.1 gives a breakdown of Japan's newspapers by type.

General daily newspapers can be divided into three types: national, block/regional, and prefectural/local.

Table 7.1
Newspapers in Japan, by Type

Type of newspaper	Number
Nationwide	5
Block	4
Prefectural	75
Sports	14
English	5
Trade	654
TOTAL	757

First there are the national daily newspapers based in Tokyo or Osaka (with daily circulations in the millions). These papers have printing plants in strategic regional locations throughout Japan. The location of these printing centers allows the national dailies to publish local editions. Advertisements can be placed either nationwide or in selected regions. Advertising rates for regional editions are determined by local circulations. *Nihon Keizai Shimbun* (a nationwide financial newspaper) is the only national daily that will accept local ads for real estate and publishers.

There are four major national general daily newspapers and one national business daily. The general-interest dailies are the *Yomiuri Shimbun, Asahi Shimbun, Mainichi Shimbun,* and *Sankei Shimbun*. The business newspaper is the *Nihon Keizai Shimbun*. All five national dailies print both morning and evening editions. Together, they account for about half of Japan's total daily newspaper circulation.

Japan's largest daily newspaper in terms of circulation is the *Yomiuri Shimbun* (established in Tokyo in 1874), which in 1997 had a national circulation of 10.15 million for the morning edition and 4.39 million for the evening edition.

Asahi Shimbun is the second largest newspaper. Established in Osaka in 1879, it has a morning circulation of about 8.36 million and an evening circulation of about 4.38 million.

In third place, the *Mainichi Shimbun* (established in Osaka in 1882) has a morning circulation of about 3.97 million and an evening circulation of about 1.89 million.

Trailing the top three general-interest newspapers, the *Sankei Shimbun* (established in 1933 in Osaka) has a morning circulation of about 1.9 million and an evening circulation of about 958,000.

The fifth national newspaper is the business-oriented *Nihon Keizai Shimbun* (established in Tokyo in 1878), also known as the *Nikkei*. In terms of circulation, it ranks fourth, with a morning circulation of about 2.99 million and an evening circulation of about 1.65 million.

All five nationwide dailies publish national and regional editions. All publish editions for Tokyo and Osaka, and, with the exception of the *Sankei Shimbun*, all print special editions for Hokkaido, Nagoya, and Kyushu (including western Honshu).

In addition to the national daily newspapers, Japan has three block (or regional) newspapers. Each block newspaper is based in a large regional city, and has a circulation that covers several surrounding prefectures.

The *Chunichi Shimbun* (covering the Nagoya area) and the Kyushu-based *Nishi-Nippon Shimbun* fit the definition of block newspapers. *Chunichi* has a morning circulation of 2.44 million and an evening circulation of 739,000, while the *Nishi-Nippon* has a morning circulation of 845,000 and an evening circulation of 194,000.

Although not meeting the "technical" requirements of block newspaper status, the *Hokkaido Shimbun*, which covers the island of Hokkaido (geographically vast but a single prefecture), is usually treated as a block newspaper. It has a morning circulation of 1.2 million and an evening circulation of 759,000.

In addition to the above three, the *Tokyo Shimbun* is often counted as a fourth block newpaper, although it is published and owned by the *Chunichi Shimbun.* The *Tokyo Shimbun* has a morning circulation of 700,000 and an evening circulation of 425,000.

The last type of general newspaper is the prefectural newspaper (sometimes called local newspaper). Most are based in their prefectural capital, and are circulated only within their prefecture. Local newspapers' circulations average around 200,000, although they vary between 50,000 and 700,000. Each of Japan's 47 prefectures (with the exception of Shiga) have at least one local newspaper. Several of the larger prefectures, such as Fukushima, Fukui, and Okinawa, have more than one local newspaper. Some of the prefectural newspapers' readership spills over into neighboring prefectures. Many of them print both morning and evening editions.

Local newspapers attract advertising from major Japanese corporations because of their loyal readership, which gives prefectural newspapers a share of from 55 to 70% in their prefecture. This is compared with a usually less than 20% share for the national dailies. In each prefecture, at least one local newspaper has larger sales than any of the national newspapers.

Japan also has several types of specialized newspapers: sports, free, trade, tabloid, and English.

Sports newspapers are an important category. Japan's first sports newspaper, the *Nikkan Sports*, was launched in 1946. However, it was not until the 1964 Tokyo Olympics that circulation of sports newspapers really began to grow.

Four of the nationwide general-interest dailies each own a sports newspaper. *Asahi* owns *Nikkan Sports*, *Mainichi* owns *Sports Nippon*, *Yomiuri* owns *Hochi Shimbun*, and *Sankei* owns *Sankei Sports*. In addition, three daily block newspapers, *Chunichi*, *Nishi-Nippon*, and *Hokkaido*, each own a sports newspapers.

In total, Japan has 17 sports dailies, all of which have branched out from their original sports-only focus. Since the early 1990s, the sports newspapers have carried articles on domestic elections and political scandals, as well as overseas news, in a format that is easier to read than that of the major dailies.

Sports newspapers in Japan, with their liberal use of color, splashy headlines, and erotic stories, illustrations, and photos, are in a sense Japan's popular press. Three-quarters of sports newspapers are delivered to the home. However, most sports newspapers have two versions—the version delivered to homes and the *ekiban* version sold in kiosks at train/subway stations. The latter version is filled with sex-oriented articles, pictures, and ads.

An interesting category is one most foreigners are seldom aware of, the free newspapers. Free papers originated with the *danchi shimbun,* published for residents of the public housing projects (*danchi*) that began to be constructed in the latter half of the 1950s. The first *danchi shimbun* was published for about 60,000 residents of a housing development in the Tokyo metropolitan area. The paper, titled *The Key*, was delivered by housewives living in the *danchi*. Its success led to the publication of similar papers for *danchi* across the country.

Prompted by the success of *danchi shimbun*, local free papers were launched in the 1960s. The pacesetter was the *Sankei Living Shimbun* (affiliated with the *Sankei Shimbun*). This paper, too, is delivered by housewives hired on a part-time basis. When first launched, this delivery system attracted major attention. At present, the *Sankei Living Shimbun* reaches all 43 of Japan's major metropolitan areas and enjoys a circulation of 7.3 million. The advantage for advertisers is that *Sankei Living Shimbun* allows advertisers to place ads by ward. Thus, if an advertiser wants to target eight of Tokyo's 23 wards, it can do so. Although major Japanese corporations place ads in the *Sankei Living Shimbun*, the majority of ads are placed by local retailers.

Like so many countries, Japan has tabloid newspapers. The two national daily tabloids are *Nikkan Gendai* and *Yukan Fuji*, both evening newspapers with claimed circulations in the 2.5 million range.

Japan has business newspapers, many of them dailies, focusing on a particular industry. The major papers are the *Nihon Kōgyō Shimbun* (the Japan Industrial Journal), *Nikkan Kōgyō Shimbun* (Nikkan Industrial News), *Nikkei Sangyō Shimbun* (Nikkei Industrial News), and the *Nikkei Kinyū Shimbun* (the Nikkei Financial Daily).

In addition, Japan boasts hundreds of trade papers, such as the *Denki Shimbun* (electronics), *Nikkan Kensetsu Kōgyō Shimbun* (construction), *Nihon Nogyo Shimbun* (agriculture), *Nippon Shokuryo Shimbun* (food), *Jutaku Shinpo* (real estate),

Nikkan Suisan Shimbun (fisheries), *Sen Kan Shimbun* (textiles), and *Nikkei Ryūtsū Shimbun* (commodity distribution).

Circulations of business and trade newspapers range from the tens of thousands to the hundreds of thousands.

In addition to the Japanese newspapers, there are four daily English-language newspapers. Three are published by the major national dailies: the *Asahi Evening News*, the *Mainichi Daily News*, and the *Daily Yomiuri*. The fourth, the independent *Japan Times*, was first published in Tokyo in 1897 and is the oldest English-language newspaper in Japan, boasting the largest circulation (approximately 80,000). In addition, there is one English weekly, *The Nikkei Weekly*. All the English-language newspapers have very limited circulations.

CIRCULATION, SUBSCRIPTIONS, AND SALES

Newspaper circulation in Japan is high due to an efficient home-delivery system, a high literacy rate, and a general enthusiasm for reading newspapers. It is estimated that more than 80% of adults read at least one newspaper every day, according to the survey by the Japan Newspaper Publishers and Editors Asso-

Table 7.2
Circulations of Japan's Major National Daily and Sports Newspapers

	Morning edition	Evening edition
General newspapers		
Yomiuri Shimbun	10,152,569	4,395,818
Asahi Shimbun	8,360,815	4,384,851
Mainichi Shimbun	3,979,849	1,898,852
Sankei Shimbun	1,943,409	958,475
Nikkei Shimbun	2,997,881	1,659,975
Sports newspapers		
Chunichi Sports	679,926*	—
Daily Sports	963,071*	—
Hochi Shimbun	672,037	—
Nikkan Sports	1,955,877*	—
Nishi-Nippon Sports	182,658*	—
Sankei Sports	1,356,968*	—
Sports Nippon	982,890	—
Tokyo Chunichi Sports	320,254*	—
Tokyo Sports Press	458,000*	2,095,000*

*Circulation figures represent monthly average from January to June 1997.
Source: Japan Audit Bureau of Circulation, ed., *Newspaper Publishers Report* (1998).

Table 7.3
Time Spent Daily Reading Newspaper (Hours/Minutes)

	Weekday	Saturday	Sunday
Male			
Average	00:28	00:27	00:25
10–15	00:02	00:04	00:03
16–19	00:06	00:06	00:08
20–29	00:11	00:10	00:10
30–39	00:20	00:21	00:20
40–49	00:29	00:31	00:26
50–59	00:41	00:35	00:37
60+	00:49	00:46	00:41
Female			
Average	00:20	00:20	00:17
10–15	00:02	00:04	00:04
16–19	00:04	00:05	00:03
20–29	00:09	00:11	00:08
30–39	00:16	00:14	00:14
40–49	00:24	00:24	00:21
50–59	00:28	00:28	00:24
60+	00:32	00:30	00:27

Source: NHK Survey (1995).

ciation. However, the percentage of people who read a newspaper every day is lower among the young, with only about 51.7% of those aged 18 and 19 reading a paper daily.

Table 7.2 gives the circulation figures for Japan's major national daily and sports newspapers. Newspaper circulation is audited by the Japan Audit Bureau of Circulation (ABC), an independent organization established in 1952. ABC publishes reports monthly and half-yearly.

On average, each household subscribes to at least one newspaper. About 70% subscribe only to the morning issue, even though the additional cost of subscribing to both morning and evening editions is minimal.

Because many households subscribe to a national paper and a local paper, the average Japanese home receives 1.3 newspapers. Newspapers thus provide an effective but expensive way to blanket an area with advertisements. The average daily time spent reading a newspaper is shown in Table 7.3.

Since 1990, the increase in the number of daily newspapers circulated has not kept pace with the increase in the number of households. There are two reasons for this. One is the economic slump, which has forced many companies to economize by reducing the number of newspapers to which they subscribe. The second is the growing trend of households to subscribe to only the morning edition of a newspaper rather than to the traditional set of morning and evening editions.

Overall, however, the decline in general-readership newspaper circulation has been offset by the increased circulations of sports newspapers since 1990.

Still, at the present time, the five national newspapers account for 52% of all newspapers sold in Japan, while the sports newspapers, despite their rapid growth, can claim a market share of only 12%.

The vast majority of newspapers in Japan are subscribed to. Subscription home deliveries account for over 90% of total sales of the national dailies (more than 99% for *Yomiuri Shimbun*, *Asahi Shimbun*, and *Sankei Shimbun*). Only the *Nikkei* (5.4%) and the *Mainichi Shimbun* (1.7%) rely on retail sales for more than 1% of total sales. When sports and leisure newspapers are included, an impressive 93% of all newspapers are delivered to subscribers' homes. They are delivered by breakfast time (and again in the early evening if the evening edition is also subscribed to).

Block and prefectural newspapers (morning and evening editions) are no exception to the rule, with over 95% delivered to subscribers. The exception to the rule of subscriptions accounting for over 90% of total sales is the sports newspapers. About 35% of sports newspapers' sales are single copies purchased by salarymen at train stations on their way home. The newspaper is disposed of at their home station; they wouldn't be caught dead taking home the paper, with its erotic stories and lurid photos.

Besides subscriptions, newspapers are also sold at newsstands (kiosks) and convenience stores. A breakdown of general and sports newspaper sales is given in Table 7.4.

Newspaper subscriptions are sold in Japan through delivery agents. Each newspaper has a network of sales and delivery agents who are nominally independent of the newspaper. They both deliver the newspapers and are responsi-

Table 7.4
Sales of General and Sports Papers (%)

	Home delivery	Single-copy sales	Mailed	Other
General papers	92.9	6.6	0.05	0.45
Sports papers	63.9	35.7	0.01	0.39

Source: Nihon Shimbun Kyokai (The Japan Newspaper Association), 22 May 1997.

ble for gaining new subscriptions. Newspaper delivery is a big business. In 1995 there were around 23,000 delivery agents employing about 480,000 delivery personnel. Interestingly, of the delivery personnel, 83% were adults (40% male, 43% female), and 17% were students (8% junior high school and 9% senior high school).

Most delivery agents handle a single newspaper's publications, but there are some that handle noncompeting publications. Each sales agent is granted exclusive territory in return for promising not to handle competing newspapers. The agent's main revenue source is the delivery fees (about half the cost of the newspaper subscription) and the stuffing-and-delivery fees received for handling the inserts delivered with the newspapers.

This delivery system is advantageous to Japanese newspaper companies in that it guarantees fewer returned copies than newspapers in other countries. This practice is also the major reason for newspapers' high circulations in Japan, although it is very costly to maintain.

Competition between delivery agents for subscribers is fierce. Each local market has from two to five newspapers battling for dominance. The huge circulations enjoyed by the nationwide dailies is fueled by the heated sales competition between the nationwide network of delivery agents. As a result of these huge circulations, articles are diluted to fit the taste of all readers. The most popular pages of a newspaper are the TV program schedules (66.4%), social issues (60.5%), regional news (56.7%), and sports (54.3%) pages.

VARIOUS VERSIONS OF THE SAME NEWSPAPER

In the 1980s, Japan's national dailies invested huge amounts of capital in decentralizing their printing. All the national and block newspapers with substantial circulations outside their home regions established printing facilities in their main markets throughout the nation. This move to decentralized printing was for two reasons: to reduce news lag and to facilitate localization.

Although most general newspapers publish both morning and evening editions, there are some regions where twice-daily delivery is not feasible. While Japan is physically a small country, it is very mountainous, and many roads used by newspaper delivery trucks are both narrow and crowded with traffic. In areas where delivering two editions is not possible, the newspapers typically include some of the previous evening's news in the following morning's edition, and deliver the same amount of content once a day. Thus, these newspapers daily publish morning and evening editions in most areas, and in some areas they also print these hybrid (morning and some previous evening news) editions.

Additionally, all newspapers have local-news pages for each delivery area. These pages have to be printed and folded as part of the newspaper. Complicating matters is the time it takes to deliver a newspaper from the printing plant to the subscriber. Since the morning newspaper must arrive no later than 6:00 A.M., and the evening newspaper by 4:00 P.M., transit times have to be factored into the printing schedule.

Thus, at the printing plant, the deadline for distant deliveries is earlier than that for nearby deliveries. This means that late-breaking news may not make it into the distant-delivery edition but will be included in the nearby-delivery edition. Thus, the content of the same newspaper differs according to when and where it is being delivered.

So, even though generally there are morning and evening editions of a newspaper, there are actually several morning editions, and at least as many evening editions, of each newspaper.

Japanese newspapers cost the same amount regardless of where in the nation they are bought. Government regulations forbid newspapers to charge different prices in different areas. This ensures that a strong nationwide daily cannot lower its price in one area, thus starting a price war that a locally published newspaper could not weather.

This system is called *saihan-kakaku-iji*, or legal guarantee of the fixed retail price (an exception to Japan's antitrust law). It is one of many privileges enjoyed by newspaper companies.

MONTHLY NEWSPAPER HOLIDAYS AND LACK OF SUNDAY EVENING EDITIONS

With the exception of sports newspapers, almost all newspapers in Japan have a monthly holiday on which the newspaper is not published. These holidays are mainly to give the delivery agents a day off. On these days, sports newspapers increase the press run for newsstand sales.

With the exception of the sports newspapers, none of the daily nationwide newspapers publishes Sunday evening editions. They do publish Sunday morning editions, but these have fewer pages than the weekday paper. The thick Sunday editions of the U.S. do not exist in Japan.

LIMIT ON THE NUMBER OF NEWSPAPER PAGES

Japanese newspapers have noticeably fewer pages than newspapers in many other countries, thus increasing competition for ad space.

In 1970, the major daily nationals began publishing 24-page morning editions. In 1987, three of the major dailies increased their morning editions to 28 pages.

Today, depending on the day of the week, the general national daily newspapers' morning editions average from 24 to 36 pages, and their evening editions average

12 to 20 pages. It is not possible for newspapers to publish more than 36 pages because the delivery agents refuse to deliver papers thicker than that.

NEWSPAPER ADVERTISING

Due to limited advertising space, classified ads for used goods are almost nonexistent in Japanese newspapers. The cost of a classified ad would most likely be higher than the amount the advertiser might hope to recover from the sale.

The ratio of ads to articles in newspapers is about 45:55. The ratio for the national dailies is slightly higher. Evening editions tend to have a slightly higher ratio than morning editions. The reason for keeping ads to no more than 50% of newspaper content stems from the fact that a certain amount of newspapers used to be shipped by train throughout the country in order to obtain a lower tax rate for "disseminating information." The law on "disseminating information" remains on the books.

For general newspapers, sales account for almost 50% of income, and advertising for little more than 35%. Sales account for about 60% of income of sports newspapers, and advertising for about 40%.

Newspaper advertising is dominated by the publishing, services, housing, construction materials, wholesale, and department store industries.

Types of Newspaper Ads

There are basically three types of newspaper ads:

1. Full-page ads
2. Ads in the lower half of the page, below the news articles
3. Miscellaneous announcement ads that occupy small spaces

A newspaper page consists of 15 horizontal columns (except tabloids, which have 11 columns). Except for full-page ads, advertisements are usually placed on the bottom half of the page (under the articles). This type of ad is called *kiji shita.* At extra cost (space allowing) *kiji naka* (island) ads can be placed among the articles.

The basic unit of measurement and sales for newspaper ad space is the *dan* (horizontal column). One *dan* is slightly more than 3 cm in height and runs the width of the page. *Kiji shita* ads are typically available in 3, 5, 7, or 15 *dan* heights, and range in width from 1/8 page to a full page.

Seven columns is considered a half-page. Half of a seven-column space is considered a quarter page. Discount rates for ad volume are calculated by the total number of columns rather than by the number of insertions.

One full page in a major nationwide "blanket-size" paper is 53.4 cm high and 38.5 cm wide. One column is 3.3 cm high and 38.5 cm wide. One full page in a tabloid paper is 39 cm high and 25 cm wide. One column in a tabloid paper is 3.35 cm high and 25 cm wide.

Since the number of pages in a newspaper is fixed, advertising space demand generally exceeds space availability. It is difficult to secure a guarantee of space on a specific date or page. Ad insertion schedules are always subject to last-minute changes due to editorial priorities and/or the priorities of larger/longer-term clients.

Until recently newspapers would not guarantee advertisers a specific date for their advertisement, or on which page their ad would appear. In April 1995, *Asahi Shimbun* introduced a system called SPEED, whereby the article genre and ad space are made public three months in advance, in the form of an "ad table," so that advertisers could apply for the page they prefer. Reserving ad space entails an extra "designation fee." The success of this system led the *Chunichi Shimbun* and the *Hokkaido Shimbun* to adopt similar systems. However, even space booked this way is not absolutely guaranteed.

Mainichi, *Yomiuri*, *Nikkei*, and *Sankei*, as well as the block and prefectural newspapers, are planning to install their own versions of the SPEED system.

Some positions, however, cannot be guaranteed. Ads can be bumped from a certain day's newspaper if there is a sudden increase in editorial content due to breaking news. Editors retain the final say regarding what is published in each edition.

There is in particular a tendency toward oversubscription of newspaper space in March (the last month of the fiscal year for many Japanese companies) as companies try to use up their annual ad budget allocation. There is also a rush to place orders from about the 20th of each month as advertisers try to use up their monthly budgets.

Usually the front-page ad space of the major newspapers is locked up by the major publishing firms, who have a long relationship with newspapers because they were among the earliest advertisers. The front page is considered the most prestigious space, and newspapers consider that a major publisher's ads on the front page will increase their prestige.

The Process of Buying Ad Space

In the case of national editions, application for ad space is made no later than about half a month prior to the insertion date. The exception is application for one-time special ads, such as public-apology announcements or obituary ads called "black mourning border ads" (*rinji-men*).

The advertiser's agency applies for ad space or goes through a designated agency that has an established account with the newspaper company.

The media department of the ad agency telephones the advertising department of the newspaper to place the space request. If it is accepted, written confirmation usually follows. However, contracts are not made.

In theory, newspaper ad space must be ordered one to two months in advance. But just because the newspaper accepts the space order, that is no guarantee the ad will be placed on the desired day or page, even if both were specified when the request was accepted.

The final decision on which ads are actually placed and where they will be placed in the newspaper is usually not made until a week before publication. Decisions on full-page ads are made first, followed by those on how the remaining mix of ads of different sizes will be placed.

Between the time the space order is placed and the time of final decision-making by the newspaper, the agency's media department checks whether the space is secured. These checks are handled through phone calls and frequent visits to the newspaper, especially as the deadline nears. The agency's media department personnel visit the newspaper's ad department continuously to check if their client's name is still listed to appear as scheduled by the newspaper's scheduling department.

As editorial changes are made to the newspaper, clients' names are rearranged (in terms of where their ad will be placed) or erased (bumped to a different day in favor of another client). If the client has been bumped, the agency attempts to convince the paper to reinstate the client's ad.

The newspaper scheduling department takes several factors into consideration, after editorial content has been determined, when making its final decisions regarding ad placement. It considers how early the order was placed, whether the client is of long standing, whether the ad is nationwide or regional, what price the client is paying for the space, and if the ad must be placed on this particular day.

Submission of Ad Material

After space has been booked, the ad material must be sent to the newspaper.

Deadlines for submitting regular ad material to newspapers are usually two to four working days before publication date. Newspapers will accept only film. The format and number of required materials will differ depending on the newspaper company. Only in cases of public-apology announcements or obituary ads (*rinji-men*) will the newspaper accept material other than film.

The deadline for materials for black-and-white ads is two working days before appearance. A set of one film and two Photostats, plus two gallery proofs, must be provided. For nationwide ads, one set must be provided for each of the newspaper's main offices (Tokyo, Osaka, Nagoya, and Kyushu, for example).

The deadline for color ads is five working days before appearance (one color-separated film, one black-and-white film, one set of color galleys (cyan, magenta, yellow, black), and 40 color galleys (for Tokyo). This is for advertising in Kanto only—Osaka requires 21 color galleys. Newspapers do not provide a color proof. If the client wants to see one, the agency will have to take the client to the printing plant.

For island ads (*zappo*) that are surrounded by articles, order deadline is 35 working days before the month the ad is scheduled to appear. Insertion deadline is two working days in advance of appearance. One film and two Photostats are required.

AD SPACE RATES

Newspaper ad space rates are based on the total number of columns bought during a specified period of time. The unit (per column) price is usually lower for evening editions than for morning editions. Rates also depend on the day the ad runs and the page it appears on. The "social page" (*shakai-men*) is popular among advertisers, as is the TV/radio program page, which means those pages are more expensive than others. The TV/radio program page is the most expensive.

There are basically three types of ad rates for newspaper space:

1. For one or several insertions within three months
2. For monthly insertions for three to six months
3. For monthly insertions for six months or longer

Newspaper advertising rates are determined by factors such as type of ad, distribution area, placement period, and placement volume. Discounts are available for continuous, large-volume ad placements. The longer the ad placement period and the greater the ad volume placed, the greater the discount rate.

There are other variables that the newspapers take into consideration when quoting ad rates: number of columns bought during six months; number of columns bought previously (past business relationship); whether space is bought nationwide or just for certain areas; "cooperativeness" or "noncooperativeness" of the client in the past when a promised ad was bumped from the date that was originally requested by the client.

Thus, rates for the same ad space (half-page, for example) differ from client to client.

When regular advertisements are placed in national editions, the rates differ according to the following conditions:

1. Contract details: in the case of special ads, undiscounted basic rates apply. On the other hand, ad space that has been contracted for a certain placement period and volume will receive a discounted contract rate.

2. Morning or evening edition.
3. Distribution area: whether the space is booked for a national edition, set territory issues of a national edition, each regional branch edition, set territory issues of each local edition, and so on.
4. Total number of ad columns bought during a regular period (in the case of contract ads).

For example, in the case of contract advertising calling for two full-page placements within a six-month period in the national morning edition of the *Asahi Shimbun*, the rate would be calculated at the per-column contract rate of ¥2,480,000 x 30 columns = ¥74,400,000.

The method of calculating the rate is different for a "special ad." The rate for placing a one-column ad in the national morning edition of the *Asahi Shimbun* would be subject to the standard editorial ad rate of ¥145,000 (per centimeter, per column) x 38.5 cm column width = ¥5,582,500. The price per column is higher than the contract rate.

Basic ad rates are fixed by the total number of columns bought over a specific period of time (usually half a year).

For one-time-only ads of less than one column, placed on the lower half of the page, a "basic price" (*kihon ryōkin*) is charged. This rate is usually quoted for "apology ads" (*owabi kōkoku*) and obituary ads.

For ads of one column or more, there is a "contract" rate, called the *keiyaku ryōkin*, that varies depending on the number of columns the advertiser is contracted to place during a six-month period. Discounts are offered on the basis of the total number of columns bought for a specific period of time, such as one month. Further discounts are considered if the buyer (agency and/or client) is a longtime customer.

Ad space rates are influenced by the day the ad is supposed to appear—there are expensive days, average days, and inexpensive days. A further influence on price is which regional editions (of a nationwide newspaper) the ad is placed in, and which page the ad is on.

Newspaper ad space prices also differ according to the page of the newspaper on which the ad appears, since some pages draw more reader attention (*seshoku-ritsu*) than others, and the period during which the ad is to appear (a period with lots of ads or a period with few ads).

When a request for placement of an ad on a specific page or day is made, additional charges (*shitei ryōkin*) are added to the contract rate. The *shitei ryōkin* typically average up to 10% of the contract rate.

For a color ad, special color printing costs are added. These charges vary according to the number of colors used and the size of the ad space.

Just like the regular ads, rates for small ads differ depending on the contract details, use of morning or evening editions, distribution area, and so on. For example, placing an island ad in the Tokyo morning edition of the *Asahi Shimbun* on a special one-time basis would cost ¥734,000, and on a contract basis would cost ¥633,000.

A unique way to get your ad in a newspaper quite inexpensively is what is called *tsukami*. The newspaper is given instructions to place your ad whenever an opening comes up (usually at the last minute).

DEADLINES FOR BLOCK AND LOCAL NEWSPAPERS

Technically, requests for ad space must be made by the 18th of the month prior to the month in which the ad will appear (regardless of whether the ad will appear on the first day of the following month or the last day).

One week prior to the date on which you want the ad to appear, the newspaper either confirms or denies the ad's appearance on that date. This is a result of the newspaper's weekly internal meeting, where the final decisions regarding which ads will appear the following week are made.

Ad insertions in tabloids are basically the same as for other newspapers. However, it must be kept in mind that tabloids are smaller than regular newspapers. The average tabloid page is 39.1 cm by 24.5 cm. However, tabloid sizes vary from paper to paper, with differences up to 3 cm. If ad material conforming to the average tabloid size is submitted, most tabloids will resize it to fit their page.

Newspaper Inserts

Inserts (*orikomi*) can be placed in newspapers and distributed to subscribers through the newspaper distribution system. They are not available in the evening editions, the Monday editions, or the editions after national holidays. Traditionally, March has the highest number of inserts, and August is the quietest month.

Inserts by the real estate and retail (automobiles, department stores, supermarkets, furniture stores, etc.) industries comprise about 70% of the total.

Color inserts comprise about 65% of all inserts, with the remainder being black and white. The most popular day for placing inserts is Saturday, and 60% of insert readers are housewives.

Inserts are available in five sizes: B1, B2, B3, B4, and B5. B4 inserts account for more than half the total newspaper inserts, and B3 account for around 35%.

CONCLUSION

Newspaper advertising allows advertisers to tailor their approach. They can opt for the nationwide reach of the national dailies or for the area-specific reach of the block and local papers.

Over the years, newspaper readership in Japan has been consistently high and stable, and there are no indications that this will change. A wise selection of newspaper by category, readership, area covered, circulation, and ad size and position can offer a highly effective and efficient means of targeting a specific audience. Furthermore, although newspaper ad space sells at a premium, and will continue to do so in the foreseeable future, the cost per reader of newspaper ads is much lower than that of magazines, and audience readership is consistent over time.

Chapter 8

Zasshi
Advertising in Magazines

Whether magazines can be classified as a mass medium in Japan is doubtful in some ways. Per capita, Japan has more magazines than most other countries in the world. However, this is a direct result of the steady proliferation of new magazines every year rather than of high circulations. In general, circulations are quite small.

The average Japanese consumer buys 30 magazines per year. The large number of magazines published and their specialized readerships allow an amount of market segmentation that other media in Japan cannot match.

HISTORY

Japan's first magazine, *Seiyo-Zasshi* (*Western Magazine*), was a ten-page woodblock-printed booklet published in 1867. It featured articles translated into Japanese from Dutch magazines. It was closed down in 1869 after publishing only six issues. *Seiyo-Zasshi*'s debut marked the first use of the term *zasshi* for magazine.

The first modern magazines in Japan were weeklies introduced by the dominant daily national newspapers during the 1920s. The *Shūkan Asahi* (published by the *Asahi Shimbun*) and the *Sunday Mainichi* (published by the *Mainichi Shimbun*) were launched in 1922. These magazines aimed to be the equivalent of the Sunday edition of Western newspapers, and both are still in circulation.

From their inception, magazines were an important medium for advertisers aiming at Japan's burgeoning affluent class. Yet, until the end of World War II, their circulations were limited because their readerships generally remained elitist and intellectual.

In the immediate postwar period, magazines' importance as an advertising medium was overshadowed by the emphasis on mass production and mass marketing. The result was the prevalence of newspapers, and the emergence of radio, and later of television, as the ideal media for reaching the mass market.

Postwar growth of Japan's literacy rates, however, and the expanding middle class gradually boosted magazine circulations. As the Japanese market became more affluent, and the emphasis on mass marketing subsequently lessened, interest in magazines revived as their focused readership became more attractive to advertisers. Magazines provided a means to access specific segments of the market.

A number of specialized magazine publishers emerged during this period, notably Heibon Shuppan-sha, now known as Magazine House. Publishing companies entered into the weekly magazine field in 1956, led by the *Shūkan Shincho* (*Weekly Shincho*) published by Shinchosha. Until the *Shūkan Shincho*'s launch, it had been believed that only the major newspapers could publish a weekly magazine.

As Japan's economy began to get back on its feet during the later 1950s, several women's weeklies were launched. *Shūkan Josei* appeared in 1957, followed by *Josei Jishin* in 1958. A third women's weekly, *Josei-Seven*, was launched in 1963. The end of the 1950s also saw the introduction of two general-interest weeklies, *Shūkan Gendai* and *Shūkan Bunshun*, in 1959. The 1950s marked the beginning of the wild proliferation of magazines that continues today.

The 1960s ushered in an era of magazines specifically targeted at men, such as *Heibon Punch* and *Shūkan Playboy* (*Weekly Playboy*). Many business publications, such as *Fortune Japan* (the predecessor of *President*) and *Nikkei Business*, were launched during the mid- and later 1960s.

To meet the needs of Japan's postwar baby boomers, the 1970s saw the introduction of magazines aimed specifically at young adults. In 1972, *Pia*, an entertainment guide for young people, was launched and became an immediate success. This was closely followed by fashion magazines such as *an an* and *non-no*, targeting young women. The mid-1970s saw the entry of magazines aimed at young men. The first successful magazine aimed at young men was *Popeye*, which cataloged the latest products and lifestyles for young men. *Popeye*'s popularity led to the launch of rival *Hot-Dog Press* in 1979.

The 1980s saw a second boom in new magazines aimed at specific target segments. Magazines dedicated to the latest trends (*Dime* and *Nikkei Trendy*) were the first to be launched. Then, daily-life-oriented magazines aimed at homemakers were published, such as *Orange Page*, *Lettuce Club*, and *Saita*. In addition, several magazines dedicated to gourmet-oriented young women, such as *Hanako*, were launched at this time. Finally, *Focus*, a photo-editorial magazine, opened a new genre of journalism in Japan. It was closely followed by *Friday*.

Table 8.1
Magazines by Periodicity (%)

Monthly	63.9
Not periodical	15.9
Bimonthly	9.5
Seasonally	5.2
Biweekly	1.3
Weekly	2.8
Other	1.4
Total	100.0

Source: Japan Magazine and Book Publishers and Editors Association, *Publication Indices Annual Report* (1998).

The 1980s also saw publishers launching new magazines through line extension. As readers grew up, publishers offered them new magazines that catered to their changing needs and interests. Magazine House launched *Olive* for young women who had graduated from *an an*. The young men who made up *Popeye*'s readership were offered *Brutus* as their tastes changed.

There was also a flurry of "sister"/"brother" magazines. Shueisha, a major publisher, launched *Men's non-no* (a "brother" magazine to Shueisha's existing women's magazine, *non-no*). Shueisha also introduced *More for Men* (based on its popular women's magazine *More*). Kobunsha launched a men's magazine called *Gainer*, a "brother" magazine for *JJ*, its women's magazine.

With the heating up of the economy, the 1980s saw the launch of many Japanese versions of foreign magazines. *Marie Claire*, *Elle*, and *Cosmopolitan* are representative examples. Unsurprisingly, the 1990s saw a proliferation of new magazine titles dedicated to computers.

Table 8.1 shows a breakdown of magazines by their periodicity.

LAUNCH AND SUSPENSION OF MAGAZINES

Japanese publishers are under constant pressure to cater to the perpetually changing tastes of a highly literate population. In their never-ending search for new readers, publishers are continuously launching new magazines. This is done with the knowledge that only a handful of them will be successful.

While they relentlessly launch new titles, publishers do not hesitate to stop publication of poorly performing magazines. When a Japanese publisher terminates publication of a magazine, it usually announces the magazine has been suspended (*kyūkan*) rather than stopped (*haikan*). This is solely for the purpose of saving face.

The annual number of magazine launches and failures fluctuates wildly. Only 16 out of 126 new launches survived in 1974. From 1986 to 1996 an average of 140 new magazines were launched annually, and an average of 89 ceased publication. In 1996 slightly less than half of the 200 magazines launched survived. Table 8.2 lists magazines launched and suspended between 1986 and 1996.

Overall, the number of magazine titles published increases every year. Consignment sales to retailers are the norm, and unsold copies are returned to the publishers.

Low overheads allow publishers to launch a large number of new magazines every year. *Non-no*, a bimonthly with a circulation of 1.2 million, has a full-time staff of only 30. Printing is farmed out and sales are handled by wholesalers. Some magazines even send editorial work to independent production companies. (*Shūkan Post* regularly sends pages to production companies that specialize in articles on travel, cooking, fashion, etc.) Gakken's *La Seine* is totally produced by another company, although the official publisher is Gakken.

Table 8.3 lists the total number of weekly and monthly magazine titles printed between 1988 and 1997.

Table 8.2
Magazines Launched and Suspended, 1986–96

	No. of magazines launched	No. of magazines suspended
1986	179	133
1987	126	116
1988	131	79
1989	112	56
1990	155	81
1991	165	81
1992	158	106
1993	169	118
1994	157	120
1995	202	130
1996	200	103

Source: Japan Marketing and Advertising Yearbook (1998).

Table 8.3
Number of Weekly and Monthly Magazine Titles Printed, 1988–97

	Monthly	Weekly	Total
1988	2,681	76	2,757
1989	2,700	77	2,777
1990	2,721	81	2,802
1991	2,836	89	2,925
1992	2,851	85	2,936
1993	2,896	83	2,979
1994	2,942	81	3,023
1995	3,035	81	3,116
1996	3,177	80	3,257
1997	3,226	92	3,318

Source: Japan Magazine and Book Publishers and Editors Association, *Publication Indices/Annual Report* (1998).

MAGAZINE BACKGROUND

There are 4,002 (weekly, monthly, quarterly, annual) magazines available in Japan. Over 3,200 are monthlies. About 100 are weeklies, 150 are published every ten days, and 20 are published twice per month. The remainder are bimonthlies, quarterlies, biannuals, and annuals.

The bulk of Japan's 4,000 magazines are aimed at specific audiences and have limited circulations in the tens of thousands.

Most major advertisers concentrate their magazine advertising in about 200 major weekly and monthly magazines. The major Japanese magazines have readerships in the hundreds of thousands, with only a small handful either reaching or coming close to the million mark (e.g., *Ie no Hikari* and *The Television*). Japan does not have magazines with megacirculations like the U.S.'s *Modern Maturity*'s 22 million. The Japanese edition of *Newsweek* counts its circulation at about 150,000; the U.S. edition has 3 million readers.

Magazines normally distribute the same edition nationwide. Exceptions are publications that are area-specific, such as *Hanako* and *Pia* in the Kanto area. However, some nationwide magazines with large circulations alter their editions by territory, such as by offering a Kanto region edition or Kansai region edition. This is partially to compensate for the fact that magazine advertising typically does not lend itself to geographical segments.

In 1995 the average total monthly sales of all monthly magazines combined was 189,655,833 (or 2,275,870,000 annually). Total annual circulation of all monthly magazines combined was claimed to be 3,120,510,000. The average total weekly sales of all weekly magazines combined was 31,437,115 (or 1,634,730,000 annually) in 1995. Annual claimed circulation of all weekly magazines combined was 1,942,650,000. The discrepancies are due to several factors, such as copies returned by retailers and estimated pass-along readership.

In general, the ratio of advertising revenue to total revenue for consumer magazines is 20–30%. It increases to 50% for business publications.

Interestingly, more than 30% of all reported magazine sales are comic sales. The majority of publications in Japan that have a circulation in excess of 1 million copies per issue are comic magazines, known as *manga*. Fifteen of them have circulations exceeding 1 million. *Manga* are not aimed just at children; they are also avidly read by adults. There are more than 500 categories of *manga* released weekly or as monthly serials, in all known genres. The total *manga* readership is an estimated 30 million, about one-quarter of the population of Japan.

The largest-circulation magazine is the comic magazine *Weekly Shonen Jump* (estimated at around 5 million).

TYPES OF WEEKLY MAGAZINES

Weekly magazines can be broadly separated by content into four groups. The first group is weekly magazines for men, such as *Shūkan Playboy* (Shueisha Press), which is aimed at younger men, and *Shūkan Gendai* (Kodansha Press) and *Shūkan Post* (Shogakukan Press), which are mostly for salarymen. The latter two are commonly among the in-flight magazines carried by airlines, and/or are provided as free reading material at coffee shops and barber shops.

The second group of weekly magazines, such as *Shūkan Shincho* (Shinchosha Press) and *Shūkan Bunshun* (Bungei Shunjusha Press), are targeted at both men and women. They cover social and political matters, and are usually quite conservative. They attract more mature readers than young readers.

Weekly magazines for women such as *Josei Seven* (Shogakukan Press) and *Shūkan Josei* (Shufu-to-Seikatsusha Press) belong to the third group. They are similar to TV talk shows (commonly referred to as "wide shows" in Japan), packed full of human-interest stories. Their major topics include scandals among celebrities, the latest news on the Japanese royal family, and articles on dieting.

Friday (Kodansha Press), *Focus* (Shinchosha Press), and *Flash* (Kobunsha Press) are representative of the fourth group of weekly magazines. These magazines are composed mostly of gossip articles exposing the secrets of Japanese celebrities (or politicians), with accompanying "incriminating" photos that inevitably spur controversy.

Weekly magazines, with the exception of comics (*manga*), do not sell in the order of millions. According to the Japan Audit Bureau of Circulation, as of 1996 the weekly magazines enjoyed circulations ranging between 400,000 and 900,000.

All four types of weekly magazines tend to carry sensational stories to some extent. Also, many weeklies, whether aimed at men or both men and women, regularly contain pages with photos of nude young women. Foreign advertisers whose head offices have a problem with this should check before placing ads.

The weekly magazines can also be categorized by their publishers. The weeklies mentioned earlier are all published by regular publishing companies. Others, such as *Shūkan Asahi* (Weekly Asahi), *Shūkan Yomiuri* (Weekly Yomiuri), and *Sunday Mainichi*, are published by the major national newspaper companies. These tend to be more news-oriented.

Two of the most consistently popular and widely read young women's fashion magazines, since their launches in 1970 and 1971, are *an an* and *non-no*. *Non-no*, with a weekly circulation of 1,500,000, is targeted at young women between 17 and 23. *An an* circulates 650,000 copies every 15 days and is targeted at slightly more sophisticated women of 18 to 25.

In 1989, Sekai Bunkasha, publisher of *Katei Gaho*, a magazine for mature housewives, launched *Miss Katei Gaho*. While *Katei Gaho* is more focused on Japaneseness and/or the Japanese interpretation of Western fashion, cooking, and cosmetics, *Miss Katei Gaho* makes concessions to the Western lifestyles of younger women (the word "miss" is written in English next to the *kanji* for *Katei Gaho*). *Miss Katei Gaho* is aimed at nurturing young women as potential readers of *Katei Gaho* when they get older.

The 1980s saw the launching of cheaper magazines like *Lettuce Club* and *Orange Page*, aimed at working women. *Hanako*, launched in 1988 by Magazine House, specializes in providing detailed information about trendy aspects of the urban scene both in Japan and abroad, and contains detailed descriptions (with maps) of new boutiques, restaurants, and coffee shops.

MAGAZINE SALES

For the advertiser in Japan, trying to figure out the real circulation of a magazine is a problem. Only about 3% of magazines are audited by the Audit Bureau of Circulation (ABC).

Aside from the few magazines audited by the ABC, it is difficult to determine if publishers' claimed circulations are based on actual sales, total readership, print run, or wishful thinking.

Using publishers' claimed circulation figures is to be avoided. Often, a publisher will concentrate on readership figures, rather than circulation figures (which, for nonaudited magazines could mean print-run figures or estimated potential sales figures), to convince a potential client to place ads in a certain magazine. This method of calculation would result in lower cost-per-thousand (CPM) figures.

As a result, ad agencies commonly depend on Video Research's annual *Audience and Consumer Report* (commonly known in the Japanese ad industry as ACR). ACR provides information on the percentages of respondents reading about 230 leading magazines, and analyzes the reader compositions. The ACR data come from an annual survey based upon a random sample of about 12,000 people, 12–69 years old, in seven major markets.

Data provided by the ACR include media exposure, demographics, lifestyle, leisure activities, hobbies, attitudes, and ownership or use of over 200 products, as well as purchasing behavior. This survey is not limited to magazines, but also covers television, newspapers, radio, transit advertising, and free newspapers.

In Japan, the majority of magazine sales are single copies bought at bookstores, convenience stores, kiosks, and newsstands. Subscriptions are all but nonexistent for general magazines. The 26,000 retail bookstores account for 66% of sales, and the 49,000 convenience stores nationwide account for 18%. Table 8.4 shows the percentage shares of magazine retail outlets.

Thus, a problem in using magazines as an advertising medium is that their readerships are a moving target. While close to 80% of U.S. magazines are sold by subscription, only a minuscule percentage of Japanese magazines are. Subscriptions in Japan do not offer substantial price discounts.

Table 8.4
Magazine Retail Sales

Outlet	%
Bookstores	66.3
Convenience stores	17.8
Subscriptions	9.0
Cooperatives	2.1
Kiosks	2.0
Newsstands	1.2
Other	1.6
Total	100.0

Source: Publishing News Company, *Publishing Annual* (1996).

Since readers buy virtually every issue of a magazine from retail outlets, publishers confront severe problems in maintaining circulation and sales. It is a constant challenge to gauge and maintain reader loyalty. Because subscriptions are basically nonexistent for mass-audience publications, Japanese magazines have to attract reader interest with every issue. Magazine publishers depend heavily on advertising to accomplish this. One of their preferred media is newspapers. By category, publishers (of books and magazines) have traditionally been one of the largest advertisers in newspapers. The other advertising medium regularly used by publishers is hanging posters (*nakazuri*) in trains and subways.

Japanese consumers may buy a different magazine (on the same subject—fashion, for example) each month. Which magazine they buy is determined after seeing the newspaper or transit ad for the next issue. But the final purchase decision is made by reading the tables of contents and skimming through the magazines available. Japanese bookstores and convenience stores allow people to browse the magazines for long periods of time. Retailers can afford to allow this, since they receive the magazines on consignment and can return unsold copies. The ratio of unsold magazines returned to publishers remains steady at slightly over 20%.

Viewed in a positive light, single-copy sales mean that readers make a special/active effort to select and buy magazines, motivated by their specific interests and information needs. On average three persons read each magazine. This is another competitive advantage of magazines in Japan.

Magazines in Japan experience seasonal fluctuations in sales. As a result, agencies planning annual ad placements have to carefully consider seasonal variations of magazines' print runs. Weekly or monthly print runs are not steady in terms of numbers. Magazines sell well during periods such as *o-bon* (ancestors' festival in midsummer) and year's end/New Year. Bonus seasons (June and December) also enjoy high magazine sales and a correspondingly high volume of ad placements. On the other hand, some clients ask their agencies to try to avoid placing ads in the mid-June (*o-chūgen*) and mid-December (*o-seibo*) gift-giving seasons, when certain magazines are cluttered with gift ads.

Other periods, such as February and late August (together, commonly referred to as *nippachi*), are slack periods for magazine sales and advertisements. In general, print runs of magazines tend to be higher in the second half of the year than in the first half.

ADVERTISING IN MAGAZINES

When considering magazines for ad placement, it is important to take each magazine's editorial content into account. The diversity of editorial content in Japanese magazines, which have progressively specialized themselves, has resulted in highly segmented target readerships. When selecting magazines for advertising, it is vital to ensure that the advertised products and services, the editorial environment, and the target readership are all compatible.

Detailed information on each magazine, such as editorial content, circulation figures, readership profiles, and advertising rates, is available (from Media Research Center's "Monthly Media Data," for example). Most major publishers have English materials giving brief descriptions of their publications. There is also the annual English-language publication *Magazines in Japan*.

There is a wide range of advertising-to-editorial space ratios in magazines. Some magazines may have less than 10% of their space filled by ads, while in others more than half the content consists of advertisements.

In Japan, as in several other countries, the sale date and publication date of a magazine can differ widely. Advertisers must be careful to keep these separate and clear in their minds. A magazine might be on sale from 28 January, but the publication date (carried on the cover) might say February. In some cases, it might even say March.

Like other media, magazines in Japan will not accept an ad space order directly from an advertiser. The advertisement must be placed by an ad agency accredited with the magazine/publisher. If the advertiser does not have an agency, the publisher will introduce one that has an account with it.

There's a simple reason why publishers do not accept space orders directly from advertisers. An agency generally pays within one month of the client's ad appearing in the magazine. Clients, on the other hand, do not always pay the agency as quickly. Instead, they pay three to six months after the ad has appeared. In this sense, the ad agency acts as a creditor, and assumes all risks of nonpayment.

Most publishers rank accredited agencies in terms of their trustworthiness. Based on their experience and relationship with the agency, the publishers will stipulate when and how payment must be made.

Agencies with a history of frequently buying space in the publication do not have to pay for a space buy until two or three months after the ad has appeared. On the other hand, agencies that rarely buy space will sometimes be asked to pay in advance of the ad's appearance. This is also true of smaller agencies. Agencies that have not bought space from the publisher before are asked to have an accredited agency buy space for them for one or two years. After they have proved themselves financially stable and timely payers, they may be allowed to buy space directly.

Usually, the number of advertisements that can be carried in an issue of a magazine is fixed far in advance of its printing. Japanese magazines do not add pages as they get more requests for ad space. This makes meeting ad space booking deadlines vital.

It is very difficult to get a magazine to guarantee a specific location for an ad. If the magazine does agree to do so, it is usually more expensive. One exception is booking fixed positions such as the inside front cover. Another exception is the case of an agency that has continuously bought huge volumes of space from the publisher. An advertiser's ad may sometimes get bumped from one month (or week) to another.

Ideally, for any type of magazine (monthly, fortnightly, weekly) it is best to order space three months in advance. The farther in advance an order is placed, the higher the chance of acquiring the space desired.

As a rule of thumb, ad space is usually booked up to 60 days prior to the issue's sale date for monthly magazines. For weekly magazines, bookings are placed 50 days prior to the sale date. For popular magazines, whose ad space is always in high demand, space should be booked even earlier if possible.

Many magazines keep at least one page aside for advertising their own products, "sister" publications, and such. In a pinch, the magazine will sell this space to an agency whose client needs to place an ad in an issue that is fully booked. Publishers will offer this page because placing an ad for their own product yields no ad revenue.

On the other hand, publishers often approach agencies, asking them to find an advertiser to place an ad during a slack period (February or August, for example). They usually offer a substantial discount, which gets proportionally larger as the printing deadline nears.

Magazine advertising is largely classified by the types of pages available: "special" space and "editorial" space. Special-space pages are the inner/outer covers and the page next to the table of contents. These pages garner a high level of reader attention and are quite expensive. In popular magazines, they are quickly booked up for the entire year. Editorial space comprises all the other pages available. Editorial space ads typically are full-color, full-page ads or full-color spreads (two-page ads).

Generally, the larger the magazine circulation, the more expensive the ad. A magazine's back cover is the most expensive ad space, followed, in order, by the inside front cover, inside back cover, and the inside pages.

Space size offered in Japanese magazines allows advertisers a variety of options. Depending on the magazine, aside from full-page and double-page spreads in both standard formats and bleed, half-page, vertical two-thirds page, vertical one-third page, horizontal half-page and quarter-page formats are available.

Magazine space rates depend on a variety of variables: color or black-and-white, position (in the front half or the back half of the magazine), circulation, and production costs.

Other variables that are equally important are pass-along readership (readership of a magazine, after it is purchased and read by one person), publication prestige, number of advertisers per issue, prestige of advertisers, and overall demand.

Special rates are charged for the optimum positions of back cover (*hyō yon*), inside back cover (*hyō san*), and inside front cover (*hyō ni*). Generally (in the case of a one-page, four-color ad), the back cover is the most expensive. The inside front cover is the next most expensive space, since it is usually opposite the table of contents. This is followed by the center, especially for magazines that have saddle-stitch binding which naturally fall open at the center, or by color gravure page. Center spreads are more expensive than regular spreads because an extra cost is charged. The amount of extra cost depends on the type of binding the magazine uses. Next most expensive is a location "front of center" or on the inside back cover. Pages in the back half of a magazine are generally less expensive.

Usually the back cover and inside covers are put out for bid in the autumn. Agencies then make a bid, complete with client's name and type of product/campaign that is planned to run. The publishers look at the projected advertising amount of a potential client, the standing/prestige of the client within its category and within the market as a whole, and the type of product being advertised. Frequent advertisers are given priority. Consideration is then given to the agency placing the bid: its total volume of space bought in previous years, its record of payment, and its previous cooperation.

In some magazines, the preferred positions (back cover, inside covers) have been used by the same clients for years. Unless such a client decides to cancel its advertising, the space in question is basically locked up. When the client, for whatever reason, decides not to use the space as arranged, it is common practice for the agency to try to sell the space to another of its clients rather than hand the space back to the publisher. Weak publishers will welcome this because they are happy to see the space filled. Stronger publishers will not always accept this, and often open the space to the best offer. Or they may decide who they believe would be the best client for the space, then contact the agency that handles that client's account and inform it of the space availability.

All magazines publish card rates, which list their official charges for ad space. However, nobody actually pays card rate. All published card rates are *gross cost* (i.e., they include agency commission). Usually the agency commission is 20% of gross cost, although this varies by publication.

AD INSERTION AND PROOFING SCHEDULES

There are different deadlines for gravure pages, cover pages, and inside pages. There is also a difference in deadlines depending on whether the ad is submitted as artwork or as film. Insertion deadlines for magazines are generally earlier for artwork and later for film. Most magazines will accept either artwork or film.

Offset printing, with four-color separated positive film, is the most common magazine printing method in Japan. When preparing four-color separated positive film, the following guidelines should be followed:

Screening: 175 lines/inch for all four colors

Angles seen from emulsion side:

Magenta: 15°

Black: 45°

Yellow: 60°

Cyan: 75°

Film (color separations: magenta, yellow, cyan, and black) insertions must be accompanied by a galley proof. This must be delivered to the publication four weeks in advance of the date the magazine goes on sale. Only one color proof will be provided, usually within one week. The proof is checked by the agency and client, all final corrections are made, and the corrected proof must be returned to the magazine three weeks before the magazine goes on sale.

Artwork (or a "mechanical") is usually submitted to magazine publishers as a complete pasteup (ad artwork that can be used for making printing plates). The finished artwork is given to the printer, who sends a proof to the agency. The agency checks the proof, corrects any errors, and shows the proof to the client. The corrected proof is returned to the printer. Most magazines will provide a second/final proof if requested, and if time allows. Since a considerable number of days pass between booking, artwork submission, and putting the magazines on sale, it is not easy to handle ad development in a last-minute fashion or to deal with unexpected circumstances.

If more than one stage of color proofing is desired, this should be requested in advance and agreed to by the magazine. Specific dates for the deliveries of the first and the final proofs to the agency must be agreed upon and followed. Agreement on specific dates for returning the proofs, with all adjustments/corrections marked, to the publication should be made in advance.

When inserting artwork (*han-shita*) in a weekly magazine, the following is the usual schedule. Artwork should be provided 35–40 days in advance of sale date if two color proofs are desired. The first proof will be ready 20 days before the sale date. Any corrections/adjustments should be returned to the magazine within three to four days. The second (final) color proof will be ready ten days before sale date. Only minor adjustments will be possible. Any last-minute adjustments/corrections must be turned in within one or two days.

If the artwork is not provided until 20 days or less before the sale date, only one color proof will be possible. It will be ready ten days in advance. Again, only minor adjustments/corrections will be possible, and the proof must be returned in one or two days.

No color proof will be possible when the artwork is provided ten days in advance.

If artwork/mechanical (*han-shita*) is inserted in a monthly magazine, the following is the usual schedule. If two color proofs are desired, artwork should be provided 40–45 days in advance of the sale date. The first proof will be ready 30 days before the sale date. Any corrections or adjustments to the color proof should be returned to the magazine within three to four days. The second (final) color proof will be ready 20 days before sale date. Only minor adjustments will be possible. Any last-minute adjustments/corrections must be turned in within one or two days.

If the artwork is not provided until 30 days or less before the sale date, only one color proof will be possible. It will be ready 20 days in advance. Only minor adjustments/corrections will be possible, and the proof must be returned in one or two days.

If the artwork is provided 20 days or less before the sale date, no color proof will be possible.

A foreign advertiser using material produced by the home office should be aware that to his or her Japanese ad agency (or his or her Japanese marketing staff), the "correct" color (of a skin tone, for example) may differ from his and his home office's opinion. If material from the home office is being used, the foreign executive should be involved in checking the color proofs to avoid later misunderstandings.

For noncolor gravure and letterpress ads in either monthly or weekly magazines, the following is the average schedule. When submitting material for black-and-white ad insertions, the artwork/mechanical (*han-shita*) must be provided 35–40 days in advance of the date the magazine goes on sale.

Submissions for letterpress (*kappan*) ad insertions must be in the form of a Photostat provided 30 days in advance of the date the magazine goes on sale.

SPECIAL ISSUES AND SUPPLEMENTS

Many of the major magazines have special issues dedicated to a specific subject (travel, for example), which an advertising agency can find out about beforehand and plan for accordingly. Other magazines publish special issues devoted to new graduates. The editorial content focuses on how to groom yourself for an interview, how to dress for the interview, how to conduct yourself during interviews, and so on. Ads tend to concentrate on clothes, briefcases and handbags, shoes, and other personal items.

Many major magazines are open to creating special supplements with an advertiser. These supplements draw upon the editorial expertise of the magazines, and can be inserted in the magazine or distributed separately. Through Dentsu, Calvin Klein had a "Calvin Klein New York Book" created by *Frau*, a fashion-oriented women's magazine. The Canadian Tourist Commission had a "Vacation Planner" produced by *Blanca*, a major travel magazine. In both these cases, advertising from other companies was included to defray costs.

OTHER METHODS OF ADVERTISING IN MAGAZINES

Advertorials (*kiji-ko*) are commonly placed in Japanese magazines. These are basically ads written to look like editorial matter. There is no number on the page on which the advertorial appears. It must include the name of the company placing the advertorial. The advertiser must pay the full ad space cost (comparable to placing a regular ad). If the advertorial looks too much like a regular article, the magazine will ask the advertiser to make changes.

Editorial tie-ups (*henshū tai appu*) are also common. In them advertisers supply promotional material about their products/services for inclusion in an article by the magazine's writers.

Henshū tai appu should be requested at least three months in advance (so that the editorial staff has time to plan, and make necessary changes in the overall content of the magazine). It is usually two pages or more in length. The advertiser pays for the usual ad space cost (if it is a three-page tie-up, the advertiser pays for three ad pages) plus about ¥300,000 per editorial page (the amount depends on the magazine) as "editorial fee."

Content, layout, design, and photos are usually handled by the editorial department of the magazine. They will be shown to the client for comment. However, the final decision rests with the editorial staff. No ad message is allowed to be placed within the *henshū tai appu*, but an unobtrusive company logo may be allowed. Pages are numbered. Two copies of content (proofs) are provided, one for the agency and one for the client.

By regulation, an editorial tie-up should have a credit stating it is PR. Yet a regulation is not a law. Neither advertisers nor publishers are legally obliged to make it clear that editorial tie-ups are in fact paid for, rather than being the editor's independent point of view. However, most magazines do make an effort to indicate that a certain article has been contributed by a certain company, although this may consist of placing the advertiser's name inconspicuously at the end of the text, in small print.

Sometimes the magazine will agree to use editorial copy created by the client's agency. In these cases, the magazine will insist that the advertiser promise not to submit a similar article to other publications.

Editorial cooperation (*henshū kyōryoku*) is also offered by magazines. In this case a magazine editorial staff writes an article focusing on an advertiser's product. In return, the advertiser provides free products that can be offered to readers by the magazine (in the article). Usually, the article will be written at no charge or for a very nominal fee. Magazines often insist that an ad be placed in the same issue of the magazine.

Paid publicity (*paido pabu*) is another technique popular among advertisers. It is similar to editorial tie-ups, but can be shorter and has more chance of being placed without placing an ad. A client pays a publisher the regular ad space rate, plus an "editorial fee," to have the company or its products or services featured in an article. The article is written by the magazine's editors; it is shown to the client, but the editors have final control over the content and how it is presented. If the advertiser insists that the article carry a heavy emphasis on its product, and an in-depth explanation of the product's benefits, the magazine usually insists that the advertiser place a one-page ad next to the article.

Magazine coupons can also be utilized. The late 1980s saw a notable change in magazine advertising regulations, with the deregulation of the use of coupons in magazines in October 1987. However, coupons are rarely, if ever, placed in magazines. Magazines resist accepting ads with coupons because other clients will not buy ad space on the back of an ad page that has coupons for fear the coupons will be cut out, thereby destroying their advertisement.

THE LIFTING OF MAGAZINE AD RESTRICTIONS

In 1994, the Japan Magazine Publishers Association eased its voluntary restrictions on ads, effective in January 1995. Restrictions were removed for the following:

1. Ads that pop up to form a three-dimensional structure
2. Ads with samples of cosmetics
3. Ads with CD-ROM supplements to magazines.

The Japan Magazine Publishers Association's ban on the types of ads listed above arose from transportation problems. The direct impetus for lifting the ban was both advertisers' greater demand for such advertising and improvements in sample manufacturing technology.

Shiseido took advantage of the easing of restrictions by running an ad that included a lipstick sample. Shiseido wanted readers to be able to try its new Pienne lipstick for themselves. To make sure its samples reached the target audience effectively and efficiently, Shiseido ran the ads in both *an an* and *More*, two of the major young women's magazines.

CONCLUSION

Japan's abundance of magazines and their low circulations allow one of the best opportunities for audience-focused advertising. Yet because each issue is individually bought, the readership is a constantly moving target.

The unabated annual launch and suspension of large numbers of magazines continues to result in the growth of the total number of magazines in Japan. These huge numbers of competing magazines per category, their low circulations, and the virtual nonexistence of magazine subscriptions, are major obstacles to consistently reaching the target audience, and necessitate a substantial budget if the necessary ad frequency is to be achieved. Japanese magazines continue to be slow to offer new advertising techniques to offset these limitations. Although the 1990s saw Japanese magazines finally allow advertising techniques such as "scratch-and-sniff" ads, coupons, and pop-up ads, the prohibitively high costs have deterred their widespread use.

Chapter 9

Rajio
Advertising on Radio

Amazingly, in the nation that flooded the world with cheap transistor radios, radio is not highly developed as a major mass medium. Although the average Japanese household owns 4.7 radios, the number of both radio stations and listeners is disappointingly low compared with other countries. Whereas the U.S. has 5,000 commercial AM stations, Japan has 47. The U.S. has 4,470 commercial FM stations, and Japan has 47. The U.S. has 1,424 public stations; Japan has three. In addition to the AM and FM stations, Japan boasts one shortwave station and two satellite stations.

Although there are seven AM stations, one shortwave station, and seven FM stations (including NHK's) in the Tokyo metropolitan area, within the city of Tokyo itself there are only four FM stations: NHK-FM, Tokyo FM, InterFM, and J-Wave.

In Japan, where commuting to work by private automobile is rare, radio advertising garners only 4% of ad spending, while transit ads (including posters in trains and at stations) pick up a higher percentage.

Both advertisers and ad agencies have been reluctant to consider radio as an effective medium. The traditional argument is that only housewives listen in the mornings, salesmen and taxi drivers during the day, and high school and university students late at night (while studying). Based on proper market segmentation, that argument sounds like a good reason for using radio. Among foreign companies, Coca-Cola has taken advantage of effective use of radio advertising. Toys 'R' Us's experiments with radio commercials have also been successful.

Since the advent of television in 1953, radio has steadily lost its popularity. As a result, it is the poor relation within the Japanese mass media. During the 1990s, though, there was a slight revival in radio with the launch of new FM stations.

HISTORY

Upon the successful launch of radio broadcasting in the United States, Japan became keenly interested in the new medium. In 1923, over 50 applications were submitted to the government for broadcasting licenses. Then Japan was devastated by a major earthquake.

The great Kanto earthquake of 1923 provided a major stimulus for the development of radio in Japan. The absence of information at the time caused rumors to run wild, compounding the disaster with misinformation.

To rectify that situation, the government suggested that the applicants for broadcasting licenses merge and form three independent corporations in the cities of Tokyo, Osaka, and Nagoya. This led to the establishment of the Tokyo Broadcasting Station, which began broadcasting from a makeshift station in the Shibaura district of Tokyo on 22 March 1925. In June 1925, Osaka Broadcasting Station went on air, followed in July by Nagoya Broadcasting Station. In August 1926, the government forced the merger of these three stations to form the predecessor of today's Nihon Hōsō Kyokai (NHK), Japan Broadcasting Corporation. NHK's radio broadcasting was a primary source of news in Japan from its inception to the end of World War II. (The abbreviation NHK did not come into use until 1946.)

Prior to the war, the only law regulating broadcasting was the Wireless and Telegraph Law. Under that law, NHK was subject to government control and placed under the auspices of the Ministry of Communications. It was a key component of the military government's mobilization of the national citizenry during the war. A special broadcast at 7 A.M. on 8 December 1941 announced commencement of hostilities with the U.S., and the emperor's broadcast at noon on 15 August 1945 marked the end of the war.

During the occupation of Japan after the war, Supreme Command Allied Powers (SCAP), led mainly by the United States, sought to carry out a drastic reform of Japanese broadcasting. It presented draft documents on broadcasting policy in October 1947, suggesting that a self-governing commission independent of the national government be set up to administer and manage broadcasting activities. The Japanese cabinet, however, tenaciously opposed the commission's independence from the government. The final decision to press ahead with the reforms was made by General Douglas MacArthur.

The Wireless and Telegraph Law was repealed on 31 May 1950, and replaced with the Broadcast Law and the Radio Broadcasting Law, which were enacted on 1 June 1950. The Law for the Establishment of the Radio Wave Management Commission was also enacted. This established the Radio Wave Management Commission, which was patterned after the U.S. Federal Communications Commission, in June 1951.

Under the reorganization of broadcasting, NHK was reestablished as a nonprofit corporation. Until the promulgation of the Radio Broadcasting Law of 1950 (*Denpa Hō*, 1950) on 1 June, there were no commercial radio broadcasts in Japan.

One of the Radio Wave Management Commission's first actions was the issuance, in April 1951, of provisional licenses for the nation's first commercial radio stations. Sixteen licenses were granted. The majority of applicants were backed by newspaper companies, both nationwide dailies and local papers. Even today, most radio stations have an affiliation with a newspaper.

The Radio Wave Management Commission functioned for slightly over two years. Three months after the San Francisco peace treaty came into effect (in September 1951) and Japan regained its independence, one of the government's first actions was the abolition of the Radio Wave Management Commission.

COMMERCIAL RADIO BROADCASTING

Japanese commercial AM radio broadcasting began in 1951. On 1 September of that year, the first privately owned radio stations went on air in Osaka and Nagoya. *Shin-Nihon Hōsō*, New Japan Broadcasting (NJB), now Mainichi Broadcasting, went on air in Osaka, and *Chubu Nihon Hōsō*, Chubu Nihon Broadcasting (CBC), went on air in Nagoya.

In December 1951, Tokyo finally got a commercial broadcaster, Radio Tokyo (now TBS). Founded in 1951 with Christianity Foundation support, Bunka Hōsō began broadcasting in March 1952 with a strong emphasis on cultural and educational programming, which was unusual at that time for commercial radio. The programming policy was subsequently modified and modernized to meet the needs and demands of listeners.

Radio's brief golden age was during its first half-decade (until the mid-1950s). By 1957, 40 radio stations were broadcasting. After that, the launch of television broadcasting led to radio's decline. With the invention of the transistor radio, the decline was stabilized. Radios were carried outdoors and installed in automobiles, and AM broadcasters created new program formats to encourage radio listening in these venues.

To understand the state of radio in Japan today, it is important to remember that until recently there were very few stations. For example, in the Tokyo metropolitan area, the first FM station was the public broadcasting NHK FM in 1960. It wasn't until 1970 that Tokyo got its first commercial FM station, Tokyo FM. There was then a 15-year hiatus before the second commercial FM station in Tokyo, Yokohama FM, was launched in 1985.

The 1980s saw a boom in the launches of new FM stations, beginning with the 1985 opening of eight new FM stations (bringing the total nationwide to 21). In

1986 one new FM radio station began service, and 1987 saw the launch of two. In 1988 five new FM stations were launched, including FM Fuji, J-Wave, and FM Saitama. This was followed by three new stations in 1989 (in the Tokyo metropolitan area), including FM Sound Chiba. There were three more in 1990 and one in 1991. In 1993, three "second-wave" FM stations opened. Nine new FM stations took to the air in 1995.

TYPES OF RADIO BROADCASTING

Radio broadcasts are divided into three categories: AM, FM, and shortwave.

AM (amplitude modulation) broadcasts use 535–1605 MHz. Since November 1994, it has been possible to listen to AM radio broadcasts on all Tokyo Metropolitan Government-operated subway lines (used by an average of 1.6 million passengers daily).

FM (frequency modulation) uses ultrahigh frequency (30–300 MHz). Because FM can achieve good, strong sound quality against static and interference, it is particularly suited for music broadcasts.

Shortwave radio broadcasts use a shorter wave frequency (6–30 MHz). Because shortwave can reflect off the Earth's ionosphere and travel long distances, a single station can cover the entire country. Commercially, only one station, Radio Shortwave, is broadcasting. A Nikkei affiliate, Nihon Short-wave Broadcasting, manages it. Nihon Shortwave Broadcasting was established on 27 August 1954 as Japan's first domestic shortwave radio station. Its programs are broadcast nationwide.

RADIO NETWORKS

AM and FM broadcasts, like TV, are delivered through networks. Like television networks, radio networks operate as cooperatives under the leadership of key stations.

The two major AM commercial radio broadcasting networks were established in 1965. The Japan Radio Network (JRN) is led by TBS Radio (Tokyo Broadcasting System). The Nippon Radio Network (NRN) is affiliated with key stations *Bunka Hōsō* (Nippon Cultural Broadcasting) and *Nippon Hōsō* (Nippon Broadcasting System), both of which are part of the Fujisankei Group.

Nippon Cultural Broadcasting, known by the call letters JOQR, is a key radio station in Tokyo and has 38 member stations in its national radio network.

Nippon Broadcasting System has been the acknowledged leader of Japan's radio industry since its founding in 1954. It has 37 affiliated stations across Japan.

Compared with TV networks, AM radio station networks are loosely linked and do not necessarily air similar programming. This is because AM broadcasts are very regional, and have low production costs. Each local AM station carries a

Table 9.1
Number of Radio Stations, by Region

	AM	FM	SW	Total
Kanto	6	8	1	15
Kansai	6	6	—	12
Hokkaido	2	2	—	4
Tohoku	6	6	—	12
Koshinetsu	3	3	—	6
Chukyo	4	4	—	8
Hokkuriku	3	3	—	6
Chugoku	4	3	—	7
Shikoku	4	4	—	8
Kyushu	7	9	—	16
Okinawa	2	1	—	3
Total	47	49	1	97

Source: Japan Advertising Agencies Association (1997).

high ratio of local programming (and a low ratio of network programming). On the other hand, the ratio of network programming at FM stations is increasing.

The first FM network was JFN (Japan FM Network Association), which dominates the FM industry. JFN operates a nationwide network of 33 stations with Tokyo FM as its key station. Tokyo FM distributes nearly half of its programs to other JFN stations. Members of JFN also have access to programs produced by Japan FM Network Corporation, a program supplier owned and operated by JFN.

The second FM network is the Japan FM League (JFL), with 11 stations. JFL is not a vertical relationship where a key station leads local stations; rather, it is a network of 11 equal partners.

In addition to the networks, there are independent AM and FM stations. Table 9.1 breaks down the number of radio stations by wavelength and per region.

DISTINCTIVE FEATURES OF RADIO

Radio is a personalized medium that can be used to reach certain segmented audiences: housewives, drivers, young people. For this reason, it is well-suited for deploying target-specific advertising. Radio stations are also willing to work constructively with advertisers to accommodate their wishes. As a typical example, advertisers wanting to promote sales of their products can broadcast live radio shows from a retail store. Radio media costs are low and radio cost-effectively gives advertisers direct contact with their target audience.

Radio audiences can be segmented by type of listener (student, drivers, etc.) and by geographical area. The target audience could be, for example, people listening while driving their cars. In such a case it would be important to consider the demographics and number of cars in a given area. Thus radio is used often by the service and leisure industry, foods and beverages, luxury goods, automobiles, and related products.

In general, the most popular listening times for radio are the 7 A.M. (weekday) peak, most probably people trying to get updates on the weather, road conditions, and latest news prior to going to work; the weekday and Saturday peaks of 10 A.M.; and the Saturday peak of 1 P.M.–3 P.M.

About 51% of listeners of AM (42% of FM) listen at home, about 31% (27% of FM) listen in their car, and 17% (31% of FM) listen at other locations.

Like TV programming, radio programming begins in April with a schedule that allows the broadcast of night baseball games (*naitā*). Also like TV, radio reschedules its programming in October, when the night games end.

Japanese AM stations tend to broadcast a variety of programming, whereas FM stations devote much of their broadcast time to music.

A radio station's coverage is measured by the number of households and the population within its broadcast area. AM and FM stations usually cover one or two prefectures. This excludes stations in three areas (Tokyo and the surrounding prefectures, Osaka, and Aichi) that have considerably wider reach. For example, TBS Radio's broadcast area covers one metropolis and 11 prefectures, comprising 16,474,000 households.

April 1990 saw the launch of a new radio program rating system for the Tokyo metropolitan area. This system was introduced by Video Research, which set identical standards for AM and FM stations. The results of the new survey system were a shock to the radio stations, sponsors, and ad agencies. This system forced a major review of programming by the radio stations.

Video Research's rating survey was expanded in 1993 to cover the Kansai district and Fukuoka area.

CATEGORIES OF RADIO ADVERTISING

Radio commercials are classified in the same way as TV commercials: both program sponsorship commercials and spot commercials are available.

Radio ad rate systems resemble those of television. In particular, rates are determined by the number of households (or population) within the broadcast area, and for some stations, the time slot in which the commercial is aired. In addition to these factors, rates are determined by listenership ratings, each station's business power, supply and demand relationships, and so on.

Radio time (program sponsorship) is sold in much the same manner as television time. However, radio spot rates differ greatly from those of television. The rate basis for radio spots is a per-spot price.

The two types of radio program sponsorship commercials available are

1. Network program sponsorship
2. Local program sponsorship

The standard contract term for program sponsorships is six months, but this can be extended. Sometimes a three-month contract can be obtained. Usually this is when a program is new and the station cannot find sponsors, or when a program is losing sponsors due to low ratings. Many programs are booked exclusively by national advertisers on a long-term basis. A word of warning: Because FM stations are very popular in urban markets, some popular programs have long waiting lists.

As with TV program sponsorships, the cost of a radio program sponsorship commercial consists of a time charge, a network fee, and production cost. The network fee is the cost of networking a program. Usually this is the cost of using the microcircuits of the Nippon Telegraph and Telephone Corporation (NTT). No networking fee is charged for AM radio broadcasting, for which NTT's microcircuits are not used. The production cost is the sponsor's share of the cost of producing the program.

Radio program sponsorship ads consist mostly of 20-, 40-, and 60-second slots. Depending on the program and the type of sponsorship, it is also possible to air commercials that are considerably longer.

Table 9.2 gives the allowable commercial placement volume within a radio program.

Table 9.2
Allowable Commercial Placement Volume Within a Radio Program

Radio program time	Commercial time
5 min.	1 min.
10 min.	2 min.
15 min.	2 min. 30 sec.
20 min.	2 min. 40 sec.
25 min.	2 min. 50 sec.
30 min. or more	10% of program time

CONSIDERATIONS FOR PROGRAM SPONSORSHIP

It is essential to choose a program that matches the company's image or advertised product's characteristics. The audience ratings should be high and justify the rates, which must be affordable. It is important to investigate trends in household audience ratings as well as individual audience ratings to determine whether the time slot is the most appropriate for the target audience.

Another consideration will be whether to purchase network or local sponsorship. If the program you are considering is networked, be sure to determine whether the areas being offered meet your purposes. You might also consider sponsoring the program in selected local areas if that option is offered, and better suits your needs.

Finding a program sponsorship opening is not always easy. It is advantageous to indicate as early as possible the radio program you wish to sponsor. If the program is popular, and hence expensive, you must determine if the cost justifies the anticipated returns. Popular programs often have no available openings or, due to another sponsor's buying up of the time, would-be sponsors may have to wait up to a year before being able to sponsor the program.

In cases where a number of firms vie for the same time slot, the station tends to give precedence to the sponsor with the longest relationship with the station.

Timing is a crucial factor in purchasing program sponsorship. The busiest months for existing sponsors are April and October (but the possibility of adding or dropping a program exists even in the minor reorganization months of July and January). Accordingly, between January and February and in August, radio stations and ad agencies are speculating as to what current sponsors are planning to do in the next half-year. As a result, information-gathering and timing during these months are vital.

PROGRAM SPONSORSHIPS

Many radio program sponsorships are secured by national advertisers on a long-term, exclusive basis. Every year, programming changes are made in April and October, the beginning and end of baseball broadcasts.

FM stations are particularly popular in urban markets. This results in long waiting lists for sponsorship openings on popular FM programs.

Standard contracts for sponsoring a program are for six months, but can be extended. Radio stations require notice of any changes in term length and/or contract renewal at least one month before termination.

Mini Belt programs are available. These are independent miniprograms regularly broadcast from Monday through Friday within larger programs (which include traffic reports, weather reports, etc.) that are typically five to ten minutes long. These programs can be sponsored for one-month periods.

Running a 20-second ad Monday through Friday, covering only Tokyo, typically costs from ¥2 million to ¥3 million per month.

There are also *hako* programs, or weekly series (once per week). Many of these programs are broadcast on Saturdays and Sundays. A one-hour program (360-second sponsorship) runs about ¥5 million to ¥7.5 million per month. However, when a program is specially produced on the sponsor's request, the production fees can greatly increase the total cost. Also, where open time is hard to come by, as in FM programming, costs can run in excess of ¥20 million a month.

However, being the sole sponsor of one of these programs is effective in terms of the image enhancement they provide the sponsoring company and/or its product. Single sponsorships also have the merit of strengthening the audience's understanding of the advertiser's image.

The most difficult sponsorship slots to buy are broadcasts of night baseball games. Demand for sponsorship slots on these programs is high. These broadcasts offer the following features:

1. Representative program of AM radio
2. Live, continuous radio broadcast up to the end of the game
3. Broadcast of popular local team games in each region
4. On networks, substitutions or switching of commercials is possible
5. High listenership and strong appeal (more than ten 20-second spots per game)
6. Ideal for reaching the male target audience
7. In principle, joint sponsorship by six advertisers per day

Additionally, possibilities exist to tie in an event with a radio program sponsorship. Advertisers can do more than simply sponsor a radio program; they can also hold an event, such as a live concert. It is also possible to have a program that cuts from the studio to an outside event.

The program sponsor shoulders the cost of transmission and program production. If the program is being aired through network affiliates, there will be an additional network cost.

Radio sponsorship, especially of an AM station's main program—live coverage of night baseball games—with a nationwide network, once a week (joint sponsorship with six advertisers), with ten 20-second commercials, could cost up to approximately ¥40 million per month (1996 Spring rates).

Sole sponsorship of a radio program is possible. In radio it is comparatively easier, than on TV, to produce a program that reflects the intent of the sponsor. This is especially the case with single sponsorships. Radio stations are willing to consider a potential sponsor's ideas for a program's content.

Bookings for program sponsorships should be made two to three months in advance of the air date, but sometimes can be made as little as one month in advance. The minimum period booked is six months, although on rare occasions a station will accept a three-month booking.

Commercial material must be inserted one week in advance of air date (this can be shortened to four working days in some cases). One 6mm (stereo) tape must be given to the key station.

RADIO SPOTS

Radio spot space is sold on the basis of cost per spot by time zone, not on audience rating. However, a few AM stations charge higher rates for the morning and evening commute periods, and some FM stations charge higher rates for time slots in the "leisure" zone (weeknights, Saturdays, and Sundays). Popular time zones that reach drivers or youth are usually fully booked far in advance.

Spot rates are usually determined on an annual basis from April through the following March. They do not fluctuate in price as TV spots do. There are two types of radio spot commercials:

1. Station break commercials
2. Participating commercials

Spot broadcast periods and times basically follow the client's request. If spots are ordered at a certain volume for a particular period, time slots can usually be chosen as one wishes. However, some specific time slots at some stations may be difficult to reserve due to crowding. Unlike television, there are many different time belts available throughout the week for radio spot airing (morning and evening commute hours, evening youth hours, etc.).

Radio offers the potential for developing various kinds of spot commercials. For example, live commercials, spots announcing the time (commercial with time announcement 10 seconds before the exact time), call sign spots (commercial with the station's call sign or jingle), and infomercials (conveying an ad message as a notice or report).

Spot commercials of 20 seconds are the norm, but depending on the purpose and content of the commercial, 5-, 10-, 40-, and 60-second spots can also be placed. (However, some stations will not accept commercials under 20 seconds in length.) Other stations, such as J-Wave, provide standard card rates for spots as long as 120, or even 180, seconds.

Unlike television spots, there are more regular radio spots aired continuously over a long period than campaign spots broadcast for short periods in the same time slots. These regular spots are mostly concentrated around the morning commute hours. (Being broadcast at the same times, after several weeks they can achieve a cumulative effect similar to program sponsorship.)

At key stations, there are network spots available as well as the "local" spots. Such network spots are commercialized portions of network programs, separate from the commercial zone of the programs. (For example, a program with a 60-second commercial period would be shaved to a 40-second sponsorship length, with the remaining 20 seconds being sold as a network spot.)

This is well-suited for products with national campaigns, since very low rates can be realized, compared with buying spots at each individual station. (The number of network stations differs, depending on the network program, and buying about ¥15 million worth of time from Monday to Friday can be done for around ¥5–6 million per month.) Per-month purchases are the norm.

Radio rates are quoted on a per-spot basis. Spot commercials have a time-charge only. Most radio stations charge a uniform amount for all time periods except early morning and late night.

Some stations charge the same rate regardless of the time slot; some AM stations charge higher rates for the morning and evening commuter times; and some FM stations charge more for slots in the leisure zone (weeknights, Saturdays, and Sundays). In addition, there are stations that set special unit prices for programs which have garnered a large listenership.

Rates for radio spots do not have large seasonal fluctuations in unit prices. On the other hand, because discounts can be received for volume ad placements, there can be large fluctuations in price based on total placement volume.

Rates are calculated by the number of commercials aired. The unit price for a single 20-second commercial at a key station (TBS, Bunka Hōsō, Nippon Hōsō, Tokyo FM) would run about ¥60,000 to ¥65,000 (1996 Spring rates).

Bookings of spot commercials should be made two to three months in advance of air date, but sometimes can be made as little as one month in advance. Commercial materials must be submitted to the station four days before the airing date. If the campaign consists of a series of commercials, their order must be indicated. After airing, written confirmation, proving that the commercials were aired, will be provided by the station.

As with TV, there is no minimum airtime period that must be booked (no station is going to state that an advertiser must buy air time for at least two weeks, for example). Rather, the ad agency must tell the radio station your objectives (e.g., "Within a budget of ¥_______, we want to air spots before the Christmas season, in as focused a time period as possible, and get at least 1,000 GRP"). The station will then make a proposal that will achieve those goals.

Commercials are usually submitted on 6 mm open-reel sound tape (tape speed: 38 cm/sec, stereo).

CLASSIFICATION BY TIME SLOT

Some radio stations classify commercials by the time slots in which they are aired. Some stations don't have time slots, but charge a flat rate for commercials regardless of which day of the week, and what time, they are aired. With radio stations that divide their time by slots, the actual time-slot setups differ greatly, depending on the station. For example, in AM broadcasting, TBS and Bunka Hōsō divide their broadcast day into three slots: A, B, and C. Nippon Hōsō, on the other hand, has two time slots (H and B) for Fridays, Saturdays, Sundays, and holidays, and two (A and

Figure 9.1
Radio Time Classifications

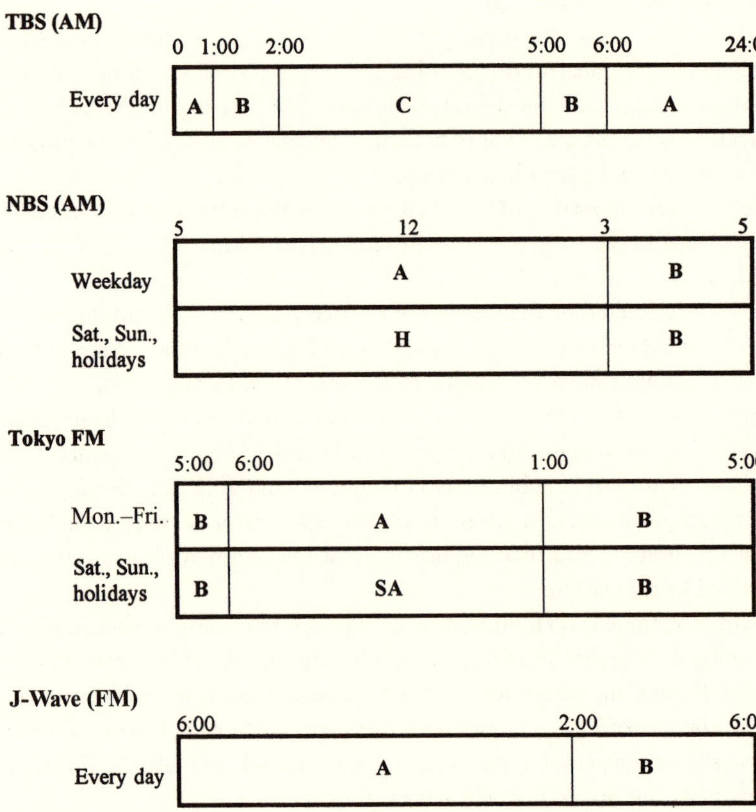

Table 9.3
Radio Listening Hours

Age	Weekday	Saturday	Sunday	Average
Male				
Average	00:27	00:24	00:17	00:22
10–15	00:05	00:06	00:03	00:04
16–19	00:11	00:23	00:26	00:20
20–29	00:18	00:16	00:11	00:15
30–39	00:32	00:25	00:08	00:21
40–49	00:31	00:31	00:19	00:27
50–59	00:37	00:31	00:20	00:29
60+	00:39	00:32	00:27	00:32
Female				
Average	00:25	00:23	00:28	00:25
10–15	00:06	00:19	00:19	00:14
16–19	00:10	00:13	00:10	00:11
20–29	00:14	00:12	00:11	00:12
30–39	00:17	00:15	00:09	00:13
40–49	00:35	00:29	00:21	00:28
50–59	00:42	00:41	00:28	00:37
60+	00:33	00:31	00:27	00:30

Source: NHK Survey (1995).

B) for the remaining days of the week (see Figure 9.1). FM radio stations use different slot rankings. Radio Shortwave doesn't divide its time into slots.

Radio's listening audience is clearly segmented by time slot, gender, age, and day of the week, so care must be exercised to ensure that commercials are aimed at the right audience. Table 9.3 shows the average listening hours for radio in general.

CONCLUSION

For all its recent revival, radio is still the poor cousin of the mass media. Both the number of stations and the number of listeners remain low. Yet radio is an inexpensive method of reaching a fairly focused target. As such, its use as a supplementary medium can be valuable.

Chapter 10

Kōtsū Kōkoku
Mass Transit Advertising

Mass transit is not seriously considered as an advertising medium in most Western markets. Overlooking it in Japan is a mistake. Within the context of overall advertising strategies, the importance of transit advertising cannot be ignored. The mass transit systems, and the media space they offer, are concentrated in the major cities with high population densities.

Mass transit in Japan is often referred to as the nation's fifth mass medium. In actuality, its share of total advertising expenditure ranks it fourth (after television, newspapers, and magazines). A review of mass media advertising expenditures in Japan shows that the percentage spent on transit advertising overtook that of radio advertising in 1988. Commuter advertising costs in 1996 added up to ¥248 billion, about 4.3% of total advertising costs.

What makes railways in Japan such an appealing advertising medium is the annual passenger volume of 358 billion, and the 27,000 km of railway lines that reach every corner of a country the size of California. Table 10.1 breaks down transit use, by purpose, in metropolitan Tokyo.

Public rail transport is readily available, and is heavily used by commuters in the major cities of Japan. It is clean, efficient, and on time. Most people with a daily commute buy one-, three-, or six-month passes. Upon entering a station, commuters have access to a diversity of destinations. In particular, the Tokyo and Osaka areas have exceptional train and subway systems. Tokyo alone has 336 Japan Railways stations, 232 subway stations, and 703 private line stations.

HISTORY

Japan's first railway was inaugurated in 1872. It was a steam-powered service that ran the 28 km between Shimbashi (now Shiodome) in Tokyo and Yokohama

Table 10.1
Breakdown of Mass Transit Users,
Tokyo Metropolitan Area

Reason for traveling	%
Commute (workers)	50.4
Commute (students)	15.1
Business	8.4
Private	26.1
Total	100.0

Source: "10,000 Person Survey," *The JR Transit Advertising Data Book* (1996).

(the present Sakuragicho station). Nine years later, the country boasted over 200 km of track.

However, not all early railways were steam-powered. Japan's first horse-drawn tram service (*basha tetsudō*), running between Shimbashi and Nihonbashi in Tokyo, was launched in 1882; and at the end of the nineteenth century, Kyoto, Nagoya, and Kawasaki had electric railways.

By 1901, rail tracks had been laid the entire length of Japan's main island of Honshu, and some tracks had been laid on each of the other three major islands. In tandem with the construction of state-owned railways, private lines were constructed.

The government initially encouraged the proliferation of private lines with tax exemptions and cash subsidies. However, in 1906 it promulgated the National Railways Law, nationalizing the nation's rail system along the lines of the Prussian model. This meant that the government purchased the main trunk lines, while private enterprise was allowed to operate the feeder lines. It was not until April 1987 that Japan National Railways (JNR) was privatized and broken up, giving birth to seven new JR (Japan Railways) companies. The two major JR companies are JR East and JR West, serving the Kanto and Kansai areas, respectively.

Even before the promulgation of the National Railways Law, the private rail companies were looking for opportunities to increase their profitability. This led to the development of transit advertising. Japan's first transit ads appeared in the carriages of Tokyo's *shidō basha* (horse-drawn trams) in 1885. These *nakazuri* were posters hung from the ceiling over the aisle of the carriages. The profitability of this first transit advertising led to Tokyo's Ueno and Shimbashi train stations allowing *e-bira* (picture poster) ads to be placed in their waiting rooms in 1889, in an effort to increase income. A sake brewery was the first advertiser to try this new medium.

Finding that selling ad space in the stations provided a nice side income, Shimbashi station built a *tachi kanban* (fixed billboard) in 1899, for which it charged a higher rate. *Mitsui Gofukuten* (the predecessor of today's prestigious Mitsukoshi department store) was the first business to buy space on the billboard.

Always the leader, in 1901 Shimbashi station sold space on the first illuminated sign. In the same year, the *Keihin Dentetsu* railway began allowing ads to be placed inside its trains. A more original approach to transit advertising was the placement of ads on train tickets. In 1903, Takashimaya (the department store) was the first advertiser to have its ads printed on the train tickets sold at Kyoto and Osaka stations. In 1906, yet another railway company, *Kyohan Densha*, allowed ads to be placed both in its trains and in its stations. Mass-transit advertising was on its way to becoming an established medium.

Japan's development of rail transport was not limited to conventional railways. The first subway in Japan was opened in 1927 with a 2.2-km line from Tokyo's Asakusa to Ueno. This private-company enterprise was the first subway in the whole of Asia. The line, now known as the Ginza line, was completed in 1939, extending 14.3 km from Asakusa to Shibuya. By the outbreak of World War II, both Tokyo and Osaka had subways in operation.

THE JAPAN RAILWAY GROUP

The JR group is made up of six passenger railway companies, a freight railway company, and several affiliated companies. It also operates the bullet train (*shinkansen*) lines. It boasts some impressive figures:

Number of stations:	1,708
Total route length:	20,251 km (1,067 mm gauge)
	18,215 km (1,435 mm gauge)
	2,036 km (double track)
	7,851 km (39%) (electrified track)
	11,737 km (58%) (regular track)
Passenger traffic:	23,731,000 people/day
	676,712,000 people/km day

JR East is the largest JR company, and runs trains in the Kanto area. In the Tokyo metropolitan area alone, JR East runs 36 train lines.

The majority of JR East's passengers have seasonal commuter passes and spend 231 minutes over five weekdays on the train and subway lines in Tokyo.

An average of 36 million people move through the nationwide metropolitan areas' railway network each day. In the Tokyo area alone, over 12 million people use mass transit daily. According to a survey of 10,000 people conducted by JR East in the Tokyo metropolitan area, 34.2% of all commuters use JR.

THE PRIVATE RAILWAY SECTOR

In addition to the JR group, there are 16 large railway companies and 58 smaller ones. Unlike JR, the large private railway companies are conglomerates that operate both trains and buses between train stations, and have built shopping centers and department stores around or above their large stations. These railway companies are at the core of large conglomerates that can include not only department stores but also concert halls, amusement parks, and real-estate development and financial services. More of their profit often comes from these strategically located businesses than from their railway operations.

Several of these companies have ad agencies as group members, as does JR. Group members can obtain priorities and discounts in their advertising; competitors may not be able to obtain ad space easily for their mass transit advertising in group members' facilities.

In addition to the 36 JR lines, there are 24 private lines operating in and around Tokyo.

SUBWAYS

In addition to Tokyo's vast subway (*chika-tetsu*) network (12 lines carrying 11 million people per day), Osaka boasts a network of six subway lines.

There are also subway systems in Fukuoka, Kobe, Kyoto, Nagoya, Sapporo, Sendai, and Yokohama. In 1994 there were some 34 subway lines totaling 560.3 km (3448.1 miles) operating in these nine cities.

There are two subway operators in the Tokyo area, the Teito Rapid Transit Authority (TRTA) and the Transportation Bureau of the Tokyo Metropolitan Government (TBTMG). TRTA started operations in 1927 with the opening of Japan's first subway, and presently has eight subway lines (*eiden*). It has a total length of 169.3 km of track, serves 155 stations, and boasts 2,401 rail cars. TBTMG began operating in 1960 and to date has constructed four lines—the Toei Asakusa line, the Toei Mita line, the Toei Shinjuku line, and the Toei No. 12 line. Together the two systems form an impressive 12-line network that is recognized as one of the world's most developed subway systems.

THE ROLE OF RAILWAYS IN DAILY COMMUTING

Railways are a primary method of commuting in Japan's major cities. The metropolises are served by the lines of the Japan Railways group, semipublic and/or public subway systems, and private commuter railway companies. Most trains and subways run from 5 A.M. to midnight.

Table 10.2
Transit Use in Major Cities (%)

	Private autos	Trains	Bus and others	Taxi
Aichi	65.5	22.4	10.3	1.8
Tokyo	20.1	66.0	11.9	2.0
Osaka	34.6	53.6	9.9	1.9

Source: "Transportation for Commuters" (population census, 1990).

There are five types of railway operating organizations: the JR companies, local government lines, private railway companies (*mintetsu*), companies invested in by local government and private companies ("the third sector"), and the TRTA.

The JR companies deal with commuter transportation trunk lines and cargo transportation in the urban areas. Private railway companies mainly deal with commuter transportation. The ratio of commuter transportation run by the JR and by private companies is about 2:1.

Japan's mass transit system is heavily used, and extremely congested during the rush-hour peaks. Use is highest in areas with the most developed systems (see Table 10.2).

Congestion peaks during the rush hours: 7 A.M. to 9 A.M. and 5 P.M. to 7 P.M. During these times, few commuters are lucky enough to get a seat. The majority are standing, packed tightly together. In order to avoid direct eye contact with the person a few centimeters in front of them, they either close their eyes and feign sleep, or look up and read the ads.

MASS TRANSIT ADVERTISING TRENDS

From the end of World War II until the 1980s, the main form of transit advertising was posters in the trains and in the stations. In a bid to boost advertising revenues, in the 1980s the rail companies began developing new ad media.

In March 1985, JNR began selling a prepaid "Orange Card" (with which to buy train tickets from vending machines) in the Tokyo metropolitan area and the Kansai district. JNR sold ad space of 57 sq. mm on these cards. In 1986, the advertising space on the Orange Card was expanded to 85 sq. mm. In November 1986, the Orange Card's distribution area was expanded to include all principal JNR (now JR) stations throughout the country.

In October 1986, Tokyu Corporation began offering the entire ad space on certain lines in Tokyo for the exclusive use of a single advertiser for a two-week period. Initially, the offer was for ad space on an entire eight-coach train on its main Toyoko line and on an entire ten-coach train on its Denen Toshi–Shin Tamagawa line. This system was quickly copied by the other railway operators and is now commonly called a "train jack."

Following Tokyu's lead, in 1987 JR East began offering the entire ad space on a train, on three train lines (the Yamanote, Chuo, and Sobu lines). Six years later, due to poor sales caused by the bursting of the bubble economy, JR East had to discontinue "set advertising" and limit "train jacks" to one line at a time. By the end of 1995, most major train companies allowed advertisers to charter an entire train for "train jack" advertising.

An interesting attempt at developing a new mass-transit medium was launched in 1990. JR East added a new car to its ten-car Yamanote line service. These new cars had six doors on each side, as opposed to the usual four doors per car. All poster spaces above the windows were removed. Instead, two nine-inch liquid-crystal color TV displays were installed above each door. The displays featured a videotext news service with 30-second spots displayed between programs. There was no sound. The service was aimed at providing information to rush-hour commuters who could not read newspapers on crowded trains.

Following in the footsteps of the in-car TV sets on the JR Yamanote line, the JR Keihin line introduced a car without poster spaces and equipped with TV displays (without sound).

By 1993, due to disappointingly low market response, the railway lines offering these special cars were compelled to cancel their contracts for the in-car video system.

With the slowdown of the post-bubble economy seriously affecting ad budgets, Japanese advertisers began to question more seriously the effect and value of transit advertising. This led to JR East's subsidiary, East Japan Marketing & Communication, compiling and issuing *The JR Transit Advertising Data Book* in October 1992. This booklet, published annually thereafter, carries data on JR passengers as well as rates of attention to transit ads, successful targeting, and so on. This marked the first publication of detailed data by a mass transit carrier.

MASS TRANSIT ADVERTISING

Until recently, mass transit advertising was often overlooked by many foreign advertisers. There are two reasons for this.

First, it is hard to explain to the home office. This is particularly true because most countries do not have a mass transit system as heavily developed as Japan's. Even if the country where the head office is located does have a mass transit system, it often conjures up images of dirty trains and stations that are not entirely safe, are covered with graffiti, and have few advertisements.

Second, many agencies find it difficult to propose transit advertising because its effect is difficult, if not impossible, to measure accurately.

While mass transit advertising is not a cure-all, depending on the objective of the advertiser's campaign, it can offer several advantages worth considering.

Nearly 70% of the people in two of Japan's most populous cities, Tokyo and Osaka, and close to 40% in the Nagoya area, commute daily on the mass transit system to their place of employment or to school (teenagers and university students). (Table 10.3 gives a vocational breakdown of holders of JR commuter passes.)

Mass transit advertising can allow a client to target specific territories/routes (e.g., train lines/stations with heavy white-collar traffic or heavy teenage/young adult traffic).

Mass transit advertising also allows the advertiser the choice of either short, concentrated bursts of advertising for the launch of a new product, or relatively long exposures to gain a high degree of attention and awareness from the target audience.

While it is inevitable that there will be some spillover in terms of target reached, the cost per thousand of mass-transit advertising can be very attractive. Furthermore, since many commuters read newspapers and magazines while commuting, campaigns that coordinate mass transit and print advertisements can achieve very strong results—especially those that utilize the print media sold at the kiosks on station platforms.

One of the characteristics of transit advertising is its high degree of repetitiveness. Greater recall and awareness of ads can be expected among regular commuters who tend to use the same station and same train line each day. Transit ads also allow advertisers to make their appeal to people who would otherwise be disinterested in ads, and the long commute times mean long advertising exposure to a captive audience. Because large ads are possible, the ads can be bold and exciting.

Table 10.3
Vocational Breakdown of Holders of JR Commuter Passes (%)

Employed males	52.5
University students	13.6
Unmarried women	15.6
Junior and senior high-school students	10.1
Working housewives	7.4
Other	0.8

Source: "10,000 Person Survey," in *JR Commuter Advertising Data Book* (1996).

There is a wide variety of transit advertising space available. The following is a partial list of the basic types of transit advertising opportunities inside railway and subway cars:

1. *Nakazuri* (hanging posters)
2. *Mado ue* (above-window posters)
3. Stickers
4. *Tsurigawa kōkoku* (ads on handle-grip straps)
5. Next-to-door stickers
6. Above-door ads.

In addition to advertising spaces in railway and subway cars, there are advertising spaces inside railway and subway stations. The major ad spaces are as follows:

1. Station wall posters
2. Illuminated billboards
3. Freestanding billboards
4. *Hashira-maki kōkoku* (pillar ad)
5. Outdoor billboards next to the train tracks, facing inward so that passengers on the platforms, not people passing by on the road, can see them
6. Joy-step board (poster above the staircase going up/down to/from the platform)
7. Megaboard (poster space behind the seats on the platform)
8. Bench ads.

Although there are many types of transit ads, the most widely used are posters inside the railcars and posters in the train stations. Both types are sold in sets.

Ads inside railcars include hanging posters, wall-mounted posters, and window stickers. The rates for these ads are determined by the number of ads, the number of days displayed, and the number of transit routes used.

Ads in train stations consist mainly of wall posters and illuminated billboards. Both are considered effective due to the amount of attention they attract. Installation rates are set by each railway and are determined by the number of stations used, the ranking of each station, the number of commuters transiting through the station, the size and number of posters, the locations of the posters within the stations, and duration of the ad placement. Ads vary from a small poster hung for a few days at a local station to a huge, permanent backlit sign at a terminal in a large city.

When considering mass transit advertising, obtaining the desired space and the timing of the space availability are crucial. Some agencies hesitate to propose mass transit ads because they don't know if they can get the space. Only 23 designated agencies can directly buy transit ad space, and of these only a few are major agencies. These agencies buy the transit ad space, and handle all the production work involved for an extra charge.

Public and private transportation companies generally do not deal directly with advertisers, and their method of assigning space is unique. First, the designated agencies apply for space for their clients, then the transportation companies conduct lotteries to determine which agencies will have the space for that period. Compared with magazines and broadcasting, transit advertising fees tend to be the same for all parties concerned, and price variations are slight.

ADVERTISING INSIDE RAILWAY/SUBWAY CARS

Nakazuri

Nakazuri (hanging posters) hang in pairs over the aisle of the train car. There are an average of five rows of two *nakazuri* in each car, depending on the rail/subway line. Each poster of the pair contains an ad for a different company. Transportation companies avoid placing competing products in a pair.

There are fasteners on the ceilings of the train cars to hold the *nakazuri*. *Nakazuri* must be designed to allow about 4 cm of extra space at the top margin for the fastening clip, to ensure that it does not cover the top of the ad.

While they are commonly called *nakazuri* these days, the official name is *nakazuri* poster. They are sometimes referred to by their old name, *shanai-zuri* or *shanai nakazuri* poster.

Standard *nakazuri* size for JR lines is usually B3 (36.4 cm high × 51.5 cm wide); the standard size for the private lines is 28.0 cm high × 51.5 cm wide.

Due to their placement over the center of the aisle, *nakazuri* posters have a wider scope of exposure and are in a more direct line of sight than ads placed over windows.

Nakazuri are also available in "wide" sizes, for which different rates are charged. These "wide" *nakazuri* are elongated horizontal posters that are double the B3 size

Table 10.4
Number of *Nakazuri* Posters in the Tokyo Area

Line	No. of posters	Exposure
JR	8,860	2 or 3 days
Subways	3,010	2 days
Private lines	7,900	2 days
Monorail	120	7 days

in width. One "wide" *nakazuri* takes up the space of a pair of two regular-size *nakazuri*. Wide *nakazuri* are utilized to capture higher attention because they are more noticeable.

Nakazuri are usually sold for a minimum of two to three days. *Nakazuri* space on the monorail in Tokyo can be bought for a minimum of one week.

Because the posters are usually displayed for only two to three days, they are suitable for newsworthy topics and appropriate for announcement advertising. Thus, *nakazuri* are used heavily to promote magazines (cover photo and contents are shown), to announce events, and to launch new products.

Table 10.4 gives an idea of the number of *nakazuri* posters in the Tokyo area.

Mado ue

The second type of transit ad in railcars is the *mado ue* (above-window poster). These posters are placed in a row above the overhead luggage racks that run down both sides of each railcar. There are an average of 40–50 *mado ue* spaces per car (half on each side), depending on the rail/subway line.

The standard *mado ue* size for JR is 36.4 cm high x 51.5 cm wide; the size for private lines is 28.0 cm high x 51.5 cm wide.

A frame holds the above-window posters in place. Posters above windows on *ei-den* trains need about 2.5 cm of blank space on the upper margin so that the holder will not obscure the poster edge. The left and right edges of the posters are held in place by transparent plastic strips that hinder clear viewing of all but the largest typefaces.

While commonly called *mado ue*, their official name is *mado ue* poster. Other names, falling out of use, are *shanai gakumen* and *shanai gakumen* poster.

Mado ue space is usually sold for at least four days on the main JR lines, and one month on subways and private lines. As a rule of thumb, they cost roughly half the price of the *nakazuri* posters.

Wide versions of *mado ue* are available at higher rates. Long-format, continuous ads are possible with displays two panels or four panels wide. Manila board is used as a reinforced backing for *mado ue* posters. This board is typically 53 kg paper stock. An additional labor fee is charged for "wide" poster arrangements in trains.

Table 10.5 gives an idea of the number of *mado ue* in the Tokyo area.

Heiretsu (parallel posters) are side-by-side B3 or wide-format posters inside trains. Two B3 free-hanging *nakazuri* posters can be put together, and four B3 *mado ue* posters can be placed together.

Poster advertising within trains is principally sold in sets for a number of train lines. These train lines are referred to as a group with the term *sengun* (for example, the Yamanote *sengun* is composed of the Yamanote line, Saikyo line, Joban

Table 10.5
Number of *Mado ue* Posters in the Tokyo Area

Line	No. of posters	Exposure
JR	5,420	4 days
Subways	3,670	1 month
Private lines	8,260	1 month
Monorail	120	1 month

line, Yokosuka line, and Sobu Kaisoku line). Long-term placement of above-window posters is sold in single train-line increments.

Additional In-Car Ad Spaces

Additional ad space in the railcars is offered in the form of posters and stickers next to the doors. These are placed on the *tobukuro*, the hollow portion of the wall beside the doors of trains, into which the doors slide when they open. *Tobukuro* are positioned on both sides of the doors.

Posters above the door are called *doa ue*. Their official name is *doa ue* poster; names falling out of use are *rankan*, *shanai hijou*, and *hijou gakumen*.

Posters on the space next to the door are commonly called *doa yoko* (next-to-door poster). The official name is *doa yoko* poster; some of the older names are *shin B gakumen*, *3F*, and *tobukuro gakumen*.

Doa yoko posters are B3 size and are placed beside the train car doors. Positioned at passengers' eye level, they are easy to spot and are held in place with metal frames.

Sets of four *doa yoko* posters per train car (one next to each of the four entry/exit doors) can be bought. This allows advertisers to use four different visuals, thus making possible an advertising series with a story line.

Doa yoko stickers are most often used for advertising personal accessories, candy, or canned drinks. Standing in the space next to the door is popular among young women because it affords some protection from being pressed against the hordes of salarymen. The stickers are placed at passengers' eye level, making them easy to see. They are 16.5 cm × 20 cm.

Kantsu is the name for stickers on the doors of the passageways connecting the train cars.

New-B are the posters positioned next to the doors connecting the cars. They cannot be placed on/next to the doors of lead and rear cars, which have the driving compartments.

Doa window (door window) stickers are placed on the door window at passengers' eye level, making them conspicuous and easy to view. They are 16 cm × 16 cm.

Advertisers using *doa* window stickers can expect repetitive awareness to increase because these stickers can be displayed for long periods of time. (Repetitive awareness refers to the way in which repetitive exposure to an ad builds up awareness of the product or service that is being advertised.)

STATION POSTERS AND BILLBOARDS

Ads can be placed in poster and billboard locations throughout a station. Both types of space come in an abundance of sizes and styles. Recently, with the advent of improved printing and photographic technology, there has been an increase in illuminated billboards. Billboards and posters are used extensively by major corporations for PR or product promotions in stations with high traffic volume, such as those of Tokyo's Yamanote line.

Station poster and billboard space is usually sold as sets, ranging from a number of placements in one station to a number of placements in several stations on the same line. Single placements in one station are also available.

With long-term placements at single stations possible and with their large size, billboards can be used for PR. They are effective for area marketing campaigns targeted at specific audiences passing through selected stations. Station billboards can be especially effective for advertising by retailers located in the station's immediate vicinity.

Due to the longer exposure time of billboards, they offer a greater level of repeat exposure to consumers. When used at stations where large numbers of passengers board and disembark, billboards can be a tool to achieve greater consumer awareness.

Station posters are known as *eki bari* in Japanese. The official name is *eki bari* poster. Then there are station billboards, or *eki date* (officially called *eki date* board). They used to be called *futsū kanban* or *boudo kaki kōkoku*. Backlit signboards are called *eki den*. The official name for these is *eki denshoku* board, although they are sometimes still referred to by their older names: *eki* sign board, *eki gakumen*, and *densou kanban*.

Eki date are billboards within the stations that are usually large (e.g., 3 m × 4 m). *Eki bari*, on the other hand, are posters in the stations. These posters are smaller (e.g., 1.5 m × 2 m). Both *eki date* and *eki bari* are printed on paper stock. *Eki den* range from poster size to billboard size and are always backlit. They are printed on an acetate sheet.

Station posters come in a variety of sizes and can be placed in a wide variety of locations within the stations. Since advertisers can place as few as one poster per station, or many more, posters are an extremely flexible medium. The right combination of size and location can be quite effective. Various kinds of poster sets can be used to enhance advertising impact and reach selected target groups. Station posters can make strong appeals, since they are a highly visual medium.

A single short-term period for regular station posters is about seven days. However, station posters can be placed for periods of three to six months or up to a year. In these cases, they can be replaced on a weekly basis, allowing for a campaign message that develops over time.

Station posters are placed both within the station and on the platforms. They are sold in sets that combine placements and stations. Cost is determined by the stations included in the set, the poster locations in the stations, and the length of time the posters will be displayed. One week is the usual minimum exposure period.

The ranking assigned to each station is used in determining ad rates for station posters. Rankings are primarily assigned on the basis of number of passengers using each station. Rankings are in alphabetical order, with A rankings being the most expensive. At JR East, ad rates are determined by station rankings ranging from A to G, and subway stations in Tokyo are ranked A to E.

The rankings of stations are as follows:

A. Tokyo, Yurakucho, Shimbashi, Yokohama, Shinjuku, Harajuku, Shibuya, Ikebukuro, Ueno, Takadanobaba

B. Osaki, Gotanda, Meguro, Ebisu, Suidobashi, Ichigaya, Yoyogi, Nakano

C. Mejiro, Shinanomachi, Higashi Nakano, Koenji, Asagaya, Nippori

D. Higashi Kanazawa, Itabashi, Okubo, Kaminakazato, Shimo-Osanankayama, Minami Senjyu

E. Kitayono, Nishi Oi, Yokosuka

Ad space for station posters is usually sold in sets. Each set consists of a combination of stations and a combination of display locations in each station. These can usually be negotiated to an extent. Selling space in sets is done by both the private railways and the JR lines.

A few non-JR lines sell space as "complete" sets (one cannot negotiate which stations will be included/excluded). This is done to avoid having display positions left empty. The Tokyo-area JR lines and the *eiden* subway sell the set package deals first; any remaining slots at individual stations are sold separately.

It is also possible to have station posters forming parts of a larger visual placed together to create an extended "large" visual. Additionally, panorama sets or long size sets are possible by placing posters in a row as a special set. This is called *kumi-bari*. An additional ¥600 fee per set is charged for assembling posters with different designs.

A popular method of attracting attention with station posters is known as *ren-bari* (the placement of posters of the same design in a continuous row).

A "wide" station poster can also be displayed. This would be a B0 (*B-bai*) size. As with placing "wide" ads inside the train cars, a special labor fee is charged for "wide" poster arrangements at stations.

The ad rate for station posters includes a labor fee for placing and removing the posters; "special work" fees become necessary when certain posters necessitate special handling. Examples include assembling a long series of interconnected panorama or mosaic station posters, or a wide-format in-train poster.

Posters made from special materials necessitate a separate disposal fee. If they are to be retrieved, a special retrieval work fee will be charged.

CONCLUSION

Mass transit advertising, whether within the train or in the station, is a medium that can be of great value to the advertiser. It is a mass medium in terms of viewers, but specific in terms of geographical location. It also has a repetitive effect on commuters who daily use the same line and pass through the same stations.

Chapter 11

Sono-ta no Kōtsū Kōkoku
Other Types of Transit Advertising

All of Japan's major cities offer two inexpensive advertising media whose reach extends throughout the city and into the suburbs. These are the fleets of taxis cruising each city and the bus services running on prescribed routes. While not considered mass advertising mediums, both taxis and buses offer opportunities that should be understood.

Depending on the product or service being advertised and the target audience, taxi and bus advertising can be an effective supplementary advertising medium when used correctly. Taxis are an underutilized advertising medium only recently being explored by foreign marketers, who have discovered taxi advertising can supplement a campaign aimed at white-collar workers. With the outright ban on cigarette advertising on television in April 1998, Western tobacco companies began utilizing taxis as an ad medium. R. J. Reynolds has been the leader, aggressively using taxi advertising to promote its Salem brand.

Buses can be valuable when targeting either a specific audience on its daily commute or an audience in a specific part of a city or suburb.

TAXI ADVERTISING

Each major Japanese metropolis has a fleet of taxis. Catching a taxi is relatively easy because they are continuously cruising the streets, and are available at stands in front of major hotels and train stations. Taxis carry a variety of passengers, although it is safe to say that the largest number are businessmen. Table 11.1 gives a breakdown of taxi passengers by occupation.

There are over 254,000 taxis and "hired cars" in the whole of Japan, although not all are in daily use. Tokyo alone boasts over 45,000 taxis, 20% of the entire nation's taxi fleet. More than 50 million people in Tokyo ride in taxis every month, which is equivalent to about 600 million passengers per year. It is estimated that each taxi in Tokyo carries about 66.7 people per day. Each of Japan's major cities boasts a taxi fleet numbering in the thousands, from 14,000 in Osaka to 1,900 in Sendai. Nationwide, 3,330 million people ride in taxis per year. The majority of fares are businessmen, and the average taxi ride is 15–20 minutes. Table 11.2 gives a breakdown of overall taxi usage by gender; Table 11.3 gives the breakdown by age.

Types of Taxi Advertising

Taxis reach a large number of consumers in the cities. However, unlike buses, which follow a prescribed route, taxis do not offer precise geographic targeting when used as an ad medium.

Taxi advertising can be broken down into two types: advertising aimed at passengers inside the taxi, and advertising on the outside of the taxi, targeting the world at large.

Internal taxi ads play to a captive audience whose sole distractions are looking out the window or perhaps, using their mobile phone.

External taxi ads are aimed at passengers as they enter the taxi, at drivers of other vehicles, and at pedestrians.

There are three kinds of internal taxi ads:

1. Ad cases
2. Door-window ads
3. Digital ads

Table 11.1
Taxi Passenger Breakdown by Occupation (%)

Businessmen (salarymen)	44
Housewives	12
Self-employed	16
Office ladies	10
Executives	8
Freelancers	8
Students	2

Source: New Mobile Media-Net, "Adrun Usage Study" (March 1998).

Table 11.2
Breakdown of Taxi Usage by Gender (%)

	Total	Business/ commute	Shopping/ other	Leisure
Male	54.5	73.5	22.4	4.1
Female	45.5	34.0	61.4	4.6
Total	100.0	55.5	40.2	4.3

Source: Tokyo Taxi Association, Research on Taxi Users (July 1998).

External ads come in two forms:

1. Rear-window stickers
2. Superstickers

"Take-one" pamphlet ad cases are available in taxis. These consist of a holder with a clear plastic cover (in which an ad is inserted) on the back of the front seat. Inside the holder are ad pamphlets ("take ones"). The ad case is directly in front of the rear-seat passengers (about 70 cm in front of their noses). The holder is 100 mm high × 200 mm wide.

Ad case(s) are usually sold in lots of 1,000, 2,000, or 3,000 taxis, for one, two, or three months, although various combinations are negotiable.

On average, about one pamphlet per taxi is removed each day. At the end of each month, the taxi advertising company checks how many pamphlets need to be replaced and submits a report to the ad agency at the beginning of the following month. Pamphlets and/or the case ad can be changed during the period booked. Pamphlets are 100–200 mm high × 190–215 mm wide, and must be three-fold A4 size.

Ad case space should be booked about 45 days in advance. After applying for ad space, it takes one week for confirmation of which taxi company will carry the ad. Artwork for pamphlets and/or case inserts take two weeks to complete (from day of submission). It then takes one week to put all the pamphlets/inserts in place.

Taxis also have door-window ad spaces. Door-window ads are actually stickers on the side rear passenger windows. They are placed on the outside of the door, but can be seen clearly from either outside or inside the taxi because they are printed on both sides. Space has to be booked 60 days in advance. Stickers can be round, square, or rectangular. Their average size is 140–160

Table 11.3
Breakdown of Taxi Usage by Age (%)

	Business/ commute	Shopping/ other	Leisure
–19	33.3	53.4	13.3
20–29	50.8	42.9	6.3
30–39	54.8	40.4	4.8
40–49	62.5	32.6	4.9
50–59	66.7	31.3	2.1
60–	40.8	55.0	4.2
Total	55.5	40.2	4.3

Source: Tokyo Taxi Association, Research on Taxi Users (July 1998).

mm high × 130–140 mm wide. The minimum is usually at least 500 taxis for at least one month.

Rear-window stickers are also used on taxis. They are usually placed on the corner of the taxi's rear window, and can be seen only from the outside (by cars behind the taxi, or nearby pedestrians when the taxi is stopped). Space has to be booked 60 days in advance. The stickers' size is 100 mm high × 400–450 mm wide. The advertising contract is usually for a minimum of 500 taxis for at least one month.

There are also taxi superstickers (TSS), which cover more than half of a taxi's rear window. They are printed on a "two-way" material, so the taxi driver can see through them but they look like a solid sheet of material from the outside. They are centered on the rear window. The size of a TSS is 250 mm high × 850 mm wide. The minimum advertising period is at least 500 taxis for three months.

Finally, taxis offer TMS (taxi media system). TMS is a digital display panel above the front passenger seat, where the vanity mirror is usually located. It was launched as a new ad medium in January 1997 and initially installed in 5,000 taxis.

TMS receives news and information from FM radio stations, and displays them as digital text. Commercials are placed between news items. One TMS cycle is 18 minutes and has about 30 ads. Within a period of 18 minutes there will be a bulletin, one CM, another news bulletin, another CM, and then a longer news bulletin, and so on.

The TMS screen is 18 mm high × 155 mm wide. Text of 12 characters (at most) can be shown at one time; there are four "scrolls" for a total of about 45 characters within 18 seconds. Scrolling can be horizontal or vertical. The digital text characters are green.

Initial indications show that 89% of passengers watch the new medium.

Taxi Advertising in Tokyo

There are several specialized agencies in Tokyo selling taxi advertising space. Nihon Taxi Advertising and JOC are two of the largest. Each agency has exclusive contracts with several taxi companies. Advertisers cannot choose the taxi company they want to use, but will be notified of which taxi company will carry their ad one week after they indicate a desire to place an ad. Advertisers' ad agencies are responsible for providing final artwork (*han-shita*). The taxi ad agency does the production work, which will be charged to the client in addition to the space cost.

BUS ADVERTISING

Buses are an inexpensive means for reaching consumers in Japan's major metropolises, each of which has several bus lines. Tokyo has an extensive bus network operated by both the Tokyo municipal government and either private railways or private bus companies.

The majority of commuters in Japan's major metropolitan areas use the system of trains and subways. Many also use a bus service. The bus services bring commuters to and from the train stations closest to their homes and to their place of work. Bus routes cover both suburban and metropolitan areas, as well as rural areas that do not possess train service.

Buses offer an opportunity to advertise to the passengers, and to the world at large. Bus advertising does not allow target segmentation in terms of demographics. It does, however, allow precise geographic segmentation within specific localities, due to the prescribed routes followed by buses. For this reason, the preponderance of bus advertising is placed by retailers located near bus routes. Bus advertising is available in two types—internal and external.

There are five types of internal bus ads:

1. Wall-mounted posters
2. Side-hanging posters
3. Ads on the back of the driver's compartment
4. Stickers
5. Ads on handle grip straps

There are two types of external bus ads:

1. Billboards on the bus sides
2. Billboards on the rear of the bus

Table 11.4
Posters in Buses, Tokyo Metropolitan Area

Bus company	No. of posters	Period available
City Bus	1,910	7 days/15 days/1 month
Tokyu Bus	711	1 week/2 weeks/1 month
Keikyu Bus	710	1 week/2 weeks/1 month
Keisei Bus	1,100	1 week/1 month
Shin-Keisei Bus	320	1 week/1 month
Odakyu Bus	445	2 weeks/1 month
Seibu Bus	682	1 week/1 month
Keio Bus	543	2 weeks/1 month
Tobu Bus	1,007	7 days/15 days/1 month
Kanto Bus	395	10 days/1 month
Kanachu Bus	1,867	7 days/2 weeks/1 month
Yokohama Municipal Bus	1,100	7 days/1 month
Nishi-Tokyo Bus	274	2 weeks/1 month

Source: Asahi Advertising, Inc. (1997).

The mainstay of bus advertising is ad posters inside the buses, above the windows. The major bus companies sell this space on each route they serve. In major metropolitan areas the exposure period for these posters is usually a week, two weeks, or a month. The exposure periods differ slightly from bus company to bus company.

Bus companies serving the Tokyo metropolitan area include Tozai, Keihin Kyuko, Tokyu, Keisei, Kanto, Odakyu, Tobu, Kokusai Kyogo, West Tokyo, and Tamagawa (see Table 11.4).

Posters on the outside of buses (one on each side and one on the back) reach consumers working or living within a certain geographical area along the bus route. The poster on the right (driver's) side is longer than the poster on the left side of the bus (where the doors for passengers are located).

Due to crowded conditions in the cities, buses are often stopped in traffic or moving quite slowly. This makes their external posters, especially those on the sides, highly visible to pedestrians. And the constant stop-and-go traffic in Japan's cities makes the posters on the backs of the buses highly visible to other drivers.

Standard bus poster sizes (Tokyo) are as follow:

"Wide version" (on driver's side): 1900 mm wide × 500 mm high

"Standard version" (on side with doors): 1200 mm wide × 600 mm high

"Rear ads" (on the back of bus): 600 mm wide × 400 mm high

CONCLUSION

Taxi advertising, whether inside or outside the cab, is not for every advertiser. The same can be said of bus advertising. However, for an advertiser with a large enough budget, placing ads on these two types of vehicles further strengthens the target's awareness of the client's core ad message. On the other hand, for an advertiser with a limited budget, these locations can be an effective part of a campaign that concentrates efforts and resources in a focused area.

Chapter 12

Shine-ado
Cinema Advertising

The potential use of cinema advertising is not often seriously considered by major foreign advertisers in Japan. They don't need to. They have budgets large enough to afford the luxury of advertising in the mass media in order to reach broad target audiences. However, advertisers with budget limitations or particular needs can make effective use of cinema advertising.

HISTORY

Japan has a long history of cinema viewing, reaching back to the first screenings in Kobe in November 1896. Japan's first movie theater, the *Denki-kan* (Electric Pavilion), opened in the Asakusa district of Tokyo in 1903, and by the early 1920s cinema's popularity was increasing rapidly. During this period both the number of cinemas and cinema attendance increased annually.

From the 1920s until the advent of television broadcasting in 1954, movies were a popular form of entertainment, attracting millions of people every year. Inevitably, the postwar rise of television led to the decline in the growth of the number of moviegoers. In 1958, cinema attendance in Japan peaked at 1.1 billion tickets sold at the 7,067 movie theaters nationwide. Since then, the decline in attendance has been constant, although the largest decrease was recorded between 1960 and 1965, when attendance dropped from 1 billion to 373 million and the number of theaters decreased from 7,457 to 4,649. This was the period when sales of television sets were booming. The advent of home-use VCRs in 1975 further spurred the decline in cinema attendance.

The number of theaters and attendance between 1987 and 1996 are given in Table 12.1

Table 12.1
Number of Theaters and Attendance, 1987–96

	No. of theaters	Annual attendance	Attendance rate per total population
1987	2,053	143,935,000	1.19
1988	2,005	144,825,000	1.19
1989	1,912	143,573,000	1.17
1990	1,836	146,000,000	1.19
1991	1,804	138,330,000	1.12
1992	1,744	125,600,000	1.02
1993	1,734	130,720,000	1.05
1994	1,747	122,990,000	0.98
1995	1,778	127,040,000	1.01
1996	1,828	119,575,000	0.95

Source: Jijieigatsushinsha (1 December 1997).

Table 12.2
Types of Movie Theaters (%)

Single screen	35.5
Five or more screens	9.1
Two to four screens	55.4
Total	100.0

Source: Sunrise Co. (1995).

The continued decrease in movie attendance in the 1980s and 1990s was a direct result of the growth of the video rental industry. With the price of renting a video being only one-third to one-quarter of the price of a movie ticket, viewers opted to enjoy movies at home. Every neighborhood has a video rental shop, and on average each shop has 2,500 videotapes in stock and a long list of rental customers.

In 1996 the total number of commercial movie theaters was 1,828, a decline of 225 since 1987. Recently however, there has been an increase in cinema complexes, video theaters, and drive-in theaters, resulting in more screens per theater (see Table 12.2).

CINEMA IN JAPAN TODAY

Today, a slight majority of moviegoers are women. About 90% are single, and 10% are married. In addition 49% go to a movie with a member of the opposite sex, 23% go with a friend of the same sex, 15% go with their family, and 5% go alone (8% are unknown). See Table 12.3.

The cinema cycle begins with movies aimed at the year-end crowd, from November to January. From March through April, movies are geared toward teenagers and children on spring break. Movies targeted at teenagers and young adults are released during April to June, which also covers the "golden week" vacation. From June through mid-August, large-scale hit movies are released for the summer vacation period. From mid-August to November, more large-scale hits are released.

Table 12.3
Frequency of Movie Viewing During the Past Year (%)

	Age					
	Total	–19	20–29	30–39	40–49	50+
	Animation					
Did not go	80.6	67.1	75.8	67.6	82.2	95.2
Went at least once	18.9	32.0	23.5	31.7	17.2	4.6
Do not remember	0.5	0.9	0.7	0.7	0.6	0.2
	Domestic Film					
Did not go	77.6	70.8	70.9	78.3	79.7	82.7
Went at least once	20.9	27.0	26.7	19.8	19.0	16.7
Do not remember	1.5	2.2	2.4	1.9	1.3	0.6
	Foreign Film					
Did not go	57.8	42.4	37.3	60.4	62.1	73.1
Went at least once	40.7	55.9	61.1	37.4	36.6	25.8
Do not remember	1.5	1.7	1.6	2.2	1.3	1.1

Source: Video Research Co., Audience & Consumer Report (1998).

FOREIGN MOVIE RELEASES

Foreign movies account for more than half the movies shown in Japan. In general, about six months to a year elapses before major non-Japanese movies appear in theaters in Japan. Hollywood films appear in other countries, or even as airline in-flight movies, before they appear in Japanese theaters.

Contrary to popular opinion, the delay in the screening of foreign films in Japan is not due to time required for subtitling, which can be handled in a matter of weeks. (Most foreign films are shown in their native language, with Japanese subtitles.) Domestic distributors claim promotion (preparation of posters, ad campaigns, etc.) is what takes time. Particularly time-consuming is the preparation and execution of merchandising agreements.

Another promotional consideration is the timing of a film's release. Hollywood films released for the U.S. summer season are not necessarily timed right for the Japanese market (summer break in Japan is much shorter than in the West). Local distributors aim for release during the peak Japanese moviegoing seasons: holiday periods such as "golden week," spring break, summer vacation, and New Year's.

Waiting for a film to be released in the U.S. and prove itself allows domestic promotions to announce the film as *zen-bei dai-ichi* (no. 1 in the U.S.), virtually guaranteeing its success in Japan.

A few films, usually those starring major Hollywood stars who regularly appear in Japanese TV commercials, are released earlier due to the stars' popularity in Japan. Films by Arnold Schwarzenegger and Jodie Foster typically are released in Japan within a month of their U.S. debut, since they are certain to draw crowds.

Another factor inhibiting the early release of Hollywood films in Japan is the dearth of screens available. The U.S. boasts more than 12,000 cinemas nationwide, many of them multiscreened. Japan has only 1,828 cinemas. Not only is it difficult to get a film to screen in Japan, but if a film is successful and its run is extended, films scheduled after it are delayed.

While the above is true for major Hollywood releases, many Asian and French releases, as well as minor U.S. releases, are screened quite quickly in Japan. A very few are shown in Japan before they are released in the U.S.

For the astute foreign advertiser and his agency, selection of films that have enjoyed successful releases overseas prior to their screening in Japan can help guarantee effective cinema advertising.

FREE-BOOKING AND BLOCK-BOOKING SYSTEMS

Under the free-booking system, the film distribution company negotiates a screening period for each movie with each theater chain. A decision regarding the length of the screening period is based on the perceived entertainment value of the movie, and on the potential audience size.

In the block-booking system, the film distribution company and the film exhibit company agree to a yearly screening contract, with the lineup of movies, number of screens, and release dates determined in advance. This system guarantees that the distributors will have a constant flow of movies, and the movie theaters are assured a yearlong supply of movies.

In general, foreign movies are distributed under the free-booking system, while Japanese movies are distributed under the block-booking system.

TYPES OF MOVIE THEATERS

The Japanese cinema industry is characterized by theater chains, with each chain acquiring its own movies. Four major companies operate chains of wholly owned and affiliated movie theaters. They are led by Japan's three major film studios: Toho, famous for its Godzilla movies; Shochiku, which produced the hit *Tora-san* series; and Toei, famous for its animations and action movies. The fourth company is Tokyu Recreation, which is part of the Tokyu Group conglomerate.

There are three basic categories of movie theaters in Japan.

1. Road show theaters are located in city centers and in the major railway terminals; they are frequented by couples on dates.
2. Mini-theaters are located in upscale districts; they offer art/cultural films, rather than blockbusters, and have limited seating.
3. Cinema complexes are family-oriented theaters offering several screens. Located in the suburbs, these theaters are the fastest-growing segment of the theater industry. As of mid-1998, Japan had 52 cinema complexes with a combined total of 344 screens, and 12 more complexes were planned to be completed by year's end. A further 24 complexes were planned for 1999.

CINE ADS

Also known as "ad movies" or "cine spots," cine ads first appeared immediately after World War II. At the time, they consisted of color slides. Today, cine ads are made on 35 mm film (either standard or VistaVision size) and are available in 15-, 30-, or 60-second lengths. One "unit" of 15-second cine ads runs for four weeks, and a unit of 30-second cine ads runs for two weeks. Both units are equal in price. Sixty-second cine ads are also possible, but length of runs must be negotiated.

One company controls over 75% of the total Japanese market share for cine ads. This is Sunrise, a firm that specializes in selling cinema advertising space.

Cine ads allow target focus through the genre of movie chosen. A marketer aiming at young males would probably choose action movies, for example. Cine ads can be run nationwide or in selected geographical areas. Thus advertisers can either choose to run a cine ad before a certain movie (*Die Hard* in six theaters, for example) or to run it in certain areas (all movie theaters in Ginza, regardless of the movie being shown, for a two week period, for example).

An advantage to the marketer is that hit foreign movies are released very late in Japan. This allows plenty of time for planning. Also, the major studio-run theater chains know which movies will be running in their theaters six months in advance, and make this information available to ad agencies upon request.

To run cine ads before one selected movie (at about 80–100 theaters nationwide) costs from ¥9 million to ¥12 million. If cine ads are being run in only ten major cities (18–25 theaters), the cost will be between ¥2 million and ¥3 million. Running cine ads in one city (three to six theaters) further reduces the cost to between ¥500,000 and ¥1 million. A cine ad can also be screened at just one theater.

The cost of turning your fifteen-second television commercial (usually made on 3/4-inch videotape) into a 35 mm cine ad is about ¥4 million.

It is possible, in some of the bigger theaters, to offer product samples in the theater lobby, but this must be negotiated. Some theaters also offer ad space on billboards.

Some basic facts and figures regarding cinema advertising are the following:

No. of theaters in Japan: 1,884 (1997)

Annual audience: 125,600,000

Cost for 30-sec. spot: ¥60,000–¥300,000 (per two-week period, depending on the rank of the theater)

Cost per 3 m × 4 m billboard, four-week contract period = ¥100,000–¥220,000 (depending on the location).

There are three types of cine ads:

1. Color slides are usually used only for ads placed by restaurants in the immediate vicinity of the theater.
2. Ad movies, specially produced for airing in theaters, take time and money to produce, but the quality is the best available.
3. TV commercials use a processed print specially produced for use in theaters, made from the mother negative of the original TV commercial film.

COMMERCIALS IN MOVIE THEATERS

There are certain basic characteristics to keep in mind when considering use of movie theater commercials.

1. Cinemas are audiovisual venues, and since viewers do not have other distractions, cine ads allow the advertiser to convey messages to a captive audience. In other words, advertisers have no worries about losing viewers' attention, as happens with TV, where viewers switch channels, turn off the TV set, or walk out of the room.

2. The majority of moviegoers are children and young adults, an influential purchasing group.
3. Advertisers can narrow down their target audience, depending on the movie being shown.
4. The adaptation and use of the advertiser's TV commercials achieves a synergy with the TV commercials' exposure.
5. Advertisers can further support their cine-ad campaign by providing printed materials on program brochures, cinema invitations, displays in the cinema lobby, and so on.
6. Cine-ad messages are well-received in the relaxed venue of a movie theater, where people are receptive and in the frame of mind for entertainment.

Space booking for cine ads should be at least one month before the screening date. However, for the New Year and summer vacation peak seasons, bookings should be much further in advance. Also, for hit foreign movies, booking deadlines are set well in advance of the screening dates.

The minimum period to be booked is one *kūrū* (unit). However, movie theaters use two different definitions of how long one *kūrū* is. Some theaters say it is two weeks; others say it is four weeks. Thus, a careful check must be made of which definition is used by the theaters the advertiser will be using.

Material insertion deadline for cine ads is ten days in advance of screening. The material must be 35 mm *shukushō vista* (standard size or VistaVision). Sound is monoaural.

One or two copies of *shukushō vista* must be given to each theater, plus four extras.

CONCLUSION

Properly used, cine ads can be a strong tool for getting an advertising message to a specific target. They allow advertisers to present their message in a spectacular format, to a specific audience, during a concentrated period. Best of all, cine ads are viewed by a captive audience looking forward to being entertained.

Chapter 13

Sono-ta no Kōkoku
Other Non–Mass Media Advertising

Advertising is no more limited to mass media in Japan than it is in any other country. There are an endless number of non–mass media advertising opportunities available in Japan. Some are similar to those found in other markets, while others are unique to Japan. Often inexpensive and offering flexibility in terms of placement periods, these alternative media can offer valuable support for mass-media ad campaigns. This chapter briefly describes some of the most commonly used alternatives.

SHINKANSEN ADS

Advertising on the *shinkansen* (the "bullet train") is useful for reaching businessmen traveling between the major metropolises of Japan, and domestic vacation travelers.

The *shinkansen* lines, all of which are operated by JR (Japan Railways), offer a quick and less expensive alternative to flying between Japan's major cities. The Tokaido *shinkansen* covers the 552.6 km between Tokyo and Shin-Osaka stations in only two and a half hours, and the Sanyo *shinkansen* takes only 2 hours and 17 minutes to cover the 623.3 km between Shin-Osaka and Hakata stations. On both the Tokaido and Sanyo *shinkansen* lines, there are 400 intercity train trips each day. The average 16-car *shinkansen* train (400 m long) is able to carry approximately 1,300 passengers.

The busiest times of the year for *shinkansen* travel are the holiday periods, when many people go from the metropolises to visit their relatives in the countryside. During the travel peaks, some trains may run at up to 200 percent capacity (i.e., up to 100 people standing in each car), despite the provision of extra trains. The heaviest holiday traffic is during "golden week" (28 April–6 May), the summer (21 July–31 August), and the year-end period (25 December–10 January).

The major *shinkansen* lines (Tokaido, Sanyo, Tohoku, and Joetsu) offer a variety of advertising options, which can be combined in sets.

There are in-cabin wall poster spaces available, one per wall, at each end of each car (excluding the dining car). The size of the poster depends on the model of *shinkansen* car. Poster sizes on lines using older cars are half A2 size (210 mm × 297 mm). On lines using newer cars, poster sizes are half B2 size (257 mm × 364 mm). Ad space is sold for one-month periods, usually from the first day of the month to the last.

The number of poster spaces available runs from 700 to 1,500, depending on the lines used and the model of the cars on those lines. If preferred, it is possible to buy ad space in all cars or in odd- or even-numbered cars.

In-cabin wall poster ad spaces are not usually sold alone, but as part of a *shinkansen* compo (i.e., a set package with other *shinkansen* media). In-cabin wall placards are sold independently only when there are not enough orders for the *shinkansen* sets.

Sets of large ad poster panels, one per station serving the *shinkansen*, are available. Advertisers have a choice of two groups of stations that offer these ad panels.

The A group consists of the Tokaido and Sanyo lines: Tokyo, Shin-Yokohama, Odawara, Shizuoka, Hamamatsu, Toyohashi, Nagoya, Kyoto, Shin-Osaka, Shin-Kobe, Okayama, Hiroshima, Kogura, Hakata (14 stations, 14 panels).

The B group consists of the Tohoku and Joetsu lines: Ueno, Omiya, Koriyama, Fukushima, Sendai, Morioka, Takasaki, Nagaoka, Niigata (nine stations, nine panels).

The posters are 1,850 mm high × 2,400 mm wide, and can be placed during any of four three-month periods (April to June, July to September, October to December, and January to March).

Sets of station wall poster spaces can be bought at stations serving the *shinkansen*. Again, there are two groups of stations that can be chosen from.

The A group consists of the Tokaido and Sanyo lines: Tokyo (two posters), Shin-Yokohama, Odawara, Shizuoka, Hamamatsu, Toyohashi, Nagoya, Kyoto, Shin-Osaka, Shin-Kobe, Himeiji, Okayama, Fukuyama, Hiroshima, Kogura, Hakata (16 stations, 17 posters).

The B group consists of the Tohoku and Joetsu lines: Ueno, Omiya, Koriyama, Fukushima, Sendai, Morioka, Niigata, Takasaki, Nagaoka (nine stations, nine posters).

The posters are 1,030 mm high × 1,456 mm wide. Space is sold for two-week periods.

Backlit ad spaces in the *shinkansen* "green" cars (reserved seat cars) are sold in a variety of sets. These are available on the Tokaido and Sanyo lines.

Ad space is sold for one-month periods. The spaces are 420 mm high × 594 mm wide. The ad surface is a color transparency for backlighting.

Backlit ad spaces above the entrance to the *shinkansen* dining car are available on the Tokaido and Sanyo *shinkansen* lines. They are sold for one-month periods.

The spaces are 360 mm high × 1,410 mm wide.

Each of the above is combined into 20 mixed-media groups and sold to ad agencies as a *shinkansen* set.

Finally, there is a *shinkansen* magazine, *Train Vert,* in which ad space can be bought. Each *shinkansen* train has two or more green cars with reserved seats. The pocket on the back of each seat holds the magazine.

AIR TRANSPORT ADS

There are three types of advertising available with regard to air transport in Japan: internal ads, external ads, and ads in the airports.

Internal ads include seat cover ads (an ad is printed on the headrest cover), onboard video commercials, and in-flight magazine ads.

Most airlines, both domestic and international carriers, offer an in-flight video service consisting of a variety of short programs. Advertisers can place commercial messages within these programs to promote their products.

Usually, commercials either 30- or 60-seconds long are accepted, although conditions vary from carrier to carrier. Space is usually sold for one month.

All carriers, whether flying international or domestic routes, offer their passengers complimentary in-flight magazines. These magazines accept advertising.

In a new twist in transportation advertising, September 1997 saw Japan's first instance of an airplane featuring a paid advertisement painted on its exterior. The advertiser, Otsuka Pharmaceutical Co., had an ad for its sports drink, Pocari Sweat, painted on the body of a Japan Air System plane. The plane, which flew domestic routes, carried the advertisement for one year.

The ad, consisting of Pocari Sweat emblazoned in white letters on a blue background, was situated on the midsection of the plane, where the name of the airline is usually found.

One year later, in September 1998, a new domestic carrier, Skymark Airlines, advertised the provision of in-flight entertainment from the satellite broadcaster DirecTV by having DirecTV painted prominently on the side of its aircraft.

The cost of this type of advertising is rumored to be several hundred million yen.

Finally, airports offer a venue to place a variety of ads aimed at both departing and arriving passengers. The media that airports provide for ads include illuminated billboards, wall-mounted billboards, show windows, showcases, posters, ashtrays, boarding tickets, and luggage trolleys.

"LIMOUSINE" BUS MAGAZINE ADS

Tokyo, Yokohama, and Osaka have "limousine" bus service to and from downtown locations and major hotels and their respective international and domestic airports. These buses provide a complimentary magazine (in the pocket on the back of the seat) that accepts advertising. Some advertisers find this medium an inexpensive method of reaching travelers. This is especially true of companies whose products are sold overseas, particularly in duty-free outlets.

Tokyo's limousine bus magazine, VIA, is an A4 size quarterly with a claimed circulation of 150,000. VIA offers a variety of ad spaces from 84 mm × 185 mm to full-page (285 mm × 210 mm). It is placed on the Tokyo metropolitan area buses serving both Narita (international airport) and Haneda (domestic airport).

Osaka's limousine bus magazine is the B5 size *Attention*. This bimonthly is found on the vehicles of the main bus company serving the airport, and is also available in some hotels in the Osaka area. *Attention*'s claimed circulation is 200,000. Ad sizes range from 51 mm × 160 mm to full-page (257 mm × 182 mm).

FERRY ADVERTISING

Since it is a nation of many islands, ferry services are common in Japan. All ferry services provide opportunities for advertising, both in the ferries and in the terminal waiting rooms.

Ad spaces available on the ferries include showcases, wall billboards, and posters. In the waiting rooms, ad spaces consist of billboards, posters, illuminated billboards, and benches.

MOBILE ADVERTISEMENTS

Mobotron is a specially built advertising truck featuring a built-in large television screen. Television commercials can be continuously displayed on the screen. The screen is 2.5 m high × 4.2 m wide. Rental is usually on a per-day basis.

Hiring one truck for a nine-hour day costs about ¥1 million on a weekday and ¥1.2 million on a weekend or holiday. If the Mobotron is to be used far from Tokyo, additional fees will be charged.

Also available is a car with billboards mounted on the side (roof mounting can be negotiated) and speakers playing a commercial song as the car drives through neighborhoods. Since the car's route can be chosen freely, this advertising medium is well-suited for targeting a specific locality. Thus, it is often used to publicize special events such as the opening of a local store or a special sale. Since the car is subject to traffic laws and noise restrictions, a permit must be secured from the National Police Agency.

The rate for hiring one driver and car for six days (eight hours per day) is about ¥250,000. Permit costs vary by location, and billboard production costs depend on quality demanded. When arrangements are made for areas far from Tokyo, extra costs such as accommodations for the driver and operating permits will be involved.

FIXED OUTDOOR ADVERTISING

There are thousands of permanent billboard spaces available in Japan's major cities. At one time or another, all of Japan's major advertisers use billboards. While the variety of billboard sizes available is almost unlimited, there are eight standard sizes, of which 3 m high × 4 m wide is the most common. Cost varies according to size, location, and type of billboard (lit at night, not lit, etc.).

Most of the billboard sites are owned by companies that specialize in selling billboard space. In Tokyo's 23 wards, there are about 3,000 billboard sites owned by these companies. The remaining sites are privately owned by either the building or the property owners.

Electric/moving neon newsboards are also available for advertising. These electric boards, which flash news text, usually are installed on the walls or rooftops of buildings adjacent to major intersections or train stations. Commercials are typically run between the news headlines.

Newsboard ads are not a long-exposure medium; they are as transient as TV or radio ads. They require the viewer to read the ad message quickly, and thus have never gained strong popularity among advertisers.

The Asahi electric newsboard, installed at the busy Ginza 4–Chome intersection, displays text news and ad messages. From 10 A.M. to 11 P.M. daily, ad messages 15 seconds long and displaying 30 characters can be shown about 180 times.

Q-boards are another type of fixed outdoor ad space. These are computer-controlled boards that use four-color magnetized rotating cubes arranged in various mosaic combinations to form letters and pictures. A representative example is the Shibuya City visual board in Tokyo. Its 7.5 m height × 9.6 m width displays pictures and text composed of red, white, blue, and green cubes.

The Shibuya City visual board is run daily from 7 A.M. to 12 midnight. Ad display time is nine seconds, with a one-second transition between ads. Ads are displayed 170 times per day, and the contract period is usually one year.

Large outdoor television screens are commonly used for advertising. Several of Japan's major cities have such television screens, placed in areas with heavy pedestrian traffic, on which commercials can be shown. Since the screens are placed high on a building, sound usually cannot be used.

The Shibuya 109 Forum Vision in Tokyo is a typical example. The display size is 8.6 m high × 8.8 m wide. Commercials are broadcast daily from 11 A.M. to

11 P.M. Usual contracts are for a 30-second commercial to be aired 24 times per day during a 15-day period.

Finally, there are town media ad spaces on the sides of buildings and other structures. The advertisement is painted on, pasted on, or hung on the side of the building. Although they are by no means widely available, many Japanese cities have a scattering of such sites.

An example is Tokyo's Shibuya Parco store, which allows an ad to be painted directly on the store's outer wall or a large banner to be suspended from the roof to cover the wall. The size allowed for the painting is 2.4 m high × 14 m wide. The display period is usually one month. Advertisers can also negotiate to obtain space in and around the store for events and exhibits.

OTHER MEDIA

In a nation of baseball fanatics, major advertisers commonly place ads on billboards in the baseball stadiums. A great advantage of these billboards is that they are picked up by the television cameras broadcasting the game.

Coveted locations are the area directly behind home plate and those near the scoreboard, both of which receive heavy television coverage.

Ad rates at baseball stadiums vary according to the yearly number of spectators, the facilities, the size, and the ad location. Annual fees can range from as little as ¥10 million to as high as ¥800 million.

A unique ad medium is the roadside disposable message boards. These are simple message boards that can be attached to telephone poles, streetlamps, or guardrails along the streets. They consist of a simple wooden frame with an ad message printed on either cloth or paper stretched over it. Commonly, these boards advertise a movie or real estate, and are often used when a store is having a grand opening. However, there have been cases of major advertisers testing this medium. Coca-Cola has placed these boards near its vending machines. Such ads can achieve a remarkable effect when used in great numbers.

The cost depends on the number of boards, number of printing colors, quality, area covered, and method of installation, but it generally runs about ¥1,000 to ¥4,000 per board.

Finally, while it is still far from systematized, poster advertising is possible in many private and chain beauty salons, coffee shops, and sports clubs.

BROADCAST ADS

First, there are in-store broadcast ads. These typically take advantage of the background music broadcast within department and retail stores. These broadcasts are also heard in coffee shops, restaurants, and banks, and often include an ad message for the store.

Usually these broadcasts include messages that disseminate the store's own information, and thus are not easily converted to a true advertising medium. However, there have been cases where "outside" advertisers have successfully had their ad messages inserted into these broadcasts.

Then there are street broadcast ads. Speakers can be installed in a selected shopping area, and commercials can be played to advertise either local retailers or products on sale in stores in the immediate vicinity. This medium can also be used by a manufacturer's own retail outlets. For most foreign firms, this medium would probably be useful only as part of an overall product launch campaign.

ADVERTISING IN THE AIR

Blimp advertising is a medium that delivers immediate publicity. The RC blimp, a privately owned and operated dirigible, is managed like an aircraft and thus requires Civil Aviation Bureau approval. It is an unmanned, helium-filled blimp (dirigible) operated by wireless remote control. The RC blimp has been used by many major marketers, such as Kodak, Fuji film, Konica, and Asahi beer. It does not operate when weather is not favorable or the wind exceeds 6.5 m per second.

Ad space dimensions are 2.3 m high × 9 m wide, and are available on both sides of the blimp.

A one-day contract consisting of two flights (each flight lasts for 120 minutes) is about ¥1.5 milllion (launch pad usage fee excluded).

For ad balloons, an ad message (text only) is printed on a banner that is suspended vertically beneath a helium-filled balloon anchored to the ground by a long cable. A permit is required from the fire station with jurisdiction in the area where the balloon will be used, since helium is flammable. Also, the balloon cannot be used on days when winds would cause it to lean at an angle of 45 degrees or more.

Since the balloon has a diameter ranging from 2.6 m to 3 m, rooftops, plazas, or parking lots with enough space to accommodate it must be selected. Due to the balloon's tendency to incline in even a gentle breeze, sufficient caution must be exercised so that it will not come into contact with electric wires or nearby buildings. Most areas that allow ad balloons permit them to be displayed only from 9 A.M. to 5 P.M.

The ad banner is from 1.2 to 1.5 m wide and 12–15 m long. Since ad balloons are usually viewed from a distance, the message length is limited by the size of the letters that can be easily viewed.

Rates for ad balloons are extremely low by Japanese advertising standards, usually a daily charge of about ¥50,000 per balloon. This excludes production costs of about ¥5,000 per balloon. For advertisers who worry their ad text will not be readable in the waning light of evening, electric light ad banners, whose text message is written in lights, are available. However, their rates are much higher than the regular ad balloon rates.

OTHER POSSIBILITIES

Advertising can be placed in pamphlets or entrance tickets for sporting events or exhibits. In many cases the sponsors of these events/exhibits sell advertising space on the pamphlets or tickets to offset the cost of printing them. A further example of offsetting printing costs is the ad space that is sold on the backs of airline ticket holders or train ticket covers.

Another promotion method frequently used in Japan is handing out leaflets to passersby in front of the entrances to train/subway stations or stores, or on street corners with a lot of pedestrian traffic. Most often, such leaflets are contained in packets of tissues, which are eagerly received by consumers. When affordable, advertisers provide a costume for the staff handing out the leaflets. The simplest costume is a windbreaker with the company, or product, name and logo displayed prominently.

Besides the leaflet production and printing costs, charges are made for hiring staff (usually young women) to hand out the leaflets, their costumes, and, sometimes, permission to do the handing out in certain locations. Some of the major train stations levy a charge for the privilege of passing out leaflets in front of them.

CONCLUSION

Whether to supplement a core mass media advertising campaign, target a specific group, or make the most of a thin ad budget, an almost unlimited number of alternative advertising activities are available in Japan. Those mentioned are just a representative selection.

Chapter 14

Intanetto
Internet Advertising

Although internet advertising, as a percentage of total advertising expenditure in Japan, is so small that it barely registers, it is experiencing phenomenal year-on-year growth. Both the boom in home ownership of personal computers that began in 1995 and the rapid increase of Japanese companies giving their employees access to the internet have fueled the initial growth of the internet in Japan.

The state of internet advertising in Japan is changing so rapidly that much of what is written here will be outdated by the time of publication. Nevertheless, it should give a good basis for understanding internet advertising. As many Western companies have discovered, placing banner ads on Japanese web sites, particularly search engines, is an inexpensive method of entering the Japanese market.

BACKGROUND

While the development of the internet in Japan began in the latter 1980s, the hosting of INET '92, the world internet conference, by Kobe marked its real beginnings. The following year saw AT&T launch Japan's first commercial internet access service. The Japanese government, seeing the internet as a means of helping the country out of the recession, has been a positive force in the promotion of internet growth. In 1994, the prime minister's official residence set an example by establishing a home page. The Ministry of Foreign Affairs, Ministry of International Trade and Industry (MITI), and the Ministry of Finance soon did likewise. Local prefectural governments followed suit.

In tandem with the lead of the government, most major Japanese corporations established their own web sites. These sites, which originally focused on the presentation of corporate and product information, now include advertising and promotion of goods and services as well as technical information.

Japan's mass-media companies, led by the national newspapers, also set up web sites in the mid-1990s. Most of these contain a synopsis of the day's news and weather. The majority of the sites are free of subscription charges because advertising revenues cover the cost of operations.

In the mid to late 1990s, the U.S. search engines, sensing a market opportunity, began establishing footholds in Japan. These usually took the form of a joint venture. Yahoo! established itself in early 1996 through a joint venture with Softbank. AOL launched its Japanese joint venture in April 1997.

In the mid-1990s Dentsu and Softbank established a joint venture, Cyber Communications. The new company specializes in handling internet advertising.

In the autumn of 1997, DoubleClick Japan began a commercial service targeting internet service providers. During the same period, Infoseek entered the Japanese market.

According to Dentsu, during 1996 internet advertising expenditures in Japan reached approximately ¥1.6 billion. This figure included costs for both placement and production of ads. The following year, the figure reached ¥6.04 billion. That figure grew to ¥11.39 billion in 1998. That increase came as overall advertising expenditure decreased by 3.8%. Even so, internet advertising still represents only about 0.2% of overall advertising expenditure in Japan.

By the end of 1997, it was estimated that Japan's internet user population was second only to that of the U.S. Two-thirds accessed the internet from their homes in 1997, compared with only about a quarter of them in 1995. Overall, it was estimated that in 1997, Japan had 6.7 million internet users, with 6.4% of households having internet access. By the end of 1998, both figures had nearly doubled. The number of internet users grew to 11.5 million, while the figure for households with internet access increased to 11%.

Although the Kanto area of Japan contains less than one-third of Japan's total population, it has almost half of its internet users. Men in their twenties and thirties account for over 50% of Japanese internet users. There are still relatively fewer women accessing the internet in Japan compared with other developed countries. Most estimates put the number at approximately 12%.

Japanese internet users tend to be very conscious of their time online, since they must pay ¥10 per three minutes for daytime local telephone calls. This high cost is probably the biggest impediment to growth of internet use in Japan. As a result, more than 70% of Japanese homes with internet access use modems that are 28.8K bps or faster, a significantly higher proportion than in most other nations. Due to the high charges levied by NTT (Nippon Telephone & Telegraph), the local telephone monopoly, fast-loading web pages are an absolute minimum requirement for capturing the attention of Japanese web surfers. Memory-intensive, slow-loading pages are not tolerated. Internet users tend to go directly to favorite sites, and to switch quickly between sites. They spend the minimum amount of time possible on a site, saving or printing out pages to be read later.

Since Japanese users are so highly conscious of the time they spend surfing the internet, advertisers are continuously searching for effective techniques to catch their attention. One result of this battle to get web surfers to click on a banner is the heavy use of sweepstakes and promotions in internet ads. Surveys suggest that while only half of Japanese internet users often click on banner ads, fully two-thirds of those who do so admit to clicking on a banner that displays an opportunity to win a prize.

Due to the unique characteristics of the Japanese internet market and its rapid development, new uses and techniques for internet advertising are constantly being experimented with. In an interesting attempt to garner attention and build its image, Coca-Cola Japan made a deal with Excite Japan to display its logo as part of Excite's page background.

BANNER ADS

The majority of internet advertising in Japan consists of banner ads (rectangular ad spaces about 25 mm × 50 mm). A click on the ad takes the user to the advertiser's web site.

The most popular sites to place banner ads are on Japanese search engines such as Yahoo! Japan, Infoseek Japan, NTT's Goo, Fresh Eye, Open Text, Excite, and Webdew, and even on U.S. search engines. Placing ads on the web sites of Japanese newspapers and magazines is also effective.

As with mass-media advertising, the purpose of some banners is the building of awareness of a product or service, while the goals of other banners are strictly focused on sales. Regardless of its purpose, creating an attention-gaining banner is as difficult in Japan as it is elsewhere.

Since the majority of Japanese internet users are not fluent in English, it makes sense to place banner ads, in Japanese, on Japanese sites. Obviously, a banner in Japanese can be read more quickly than one in English. This is not to imply that banner ads are solely in Japanese. Often English text is utilized, but its inclusion is usually as a graphic design element. Again, to avoid losing the user's interest, the banner must be as quick-loading as possible. Many major sites place memory limitations on banner ads for this reason.

Internet advertising rates are based on two systems. The predominant system is a straightforward flat charge per length of exposure, such as ¥500,000 per month. The other system is based on the number of times the ad is exposed. In this case, the advertiser is charged a set fee for a set number of exposures. An example would be ¥500,000 per 100,000 exposures.

Of course, internet ad rates also vary with the popularity of the web site selected and the location (the page within the web site where the banner is placed). Typically, placing a banner on one of the popular search engines, with their high traffic, is the most expensive option.

In order to place banner ads on the highest-traffic servers in Japan, it is necessary to approach one of the leading internet advertising agencies. All these agencies are affiliated with the largest traditional mass-media agencies.

Japan's leading mass-media advertising agencies were not slow to grasp the potential of the internet as a new advertising medium. As a result, they were quick to enter internet advertising, usually in joint ventures. As mentioned earlier, Dentsu, the largest agency in Japan, formed Cyber Communications in 1996 in a joint venture with Softbank. Cyber Communications' main banner-hosting site is Yahoo! Japan. Soon afterward, Hakuhodo, Japan's second largest ad agency, was involved in the establishment of Digital Advertising Consortium (DAC). Several partners, including Yomiuri Advertising, joined Hakuhodo in this effort. DAC's main banner host site is Infoseek Japan.

Compared with the U.S., expenditures on internet advertising in Japan remain minuscule, yet continue to expand rapidly. Foreign firms, particularly those without a physical presence in Japan, account for a significant portion of Japan's total internet advertising expenditure. It is generally agreed that internet advertising will continue to grow in popularity in Japan. Not only does it allow target segmentation by selecting web sites most likely to be visited by a particular audience, but it is highly flexible in terms of length of time the banner is exposed, and its results are measurable.

At the time of this writing, the Japanese banner market remains a buyer's market. Most web sites have "inventory" (a number of unfilled banner slots) available at all times.

Though banner ads are the mainstay of internet advertising in Japan at present, E-mail ads are beginning to be utilized, and are enjoying increasing success as an advertising vehicle. Advertisers, particularly mail-order firms, have discovered how cost-effective E-mail ads can be. Recipients simply click on a link embedded in the message that instantly takes them to the marketer's web site.

MEASUREMENT

The methods of measuring how often a banner ad has been read differ among the various web pages and search engines. In general the concept of "hits" has been used. Since every object transferred from a server (icons, photos, etc.) is counted as a hit, the usual practice is to divide the total number of hits by five (the average number of hits per access). The result gives an approximation of the true number of accesses (number of pages transferred from a server).

"Clickthrough," the number of times a certain banner is clicked, as a percentage of total number of impressions (the number of times the audience is exposed to the banner), is also utilized as a form of measurement. A clickthrough rate of almost 2% was considered average in Japan until recently. Today, due to tremendous increase among competing web pages, even this percentage is difficult to achieve.

Another method of measurement is "page view," the number of times a certain page is displayed to a viewer. Since many pages do not contain the advertiser's banner, this method is not very accurate unless limited to pages containing the banner. In addition, search engines can record the number of times information is retrieved as an indication of an ad's effectiveness. A few web sites have begun using software that tracks page view and clickthrough rates.

Video Research, Japan's leading TV and radio rating service, has expanded to cover the internet. This was made possible through a business agreement with IPRO, a U.S. internet advertising-rating venture.

Video Research, a subsidiary of Dentsu, uses technology developed by IPRO to measure the effectiveness of advertising in cyberspace. The system involves attaching a counter to an advertiser's web server that records how many people saw the pages and ads. The system records statistics that can then be reported to the advertiser.

CONCLUSION

With the tremendous growth in Japanese computer ownership and internet access, internet advertising will be increasingly important in the overall advertising programs of many companies targeting the Japanese consumer. Since the industry is still in its infancy, now is a perfect time for marketers to experiment with the new advertising medium in order to develop the most efficient advertising models possible.

Conclusion

Understanding the consumer is vital in any market. This is just as true in Japan as elsewhere. For the non-Japanese marketer attempting to learn how to get the most out of advertising in Japan, the first step is discarding stereotypes that only compound the confusion regarding the Japanese and Japan. It is also necessary to dispense with any preconceived notions of what is "good" advertising, regardless of how successful it was "back home."

While it is easy to try to run advertising campaigns in Japan that were successful in other countries, or to evaluate an advertising plan based on what worked in the home country, such efforts inevitably result in failure.

In the same vein, foreign marketers must always remind themselves that what looks good to them doesn't always look good to the Japanese consumer. For example, a common complaint among Japanese consumers is that Western ads aired in Japan (with a Japanese sound track) are "dark." Usually, until this is mentioned, the Western marketer has never considered the brightness or darkness of commercials.

Probably the simplest, yet most often overlooked, method of creating great advertising in Japan is to decide what message you want the target consumers to take away from the ad, and then check to see if the ad accomplished its purpose. Unfortunately, too many Western marketers get stuck in the details of execution, trying to change the look of the ad to conform to their expectations, or reworking the English translation of the Japanese copy. To these people I can only say, "Never forget that you are not the target audience."

On the other hand, it is all too easy to fall into the trap of believing that Japanese advertising is somehow "different." It's easy and convenient to label any Japanese ad that is not easily understandable as "mood advertising." However, subtle as they may be, inevitably there are forces at work in the ad that get a specific message across to the consumer. It is worthwhile to find out what those forces are, and how they interact with the consumer to make the ad successful.

Overall, I've found that among the expatriates I've worked with on the client side, those who have no direct experience with advertising outside of Japan are usually the quickest to grasp the basics of successful advertising in Japan. A lack of preconceptions regarding what advertising should look like, or how it should work, seems to help a quick grasp of the essentials. More than anything, being able to accept Japanese culture, without judging it by Western values, remains a key to success.

For all the changes Japanese society is going through, understanding the importance of conformity and the value of the group remains an important factor in creating successful advertising. However, these cultural influences should in no way hinder efforts to make a product or service stand out from the pack. It's just the methods employed to differentiate a product from competitors' products that are different.

At the same time, the commonly perceived limitations of Japanese media are a hindrance only when based on a comparison of how media work in other countries. If time is taken to understand how media in Japan works, the smart foreign marketer can take advantage of its many strengths. Rather than trying to import successful uses of media from the West, the smart marketer should look at successful uses of media in Japan. There are countless examples that, unfortunately, are ignored.

Obviously I'm biased, but I truly believe that a Western marketer with a solid comprehension of how advertising works in Japan will have an advantage over his competitors. For while marketing encompasses many components, in the end it is advertising that gives the marketer the chance to speak directly to the consumer. Although advertising is just one component of successfully marketing products and services to the Japanese, it is vital to get it right.

Glossary

ai (n.) love; affection; fondness; attachment

aisatsu (n.) greeting; civilities; salutation

aisu (n.) ice

akusesari (n.) accessories

baitai (n.) a medium

bangumi (n.) program

basha (n.) horse-drawn carriage; coach; wagon

beikoku (n.) the U.S.

betsu (n.) distinction; difference (pron.) another

biru (n.) building

bīru (n.) beer

chika-tetsu (n.) subway

dabingu suru (v.) to dub; dubbing

dai-ichi (n.) no. 1

dairi-ten (n.) agency

dan (n.) column

danchi (n.) public housing development; apartment development; housing/apartment complex; public housing compound

denki (n.) electricity

denpa (n.) electric wave; radio wave

densha (n.) train run by electricity

denshin (n.) telegraph; telegram; wire

denshoku (n.) (decorative) illumination

densō (n.) electrical (wireless) transmission

denwa (n.) telephone

depāto (n.) department store

doa (n.) door

dorai (adj.) businesslike; devoid of sentiment

ea-kon (n.) air conditioner

e-bira (n.) picture poster

egao (n.) smiling face

eigyō (n.) business; trade; commercial pursuits

eki (n.) railway station

erebētā (n.) elevator

fakushimiri (n.) facsimile; fax

futsū (adj.) ordinary

gaijin (n.) foreigner; alien

gakumen (n.) wall poster (in train)

garasu (n.) glass; plate glass; pane

gāru (n.) girl

gendai (n.) the present age (day, generation); modern times; today

genkin (n.) cash

gera (n.) galley proof

Gochiku (n.) Gothic type; a black [bold(faced)] letter

gurasu (n.) glass; glass; glasses

gurēpu-jūsu (n.) grape juice

gyōkai (n.) business world; industry; trade

haikan (n.) discontinuance (of publication) (v.) to cease publication

hairu (v.) enter; come (go/get) in; come (go/get) into (a house)

hankachi (n.) handkerchief

han-shita (n.) block copy; artwork

hashira (n.) pillar; column

heiretsu (n.) arrangement in a row/line

henshū (n.) editing; compilation

hi (n.) day

hijōu (n.) emergency

hiragana (n.) cursive ***kana*** characters

hō (n.) law; rule

hōsō (n.) radio/television broadcast; telecast

hoteru (n.) hotel

iji (n.) maintenance; upkeep; preservation; support

iku (v.) go

imēiji (n.) image

intanetto (n.) internet

ippon (adj.) one

ji (n.) letter; character

jinji (n.) human business; personal affairs; personnel (section)

jishin (n.) self-confidence; confidence in oneself

jōdan (n.) joke; jest; fun; witticism; gag

josei (n.) womanhood; femininity; woman (women)

jōyō (n.) common, habitual, ordinary use; daily use; everyday use

kaikiri (n.) reservations; buying up

kaisatsu (n.) examination of tickets; (platform) wicket; ticket barrier (gate)

kakaku (n.) price; cost; value

kake-ne (n.) overcharge

kami-san (n.) wife

kana (n.) Japanese syllabary (alphabet)

kanban (n.) signboard

kanji (n.) Chinese character (ideograph) used in Japanese writing

Kansai (n.) Kansai district; Kyoto–Osaka area

Kantō (n.) Kanto district (area)

kappan (n.) letterpress

katakana (n.) square form of ***kana***

katei (n.) home; family; household

kāten (n.) curtain; drapes

kau (v.) to purchase; to buy

keigo (n.) honorific (expression/word); term of respect; used in polite expressions

keiyaku (n.) contract

keizai (n.) economy; economics; finance

keshō (n.) makeup

kihon (n.) foundation; basis; standard

kiji (n.) article; news story

kiji-ko (n.) advertorial

kinyū (n.) money

kiro (n.) kilo; kilometer

kitsune (n.) fox

kōgyō (n.) industry; manufacturing industry

kōhō (n.) (public) information; publicity; public relations (PR)

kōkoku (n.) advertisement

kopī (n.) copy

kōtsū (n.) traffic; communication; transport; transportation

kōza (n.) account

kudoi (adj.) tedious; verbose; lengthy

kujira (n.) whale

kun (yomi) (n.) Japanese rendering (reading) of a Chinese character

kūrā (n.) air conditioner

kyoku (n.) broadcasting station

kyōryoku (n.) cooperation; collaboration; working together

kyūkan (n.) suspension (discontinuation) of a publication

mado (n.) window

manga (n.) comic; cartoon

masukomi (n.) mass communications; mass communications media

meiku (appu) (n.) makeup

Minchō (n.) Ming (-style) type; the Ming dynasty

minkan (n.) commercial broadcast; commercial station

mintetsu (n.) private railway

momiji (n.) maple leaf

naitā (n.) night baseball game

naka (n.) interior; inside

nakazuri (n.) hanging poster (in train)

nama (adj.) raw; fresh; in the flesh

nashi (prep.) without (sans, minus)

nemawashi (v.) to dig around the root of a plant (before transplanting); to lay groundwork (for obtaining objective)

ni (adj.) two

nihon (adj.) two

Nihon (n.) Japan; Nippon

nippachi (n.) February and August (together)

nomu (v.) drink; take; have; taste; get a drink

noren (n.) shop (sign) curtain

nyōbō (n.) wife

o-bon (n.) Bon Festival; Lantern Festival; Festival of the Dead; Buddist All Souls' Day

o-chūgen (n.) fifteenth day of the seventh month of the year according to the lunar calendar, last day of Lantern Festival; midyear (summer) present/gift

oishii (adj.) nice; savory; tasty

o-kami-san (n.) wife; landlady (of an inn)

oku (n.) interior; inner part; innermost recess

okugata (n.) wife of a nobleman; lady

oku-sama (n.) married woman; lady of the house; wife

oku-san (n.) wife

on (yomi) (adj.) to read Chinese characters phonetically

ōpun kā (n.) convertible (automobile)

orikomi (n.) insertion; foldout

o-seibo (n.) end (close) of the year; year-end gifts

paido pabu (n.) paid publicity

pantsu (n.) underpants; drawers; panties

pasokon (n.) personal computer

posutā (n.) poster

rajio (n.) radio

renmei (n.) league; federation; confederation

ringo (n.) apple

roke-han (n.) location hunting

rōma-ji (n.) method of writing Japanese in Roman characters

ryōkin (n.) charge; fee; fare

ryūtsū (n.) distribution

sābisu (n.) service; bargain special (adj.) free of charge; with compliments

saihan(bai) (n.) resale; resale price maintenance; retail price maintenance policy

sakura (n.) cherry tree; cherry blossoms

san (adj.) three

sangyō (n.) industry; primary industries

se-biro (n.) sack coat; sack (business) suit

seikatsu (n.) life; existence; livelihood; living

seiri-bu (n.) copydesk; copy editor

seiyo (n.) the West; the Occident; Europe; Western civilization

senden (n.) advertisement; advertising campaign

senden-hi (n.) advertising expenses

senzoku (n.) exclusive jurisdiction; tender (v.) to belong exclusively to; be regularly detailed to/assigned to; to be under the exclusive control of

seshoku-ritsu (n.) contact rate

shakai (n.) society; world; the public

shanai (n.) inside of a car

shidō (n.) city (municipal) road; private road (path)

shimbun (n.) newspaper; paper; journal; gazette; the press

shine-ado (n.) cinema ad

shinkansen (n.) bullet train

shita (prep.) under; beneath (adj.) lower

shitei ryōkin (n.) designated price

shōnen (n.) boy; lad

shūkan (n.) weekly publication; weekly periodical

shukushō (n.) reduction; scale-down

shuppan (n.) publication; publishing

sono-ta (pron.) others (n.) the rest

soto (n.) outside; exterior

sūpa (n.) superimposition; supermarket

supōtsu (n.) sports

suru (v.) do; perform; try; attempt

sutando-purē (n.) grandstand play (v.) play to the grandstand (to the gallery)

sutē-bure (n.) station break

suto (n.) labor strike (***sutoraiki***); partial strike

sutoraiki (n.) labor strike; walkout

sutoraiku (n.) strike (in baseball); strikeout

tanpatsu bangumi (n.) single person

tarento (n.) talented person; television personality; young talent

teikyō (v.) to sponsor a program

terebi (n.) television

teroppu (n.) superimposed text; teloption

tetsudō (n.) railway; railroad; railroad line

tobukuro (n.) space into which train doors slide

tori (n.) bird; fowl

tōyō (n.) present, current, contemporary use

tsūshin (n.) correspondence; communication; information; news; dispatch; report

tsūshin-sha (n.) news agency, news (wire) service

uchi (n.) the inside; one's home

ue (prep.) above

un'yu (n.) traffic (service) transport; transportation

ureshii (adj.) joyful; delightful; happy; pleasant; gratifying; glad

usagi (n.) rabbit

uta (n.) poem; song

wā-puro (n.) word processor

waido-bangumi (n.) extra-long (TV) show

waku (n.) frame; framework

wari-tsuke (n.) allotment; apportionment; assignment; distribution

watakushi (pron.) I; myself; self; me

wetto (adj.) emotional

yama (n.) mountain

yasu-uri (n.) bargain sale

yōbi (n.) day of the week; weekday

yoko (n.) side; flank (prep.) beside

yomi (n.) reading

yon (n.) four

zappō (n.) island ads placed among articles

zasshi (n.) magazine; journal; periodical

zen-bei (adj.) all-American

Source: Koh Masuda, editor in chief, *Kenkyusha's New Japanese–English Dictionary*, 4th ed., rev. and enl. (Tokyo: Kenkyusha, 1979).